CHICANO TIMESPACE

Number Three:
Rio Grande/Río Bravo
Borderlands Culture and Traditions
Norma E. Cantú, General Editor

CHICANO

The Poetry and Politics of Ricardo Sánchez

TIMESPACE

Miguel R. López

Foreword by Francisco Lomelí

Texas A&M University Press
College Station

The paper used in this book meets the minimum requirements
of the American National Standard for Permanence
of Paper for Printed Library Materials, Z39.48-1984.
Binding materials have been chosen for durability.

Library of Congress Cataloging-in-Publication Data

López, Miguel R., 1951–
    Chicano timespace : the poetry and politics of Ricardo Sánchez / Miguel R. López ; foreword by
Francisco Lomelí.— 1st ed.
        p. cm. — (Rio Grande/Río Bravo; no. 3)
    Includes bibliographical references (p.) and index.
    ISBN 0-89096-962-0 (alk. paper)
    1. Sánchez, Ricardo, 1941– —Criticism and interpretation. 2. Politics and literature—United
States—History—20th century. 3. Political poetry, American—History and criticism. 4. Mexican
Americans in literature. I. Title. II. Series.

PS3569.A4677 Z76 2001
811′.54—dc21   00-031661

Contents

Foreword

Ricardo Sánchez: A Whirlwind Uncontained

To delve into the poetry and poetic sensibilities of Ricardo Sánchez is to capture the essence of Chicano expression from the beginnings of the Renaissance period in 1965. This includes the various outpourings that prevailed then: from the excesses of an anti-establishment sentiment to the rhapsody of soul-searching, from the acute cultural nationalism to the quest for homeland, and from the articulation of an identity to a sense of empowerment. In many ways, Ricardo Sánchez functioned much like a barometer of his times—sometimes a lightning rod—of the cultural mood Chicanos found themselves in. He definitely attempted to keep his finger on his people's pulse while indulging in a language that brought to bear all his senses.

Miguel López's study accurately points out that Sánchez's poetry transcends what some see as limitations in protest Movement writings, while playing a central role in creating the language the social movement devoured and appropriated. His poignant language, much like an anthropological relic of a specific era of cultural politics, became synonymous with the Movement, but he also unveiled a particular discourse on the self, combining Dostoyevsky, Tin Tan, Malcolm X, Nietzsche, Ralph Ellison, and Francisco Quevedo—all filtered through a hard-core barrio graffiti and existentialism. His chronicler and troubadour qualities simply heightened the importance of his voice: a virile modality that sought tenderness juxtaposed with a deep commitment toward a social struggle for justice. Most of all, he operated as an enlightened conscience prepared to confront the larger and abstract forces gnawing at his existential being.

Ricardo Sánchez stands out as a giant among his peers, primarily due to his presence as a poet who lived poetry. Miguel López's groundbreaking critical study presents the broad spectrum of the person and his poetic impulse. For the first time in Chicano scholarship, López examines the key cardinal points of a single poet's aesthetics, thereby portraying an author's literary production as well as an era's search for meaning and expression. Other critics have contributed evaluative overviews (Cordelia Candelaria in *Chicano Poetry: A Critical Introduction,* 1986), philosophical queries (Juan Bruce-Novoa in *Chicano Poetry: A Response to Chaos,* 1982), theoretical assessments (Rafael Pérez-Torres in *Movements in Chicano Poetry: Against Myths, Against Margins,* 1995), feminist analyses (Martha Sánchez in *Contemporary Chicana Poetry: A Critical Approach to an Emerging Literature,* 1985), and stylistic approaches (Erminio Corti in *Da Aztlán all'Amerindia: Multicuturalismo e difesa dell'identita chicana nella poesia di Alurista,* 1999; Marcella Aguilar-Henson in *The Multi-Faceted Poetic World of Angela de Hoyos,* 1985). Only the last two works focus on a single author, but it is Miguel López who offers such an in-depth critical analysis of a Chicano poet's concept of language, philosophy, discourse, sociopolitical motivation, and inspiration. In some ways he combines aspects of the herein mentioned critical approaches, except that he offers a model by which to delineate at length the multiple components present in Ricardo Sánchez's works. While theory and approach are fundamental to López, he does not sacrifice the backdrop, background, and context of the writer himself for the sake of promoting a single critical stance. For that reason, the study operates within a broad sense of interdisciplinary and cultural studies with much (auto)biography, ethnography, political anthropology, linguistics, semiotics, and textual analysis.

Sánchez is well recognized for occupying a unique place in the development of contemporary Chicano poetry, grounded in its verve, angst, and daring nature. At certain times he competed for the unofficial title of Chicano poet laureate with some of the early Movement poets: Alurista, Rodolfo "Corky" Gonzales, and Abelardo Delgado. While Gonzales's *Yo soy Joaquín* (1967) and Alurista's *Floricanto en Aztlán* (1971) are generally credited for promoting and establishing an alternative poetic expression during the first stages of the Renaissance period, it is Sánchez who hoists the banner of the social movement through the exploration of a new humanism and a world view of marginalization. This subaltern poetics of racial renewal and redemption represented a force in Sánchez's writings, thanks in great part to the gut-wrenching self-portrayal of an existential psyche and politicized persona. He decried other writers' mythologies as fabrications, or their romantic sense of historicity as naïve, or their penchant for premeditated stylistic conventionalities as shackles of the spirit. He preferred a spontaneous manifestation of the moment, usually in the form of a geyser of concepts and registers molded by a language that was as much innovative and on the edge as the imagination would allow. His ultimate objective did not target perfection, or even precision, because each poem had to be a deep descent into the self. Consequently, he hoped for readers to gain a greater awareness of themselves and their circumstances by challenging the limits of language—that which defines reality. Language, as the social medium of the soul, is what he constantly grapples with, and thus he molds it, shapes it, destroys it, deconstructs it, and recreates it. His chicanismo becomes center stage as the core of his concern.

In the process of delving into the self, Sánchez was framing a construct with which Chicanos could analogously view their social plight. His prison term experienced at Soledad Penitentiary and other institutions expresses a trapped person within an unaccepting culture. He therefore felt moved to become a chronicler for such a condition, one that had become institutionalized in multiple forms. Such disenfranchisement compelled him to speak out and indict accordingly. This helps to contextualize his modes of expression: testimonials of outbursts, unleashing diatribes, inward journeys into a troubled psyche, passionate hurlings, principled moralizations on authenticity, and incursions into self-determination and identity. Sánchez's poetry did not aim to deal with aesthetics as codes of beauty, but rather, as a mirror of the human condition vis-à-vis social strictures and points of alienation. Consequently, he pushed poetry to its limits with a new language of angst, *desmadrazgos* (outpourings of anguish and otherwise uncontained, intense feelings), and hard-core barrio dude slang with clever and sophisticated neologisms. His originality was such that many copied certain words, but no one succeeded in imitating his style.

Other poets concerned themselves with the epic qualities of a social movement, but Sánchez fixed his vision on the underside of that social phenomenon, that is, on the unofficial intrahistory as it unfolded within the rebellious convulsions of the time. His concern was less to produce unforgettable textual imagery, opting instead to tap into the pathos surrounding the events and the unwritten factors contributing to the Zeitgeist he witnessed. The concept and theory of "timespace," which López examines with meticulous attention, encases his poetics as a way of bridging the intellectual world with common folk culture. The end result appears in vibrant poetry filled with much stylistic virtuosity, serving as a viable forum for those who sought to reconcile their Mexican background with their Anglo American environment. One of his greatest contributions resides in legitimating, along with Alurista and others, what had seemed an unclassifiable expression, that is, one characterized by extensive code-switching of Spanish-English. His poetry and prose—oftentimes mixed in transgeneric expressions—now represent one of the best known Chicano voices among the annals of minority literatures in the United States.

As difficult as it is to classify Ricardo Sánchez and his writings, Miguel López comes the closest to achieving that elusive function. By combining theory with critical approaches that apply distinctively to Chicanos, he manages to lay the groundwork for a theoretical foundation rarely attempted in Chicano or any other minority literary criticism. He shows how a knowledgeable and eclectic approach is required to tackle variants and criteria that interface in unexpected modalities unlike any other literary tradition. Consequently, the reader comes in contact with a universe of ideas mainstream critics have generally regarded as writings devoid of significance. Sánchez manifests his whirlwind demeanor and character while demanding a serious re-evaluation of such stereotyping. He confirms the validity of what he says and how he says it by reinscribing and reasserting the human spirit, especially one denied and relegated for so long.

In his study López especially manages to capture Sánchez in all his experiential mood swings by unveiling the complex man and artist. He shows, for example, that the poet's struggle was as much internal as external. His inner demons haunted him at the same time they nurtured his muses. While inviting controversy, he seemed to relish the exploration of the paradoxes and contradictions of contemporary society in unabated terms. His level of discomfort has been well chronicled, mainly because he could not accept such ills as marginality, exploitation, hypocrisy, co-optation, social trappings, alienation, etc. He was often merciless, even acerbic and iconoclastic, when discussing such topics, resorting to language and images that turned those concepts inside out. Poetry for him was not a verbal game, but rather a manner in which to carve a world view and a path of liberation for his people. His reality was language.

Perhaps the greatest contribution of this study is the proper explanation of the writer's core concept of timespace within the complex aesthetic precept of "entelechy" or *entelequia*. Such a principle appears as unbridled freedom of mixing linguistic codes or eclecticism in the purest sense. It represents what is commonly termed *mestizaje* today. Sánchez, then, was the most eloquent of Chicano poets to capture such notions at the time of cultural fervor. In many ways, he was indeed ahead of his times through his relentless quixotic spirit in constant pursuit of individuation.

In order to expound on Sánchez's overbearing poetics, López develops a profile of both the writer and his writings, particularly of the two works that have stood the test of time: *Canto y grito mi liberación (y lloro mis desmadrazgos . . .)* and *Hechizospells*, two Chicano classics, for they embody an unrivaled tour de force of a soul gasping for freedom. López examines every conceivable crook and cranny of such works, uncovering perhaps two of the most profound works of poetry that defy classification from a given era. Most of all, these works contain a richness of a writer attempting to regenerate and redeem himself as well as his world. Only an in-depth study of Ricardo Sánchez such as this one can reveal the multiple, even contradictory, facets and qualities that made him memorable in Chicano poetics, thought, and culture.

Francisco Lomelí
University of California, Santa Barbara

Acknowledgments

I would like to express most sincere thanks and appreciation to my esteemed colleagues and friends at Stanford University, the University of California at Santa Barbara, and Southern Methodist University, especially to Professors Francisco Lomelí, Luis Leal, Jorge Ruffinelli, Michael Predmore, Jesús Rosales, Olga López Valero de Colbert, Sam Zimmerman, Bill Beauchamp, René Prieto, John LaPrade, and Elizabeth Miller. Also to Roberto Trujillo, Gabriela Gutiérrez, Sonia Gonzales, Sue Sturgeon, and Rosemary Sánchez. Many thanks to the staff at Texas A&M University Press and to Norma Cantú, editor, teacher, poet, and friend.

Many thanks to the Sánchez family, especially María Teresa, Rikard-Sergei, Libertad-Yvonne, and Jacinto-Temilotzín.

Above all, *muchas gracias a mi familia,* especially my wife, Joyce Z. López, my parents, Miguel and Isabel López, my brothers Ernie, Luis, Xavier, and Fernando, and their wives and children. Thank you for your support, patience, and faith.

Finally, I would like to dedicate this book to the memory of the beloved friends and family members who have passed away in recent years, especially to my brother David López, my *abuelitos* Adelina and Ramón Rojo, my dear friends and teachers Ricardo Sánchez, Francisco Lopes, and Karin Van den Dool, and my mother-in-law Ming Zheng. Que en paz descansen.

CHICANO TIMESPACE

Introduction

A Critical Approach to the Poetry of Ricardo Sánchez

"I'm going to write my memoirs
before I go totally crazy. Or
totally underground."
—Oscar Zeta Acosta,
The Revolt of the Cockroach People

"I'm a city dude, ese,
un pachuco del pasiente."
—Ricardo Sánchez,
Hechizospells

The entire body of Ricardo Sánchez's life and literary work spanned spatial, temporal, and cultural boundaries, but his most powerful contribution to Chicano literature was his autobiographical poetry. His poems forge a connection to tragic genres of the past and present and establish Sánchez as the first great tragic figure of contemporary Chicano literature. Sánchez's extended personal narrative deals with issues of power and dispossession, of linguistic and cultural barriers between Anglo American, Native American, and Mexican American peoples. But these differences are not represented as strict oppositions; rather, they are seen as possible combinations, mixtures, and *mestizajes* through which individuals and cultures negotiate difference, identity, and change.

This book undertakes a reading of *Canto y grito mi liberación (y lloro mis desmadrazgos . . .)* (1971)[1] and *Hechizospells* (1976), two collections which represent the core of an extended autobiographical project written in English and Spanish, prose and verse, and literary and vernacular forms of *pinto* and Chicano border dialect.[2] Sánchez's voice emerges across a variety of literary genres: essay, personal narrative, poetry, and criticism. His depiction of Chicano male subjectivity is at times a sonorous, embracing discourse that celebrates the natural landscape, its people, and the joys and pain of family life and personal relationships. At other times the poems and particularly the essays evoke a raucous struggle to elicit meaningful expressions of *chicanismo*.

Some literary critics who are familiar with Sánchez's work acknowledge its literary and cultural importance. According to Nicolás Kanellos, Sánchez has produced more work, published more widely, than any other Chicano poet. Francisco Lomelí has rightly observed that Sánchez was "a conscience": "His poetry attempts to inscribe the dynamic elements of life speaking for those who remain silent. . . . Sánchez became an epicenter of creativity, a tornado of sensibility, and one of the most visible writers of what has been termed early Chicano Movement Poetry. As the radical zeal of the period waned, so did his popularity, but his intensity continues to be respected."[3]

Lomelí indicates that Sánchez's popularity waned, but while he lived there was also a reluctance on the part of critics to fully engage the work of Ricardo Sánchez. This reluctance may have been due, in part, to his reputation as an iconoclastic, confrontational, even outrageous individual—characteristics that have not deterred some critics from regarding Sánchez as a founder of Chicano poetry, even as others dismiss him as a "primitive" precursor of a true Chicano poetics. Luis Leal notes that Sánchez's "love of humanity is often overlooked because of the defiant nature of some of his statements."[4]

I intend to show that Ricardo Sánchez's status as a canonical Chicano poet has been compromised by a lack of understanding of his most important work and by developments in Chicano criticism that have tended to devalue his role. By analyzing selections from this contemporary poet's texts, I want to confront the past, present, and future of Chicano literature in order to explore its problematic role as a national/regional/minority literature with respect to other literatures, particularly those of Mexico and the United States.

I believe this book provides a more complete and coherent explanation than is currently available of why *Canto y grito mi liberación* and *Hechizospells* are important to Chicano literature. Of course, I do not expect mine to be the final word. There is still a need for studies of Sánchez's earlier and later work. A full understanding of temporality and tragedy in the works of Ricardo Sánchez must include his other published works as well as his unpublished manuscripts. My main rationale for an extensive study of this period of Sánchez's production is that although there are a number of critical works on both *Canto y grito mi liberación* and *Hechizospells,* most are no more than brief essays or reviews dating to the 1970s. As of this writing, except for one dissertation, there are no comprehensive analyses of these texts, even though it was *Canto y grito mi liberación* and *Hechizospells* that established Ricardo Sánchez's reputation as one of the leading Chicano poets of his generation.[5] No one, with the possible exception of the poet Alurista, was more prolific or had a bigger following than Ricardo Sánchez; no one was more committed to his craft or produced poetry that was more linguistically and thematically complex; no one was more passionate, controversial, or forthright in his expression.

I will take exception to the critical opinion of the 1980s and 1990s that Sánchez was no more than a protest poet of the Chicano Movement.[6] I argue that such a view leaves important aspects of his writing unexplored and makes our knowledge of Chicano poetry of the 1970s incomplete. The lacunae that now exist cannot be filled by a single book. Nevertheless, I try to provide an alternative view of a poet and of a period that witnessed the rebirth of contemporary Chicano literature. In the process, I rebut the arguments of critics such as Cordelia Candelaria, whose influential periodization of Chicano poetry relied heavily on arbitrary "stages" of literary development. Whereas Candelaria categorized Sánchez's work as naïve and unsophisticated, I intend to show that Sánchez was consciously contributing to or redefining contemporary literary developments.[7]

In order for Chicano literary criticism to do justice to the literature and its community of readers, it must do more than simply survey that literature. It must engage in serious and detailed readings of the whole work of individual poets. A number of Chicano poets have been publishing continuously since the 1970s, or earlier, and we need to understand their development over the past twenty or twenty-five years. Up to now, it has not been possible to study the entire output of an individual Chicano poet. Many who first published in the 1970s are not yet old, and some are still active, making it difficult for critics to construct theories, much less definitive judgments, about their individual poetic development. Soon, however, studies of individual Chicano poets will become both feasible and necessary.

While the premature death of Ricardo Sánchez means that we may regard his literary production as complete, much of his work, including notebooks, diaries, and entire manuscripts, remains unpublished and virtually unknown. These texts lie beyond the scope of the present study, but they represent an important archive of Chicano literary history that will provide valuable materials for future study. In the meantime, we should begin the task of constructing complex theories of Chicano poetry, based on the work of individual poets. As scholars and critics begin to closely examine the work of major Chicano poets, they will be creating a solid basis for the Chicano literary studies of the future.

If this book provides a stimulus for such work, much of the credit will belong to the pioneering work of Chicano scholars such as Luis Leal, who has developed the theoretical bases from which we read and understand the literature of *mestizo* authors such as Ricardo Sánchez. I also owe much to the work and counsel of the prolific Francisco Lomelí, whose collaborative effort with Donaldo Urioste, "El concepto del barrio en tres poetas chicanos," was one of the first critical studies of Ricardo Sánchez's poetry.

My inquiry into temporality and the figure of the tragic in the poetry of Ricardo Sánchez draws on the work of the French philosopher Gilles Deleuze. I am particularly interested in Deleuze's 1962 account of tragic aesthetics in Nietzsche's philosophy and his 1966 interpretation of temporality and duration in Henri Bergson. Deleuze contends that in his attempt to resolve the struggle between mathematical and metaphysical notions of time, Bergson's notion of *duré* "becomes the metaphysical correlate of modern science."[8] This position is relevant to my view of *entelequia* as a metaphysical construct, whose legitimacy was questioned by an influential early theorist of science, G. W. Leibniz (see the subsection "What Is *Entelequia?*" in chapter 2 of this book).

I have also benefited from the work of Mikhail M. Bakhtin, whose essay on literary *chronotopes* is pertinent to my discussion of Chicano composite temporality. According to Bakhtin, chronotopes are culturally specific representations of space and time in which "[t]ime, as it were, thickens, takes on flesh, becomes artistically visible."[9] We witness this phenomenon in Ricardo Sánchez's representation of time as a highly animated cell mate:

time winks again at me,
it clings to my fingers,
strokes my mind and soul,
its scabs laugh and mock me
as it slides on bars
and jiveass hops on my bunk
and bounces off the walls and floors (*Selected Poems* 36).

For the *pinto* (Chicano inmate) personified time becomes a way to deal with the excess time and solitude that he confronts in prison. But Ricardo Sánchez demonstrates that time can also be a medium through which the *pinto* creates new ways of linking his condition as a Chicano to a universal struggle for dignity and freedom, which he sees as the highest aspiration of human beings and human society. For Sánchez, this struggle will become a tragic one as he becomes aware that it cannot be fully achieved.

Although this book primarily involves literary analysis, its subject matter is a life, an autobiography. It has benefited from biographical materials obtained from the following sources: Ricardo Sánchez's literary/autobiographical texts, critical commentary regarding those texts, published interviews, the

Ricardo Sánchez papers housed at Stanford University, and my own interviews with the poet. Both Stanford University and the University of Texas at Austin maintain considerable collections of materials, including texts, manuscripts, personal papers, correspondence, and audio/video recordings which will enable scholars of Chicano literature to engage in productive research on the author's career.

The first part of chapter 1 offers a brief account of Sánchez's eventful life. After his release from prison in 1969, his participation in the Chicano Movement made him a public figure and changed his life, but it also turned him into a fierce critic of the Movement. I disagree with critics who identify Sánchez too closely with the early Movement years and fail to note that the *pinto* poet's relationship with the Chicano Movement was a difficult and turbulent one. These critics also tend to overlook clear evidence that Sánchez's prolific output changed and developed over the course of his career.

In chapter 1 I also describe the three vital *timespaces* that function as literary chronotopes within Sánchez's narrative: the prison (*la pinta*), the *barrio,* and the Chicano migrant experience. I indicate similarities and differences between these principal timespaces of Sánchez's poetry and the discursive chronotope of Aztlán, which figures less prominently in his work.

The second section of chapter 1 analyzes the critical reception of *Canto y grito mi liberación* and *Hechizospells.* I note the contributions and limitations of various reviews and critical studies, and I indicate the need for more complex theories that will adequately describe the development of Chicano poetry and the careers of individual poets such as Ricardo Sánchez. I argue that his various roles as *pinto* poet (a Chicano poet who writes about his or her experience as a prison inmate), as Chicano Movement activist and intellectual, and, finally, as dissident and critic of the Movement, mark stages of a poetic career that extended far beyond the bounds of a "social poet" or "Movement poet."

Chapter 2 situates Sánchez's autobiographical work within the context of the cultural, historical, linguistic, and literary communities from which it emerged and with which it interacted. The first section addresses characteristics of Mexican American speech which appear in Chicano poetry of the 1960s and 1970s. These include a variety of languages and linguistic levels that range from standard to popular forms of English and Spanish, to indigenous American phrases and words, to the *caló* vernacular that is prevalent in working-class border communities such as El Paso and among disaffected youth and *pintos*. In his poems and essays, Sánchez improvises on the speech patterns of marginalized Chicano youths from the barrios and prisons of California and the Southwest. He combines these popular forms with a literate discourse gleaned from his own readings and formal and informal studies. This practice, which was typical of Chicano poetry in the 1960s and 1970s, has been in decline since the early 1980s, when writers, critics, and publishers more aggressively sought to integrate the writings of Chicanos and Latinos into a new and broader concept of American literature. Chicano literature thus gained access to substantially larger English-monolingual audiences, but at the cost of having to abandon the linguistic diversity that characterized its renaissance in the 1960s and 1970s.

The second part of chapter 2 relates Sánchez's work to Chicano Movement texts such as "El plan espiritual de Aztlán," Rodolfo Gonzales's *I Am Joaquín,* and the poetic anthology *Los cuatro.* Here I note the crucial role played by Mexican thought, both pre-Hispanic and modern, on the authors of the Chicano Movement. These Mexican influences included the literature and mythology of the ancient Aztecs, particularly the myth of Aztlán and the poetics of *flor y canto,* introduced by the poet Alurista. Also important were the Mayan ethics and philosophy popularized by the director of El Teatro Campesino, Luis Valdez. Many literary texts of the Chicano Movement period reveal an abiding preoccupation with the recovery of the lost homeland of the Southwest, which was reimagined as Aztlán, the ancient homeland of the Aztecs. Also important to the revolutionary ideology of the Chicano Movement was the Mexican Revolution of 1910, particularly its agrarian movement, and the writings of Mexican intellectuals such as José Vasconcelos and Octavio Paz. But I show that in his first collection, *Canto y grito mi liberación,* Ricardo Sánchez diverges from the ideological line of the Chicano Movement. In Sánchez's analysis the circumstances of Chicano dispossession that result from U.S. occupation of the Southwest require the recovery of the timespaces of Chicano experience by cultural means, rather than the immediate political control of the land through revolution. Sánchez believed that the colonized status of Chicanos in the United States mirrored the situation of Mexicans and other peoples of the Americas and the world. He described himself as a native of "the northernmost province of the Latin American continent."[10]

In the third section of chapter 2, "Ricardo Sánchez, Chicano Poet, American Poet, World Poet," I trace the influence of Henri Bergson on Mexican intellectuals who were critical of the positivist doctrines of the Porfirio Díaz regime, just prior to the Mexican Revolution. Young philosophers such as José Vasconcelos and Antonio Caso tried to adapt Bergson's philosophy of "creative evolution" to Mexico's particular cultural circumstances. In the second half of the twentieth century this Mexican brand of Bergsonism persisted as a critique of linear temporality and the American ideology of progress. In the 1970s Ricardo Sánchez used these ideas to express his notion of the multiple timespaces of Chicano experience. I argue that during the nine years of his incarceration in the 1960s, Sánchez developed a sense of time and space that shaped his poetry and his view of the Chicano experience. For Sánchez, Chicano poetry became a universal medium of expression and communication that links Chicanos' search for collective and individual identity to the experience of other poets and other peoples in the Americas and the world.

In the section "What Is *Entelequia?*" I show that *entelequia* or "entelechy" is a universal theme that is closely related to Henri Bergson's philosophy of creative evolution. The term is Aristotelian in origin and enters Ricardo Sánchez's poetic lexicon through his interest in Bergsonism and Mexican philosophy. I argue that the notion of *entelequia* functions as a metaphor for the development of *chicanismo* as a historical process of *liberación,* and as an expression of the human condition that encompasses both tragic joy and suffering.

Chapter 3 offers a detailed study of the theory and practice of Chicano timespace for the texts in question. While concentrating primarily on *Canto y grito mi liberación,* this chapter also includes discussion of material in *Hechizospells* that is either chronologically or thematically related to the earlier collection. This analysis begins to clarify the relationship between the two texts, in anticipation of the final chapter, which demonstrates the poetic development from one text to the next, as well as the artistic unity and coherence that Sánchez achieves in *Hechizospells.*

Chapter 4 analyzes in detail the three major Chicano timespaces that figure in *Canto y grito mi liberación* and *Hechizospells: la pinta,* the barrio, and the migrant stream. Finally, in chapter 5 I examine *Hechizospells* as an example of Chicano tragic literature and show how tragic genres and Chicano timespaces function diachronically to subvert linear representations of temporal development. Rather than providing another broad survey of Chicano poetry, this book focuses on the work of an individual poet, Ricardo Sánchez, in order to reveal for the first time the important developments that occur within *Canto y grito mi liberación* and *Hechizospells.*

CHAPTER 1

The Autobiographical Project and the Movement

Who was Ricardo Sánchez? The poet assumed or invented a number of conflicting self-representations. Depending on whom one asks, or which of his works one reads, the answer may be that he was a rebel and a revolutionary, a Chicano Renaissance Man, a Kafkaesque victim of the state, a megalomaniac, a nagging scold, a family man, or a quixotic knight errant disguised as a roving troubadour.

The autobiographical works that I address in this book deal with the Chicano subject's experiences of poverty, oppression, and incarceration, which Sánchez relates to a need for collective efforts to build cultural dignity and political enfranchisement for Chicanos. The fact that books like *Canto y grito mi liberación* and *Hechizospells* represent a number of voices and personas from the barrio, the *pinta,* and the Chicano Movement has led critics to identify the poet as a spokesman for the Chicano Movement.[1] I argue, however, that these collections often contradict what is commonly considered Movement rhetoric and that Sánchez's critics have failed to account for the poet's critique of the Movement and the deeper currents within his poetry.

Ricardo Sánchez's writing is at times a lyrical response to the rhythms of America and Aztlán, their history, landscape, and cultures, from Walt Whitman and Emily Dickinson to the native and *mestizo* cultures of the Rio Grande Valley, from its *corridos,* chants, and drumbeats, to the *mariachis* and Tex-Mex *conjuntos,* to the blues and jazz and the poetry of the Beat Generation. Sánchez's innovations may strike the reader as an overwhelming, threatening flow of languages that defies conventions and confinement. His words explore Chicanos' loss of identity on the schizophrenic borderlines of American life, then proclaim "self realization through a historical/cultural/linguistic experience" (*Hechizospells* 16).

In published interviews, Sánchez speaks of his family's rural New Mexican origins. During the Depression years his parents took the large family on the road, and eventually they left New Mexico to settle in El Paso, Texas. Ricardo was born there on March 29, 1941, the youngest of thirteen children and the first member of the extended family born outside the Hispano communities of northern New Mexico and southern Colorado.[2] On September 3, 1995, at the age of fifty-four, Sánchez died of abdominal cancer in his birthplace, El Paso.

Ricardo Sánchez's literary vocation became apparent at an early age. He recalls that "poetry was something that I felt as a child, something for which I had no name, just a sense of being, of singing, of understanding my world, and of exploring myself . . . by writing it. . . . My first poem was written when I was a child."[3]

Later, Sánchez's poetry bears witness to the childhood years of marginalization by teachers in the El Paso public schools. The border city was a place of alienation and cultural confrontation between the large Mexican American population and the Anglo citizens who occupied the overwhelming majority of political, educational, and law enforcement positions. In the 1930s this environment had given birth to the *pachuco* identity. At that time "pachuco" and "*el chuco*" were *caló* vernacular signifiers for the city of El Paso itself. But the sense of these terms would eventually extend to the city's disaffected exiles, most of them young males, who spread the *caló* argot and their improvised, nonconformist lifestyle into the barrios, jails, prisons, and military installations of the Southwest.[4] Pressure from Anglo authorities in El Paso pushed the pachucos westward to Arizona and California, where they were emulated by some Mexican American youth who saw them as romantic rebels, while the Anglo press and police branded them as Mexican troublemakers and juvenile delinquents.[5] The cult of the pachucos and their distinctive costume, the "zoot suit," were refined in the Los Angeles of the 1940s.[6] This was a time when the language, cultural heritage, and intellectual potential of Chicanos were disparaged by racist institutions, including schools, which, according to Sánchez, injured young Mexican Americans by treating them as potential janitors, but not as poets.[7] At Zavala Elementary School and at Jefferson High School in El Paso's Barrio del Diablo, the young Ricardo began to employ his language and writing skills to express the anger of a young man who saw the dignity and spirit of his people routinely trampled by schools, police, and even churches. Ricardo was raised among older brothers who sported the dress and speech habits of the *pachuquillos,* and these influences and experiences would mark his poetic style and language. But he refused to celebrate the life he saw in the barrio: "*El Barrio del Diablo* [was] the El Paso Eastside wherein most of the vices of urban centers proliferate, *i.e.* drugs, gangs, muggings, etc. The heroes in that *barrio* were ex-convicts newly released from prison; peer pressure demanded conformity to that way of living; and there seemed to exist no means for escape from the horrors of that existence."[8]

In the late 1950s Sánchez dropped out of high school and joined the army. Like other young Chicanos he was searching for a way to deal with the passage to manhood as well as seeking escape from the confinement of the barrio. In "The Pachuco and Other Extremes," the opening chapter of *The Labyrinth of Solitude,* Octavio Paz describes this existential moment of adolescence: "All of us, at some moment, have had a vision of our existence as something unique, untransferable and very precious. This revelation almost always takes place during adolescence. Self-discovery is above all the realization that we are alone. . . . The adolescent . . . vacillates between infancy and youth, halting for a moment before the infinite richness of the world. . . . The singularity of his being, which is pure sensation in children, becomes a problem and a question." According to Paz, pachucos and other Mexicans in the United States experience this as "a truly vital problem, a problem of life or death."[9]

The young Ricardo may have experienced something similar to what the Mexican poet describes when the U.S. Army sent him to the Air Defense School in Northern California. It was then that he began to publish his first poems. But while in the army he was arrested along with two companions. He was convicted of a felony in a case involving kidnapping, robbery, and assault,[10] and he was sent to Soledad State Prison for five years: "My first publication would be in now obscured, little, beat generation magazines that were mimeographed in San Francisco in 1959. My next publications would be in prison newspapers—*Soledad* in 1961 and *The Echo* at the Texas Prison System in the mid 1960's."[11] With the publication of *Canto y grito mi liberación* in 1971 Sánchez would become known in Chicano literary circles for this *pinto* poetry that he wrote in Soledad.

After his parole from Soledad Sánchez returned to El Paso where he hoped to make a fresh start. He met María Teresa Silva and married her in 1965. However, under the terms of his parole Ricardo found it difficult to find employment. He wanted to become a writer but opportunities were limited for an ex-*pinto* with little training and few credentials to bolster his ambitions. With his wife now pregnant, the lack of opportunities in El Paso drove Sánchez to take desperate action: his family's need drove him to commit armed robbery. He was once again arrested, convicted, and sentenced to a term in the state prison farm in Huntsville, Texas. Thus, in the late 1960s, when the Chicano Movement was approaching its height, Ricardo Sánchez was still in prison.

In prison libraries and at the local junior colleges where he took extension courses, Sánchez read voraciously on a variety of subjects. Among the poets and philosophers that he cited were Federico García Lorca, Walt Whitman, Emily Dickinson, Sigmund Freud, Albert Camus, Jean Paul Sartre, Karl Marx, and the poets of the Beat Generation, as well as a number of Chicano poets.[12] His own poetry found its way out of prison and into the hands of Chicano writers and activists on the outside. Abelardo (Lalo) Delgado recalls his reaction to Sánchez's work in this way: "It was back in 1969 or 70 when I first met Sánchez. I met him more through his writings which he had accumulated while in Soledad than as a person. He shared a whole manuscript which I took home and read that very night to the late hours. I shared tears of joy at the beauty of his expression and the clarity of his sentimientos. More than reading a pinto's poems I was reading the words of a freeman who had not been broken down by the various penal institutions he had 'visited.'"[13]

Delgado intervened as a mentor and friend in Sánchez's early career. Although not a professional critic, Abelardo Delgado was a perceptive reader of and commentator on Sánchez's poetry. His analysis, while nonacademic, was not uncritical. The first *pinto* poems that he received from Sánchez were an intense outcry in colloquial Spanish, English, and *caló* that communicated to the outside world and to other inmates the anguish of confinement. In his preface to *Canto y grito mi liberación,* "This Is (Mi Compa) Sánchez," Delgado comments on the poet's moods: "Sánchez is no exception to great writers having their yo-yo moods. . . .Watching Ricardo walk and talk and just be himself is poetry in itself for the man can, as he puts it, go through changes from the innocent perplexity of a young boy growing up in a gringo dominated society, to the pachuco 'conectando' in the alley, the young man exploring Juárez congales, the young man eating wise words of wise writers in wise books, the moody prisoner blending the gris [gray] of prison and now the husband, father, fighter of lost migrant causes and a variety of other moods passing like neon colors through a neon sign."[14]

After his parole from the prison at Huntsville in March, 1969, Sánchez began to find camaraderie and support among Chicano Movement activists in Texas, New Mexico, and Colorado. In order to avoid the perils of being paroled in El Paso once more, friends encouraged the ex-*pinto* to accept a journalism fellowship in Richmond, Virginia.[15] Sánchez agreed to this and, with his family, endured a kind of exile in the eastern United States. But on the other hand, this fellowship was his opportunity to write many of the poems that would later appear in *Canto y grito mi liberación* and *Hechizospells.*

After the birth of his second child, Libertad-Yvonne, Sánchez returned to Texas, where Abelardo Delgado offered him employment as codirector of the Itinerant Migrant Health Project in the Lower Rio Grande Valley. Sánchez and the family paid a brief visit to Denver, where he helped to edit *Los cuatro* (1971), an anthology of Chicano poetry featuring the work of Sánchez, Delgado, Reymundo "Tigre" Pérez, and Magdaleno Avila.

Los cuatro is essentially a self-published chapbook produced by Abelardo Delgado's home-based Barrio Publications in Denver. Barrio Publications was not unlike other small Chicano publishers of books, newspapers, newsletters, and magazines that served as an outlet for Chicano and Chicana writers whose work was in many cases rejected by mainstream publishers.[16] Sánchez's leading role in the *Los cuatro* project coincided with the founding of another Chicano publishing venture in El Paso, Mictla Publications. He was the principal organizer of this community-based project that relied on the support of family, friends, and student volunteers. Mictla published *Canto y grito mi liberación* in a large-format, clothbound edition, with illustrations and four-color reproductions by Chicano artist Manuel Acosta. According to Sánchez, the Mictla group "wanted to establish a hallmark for Chicano publishing."[17]

The effort succeeded in producing a first-rate, hardcover collection of Chicano poetry. The book's vivid testimonial of life in the *pinta,* in Chicano barrios and migrant camps, its attacks on the Texas and California prison systems, and its message of Chicano liberation brought Sánchez immediate notoriety. A cover story on minority publishers in *Publishers' Weekly* featured angry denunciations by Sánchez and Abelardo Delgado. They attacked a neglectful U.S. publishing establishment that they considered guilty of misrepresenting Chicanos: "All of you have been lamenting the polarizing of the races during the past decade. If your laments are valid, then you must repair or make up for the damage that your neglect of us has caused us. Because you still continue to overlook the history and reality of us, we have decided to create our own publishing venture."[18]

The piece succeeded in bringing the author/publishers to the attention of the industry, and a little more than a year after Mictla's edition of *Canto y grito* appeared, the collection was reissued in a trade edition by Doubleday's Anchor imprint, making it one of the first collections of Chicano poetry to be issued by a major publisher. In his introduction to that edition, Sánchez tells the story of its publication: "*Publishers' Weekly* ran the article on the following week . . . and this served as a strong impetus for our coming to the attention of the public" (*Canto y grito* 1973, 9).

Julián Olivares has written that autobiography is "a unique American genre" in which the autobiographer "[is] conscious that he [is] a participant in the 'building' of civilization of the United States."[19] Sánchez's autobiographical poetics offers specific instances in which Chicanos in El Paso are denied, from childhood, their account of what it means to be American. Thus, at the level of representation, Sánchez intervened in the recovery of this Chicano class identity and its cultural imagery. Through his autobiographical accounts of a boyhood in the border barrios of El Paso, and nearly a decade in Texas and California prisons, Sánchez dramatized the forces of "political transformation, social dispossession, cultural rupture and linguistic alienation" from which the politics of Chicano identity emerge.[20]

John Beverly identifies Latin American *testimonio*, or testimonial literature, as a recent form of first-person narrative in which the narrator is also the real protagonist of the events he or she recounts. According to Beverly, "the unit of narration is usually a 'life' or a significant life experience."[21] In practice, this genre tends to present the experiences of individuals who have been involved in the struggle of popular sectors in various Latin American societies, who have been persecuted by the abusive and overwhelming power of the state and have lived to tell about it. But a major problem for theorists who attempt to define *testimonio* as a new literary genre is how to distinguish it from existing forms of autobiography on one hand and from nonliterary forms such as documentary, oral history, and journalism on the other. Thus, Beverly asks, "Do social struggles give rise to new forms of literature, or is it more a question of the adequacy of their representation in existing narrative forms?" Beverly cites Raymond Williams's response to this question with respect to British working-class writers "who wanted to write about their working lives. The most popular form was the novel, but though they had marvelous material that could go into the novel very few of them managed to write good or any novels. Instead they wrote marvelous autobiographies. . . . These oral forms were more accessible forms centered on the 'I,' on the single person. . . . Indeed the forms of working-class consciousness are bound to be different from the literary forms of another class, and it is a long struggle to find new and adequate forms."[22]

I have chosen to read Ricardo Sánchez's texts as autobiographical rather than "testimonial" literature in the Latin American sense. There are a number of reasons for this approach, including the aesthetic intentionality of Sánchez's writing. In his work there is no mediator that intervenes in the production of the text, as is the case in a number of Latin American *testimonios*, including *My Name Is Rigoberta Menchú* and *Let Me Speak! Testimony of Domitila, a Woman of the Bolivian Mines*. Unlike the testimonial subject as theorized by Beverly, Sánchez does not shun the role of author. On the contrary, the Chicano poet insists on claiming the intentionality and responsibility of the author's role. According to Beverly, " *Testimonio* involves a sort of erasure of the function, and thus also of the textual presence, of the 'author.'. . . There seems implicit in this situation both a challenge and an alternative to the patriarchal and elitist function the author plays in class and sexually and racially divided societies."[23]

Ricardo Sánchez does not offer this alternative which Beverly claims to see in Latin American *testimonio*. On the other hand, the Chicano concept of *carnalismo* may be akin to what Beverly calls a kind of "fraternal/sororal" complicity between the narrator and reader. Ricardo Sánchez, as *pinto,* is the subaltern whose linguistic and cultural identity has been suppressed by a politically and economically dominant majority culture. But when he becomes a published writer and earns a Ph.D., he claims and uses an authorial voice to assert not only his own authority but also the cultural/historical experience of Chicanos. As a uniquely mestizo form of American literature, Chicano autobiographical narrative may well respond both "yes" and "no" to other, somewhat similar, literary forms and reject the either/or dichotomy set up by John Beverly's question: Chicano narrative (poetry and prose) is *both* a new form of literature and *also* (since it does not emerge in a vacuum) one that appropriates and employs existing narrative forms.

In the 1970s Ricardo Sánchez and other Chicano authors were forced to make a distinction between their work and the material and ideological demands of the Chicano Movement. From jails and prisons *pinto* voices seconded the call for revolutionary action on behalf of the downtrodden and dispossessed, but Sánchez's voice began to criticize the Movement's leaders and motives. The dispute involved a number of persons whom Sánchez considered "self-appointed leaders." Sánchez brought the dispute into the open with his personal narratives about growing up amid poverty and experiencing the limited opportunities available to poor, working-class Chicanos and their families.

After the publication of *Canto y grito mi liberación* Sánchez undertook a program of graduate study at the Union Institute in Ohio. He earned a Ph.D. in American studies and found employment as an instructor of Chicano studies and creative writing in a number of colleges and universities. These achievements were realized with considerable effort on the part of Sánchez and his family. Yet in his narrative, individual initiative and hard work—two key factors that won for him, a Chicano ex-convict, a chance at the American dream of success—are viewed, from a Chicano perspective, with skepticism. In his writing, references to American-style achievement intermingle with explicit condemnations of American society for its denial of cultural dignity and security to the majority of Chicanos and Chicanas. The working-class subject longs for the benefits that others enjoy, even as he expresses outrage and contempt for the elitism that binds him: "I wanted to prove that a Chicano from a resourceless *barrio* could make the journey from being a high school dropout, badly discharged soldier, convict, and social outcast to becoming a professor with an accredited Doctor of Philosophy degree as well as being fairly published and involved in a political movement struggling toward the liberation of the internal colony that Chicanos represent."[24]

Indeed, Sánchez would advocate radical noncooperation with the American work ethic and its dehumanizing ideology. His position is reminiscent of the bohemian Beat movement of the 1950s and the civil disobedience of the youth counterculture in the 1960s: "If enough people determine not to work, not to support the system (we support it, it does not support us!), nor defend it—the system shall fall or change" (*Hechizospells* xiv). He writes of a Chicano community in northern New Mexico (La Academia de la Nueva Raza) whose doctrine is: "THE BEST PROFESSION IS THAT OF HAVING NO PROFESSION. Their only business is life, and life is bettering the living conditions and realities with the people—not for them!" (*Hechizospells* xvii).

Inevitably, Sánchez contradicts himself on this issue, alternately denying and acknowledging complicity with the ideology and perquisites of American middle-class success. Nevertheless, his continued advocacy on behalf of Chicano cultural values led to conflicts with agencies and individuals, both Chicano and Anglo, that controlled access to academic positions, literary publication, and research grants. For the Sánchez family, the consequences of this ideological struggle within the mind and soul of the main breadwinner was a migrant existence marked by uncertainty, chronic poverty, and a series of temporary residences. Images of hunger in the community and in the household give an edge of tension and immediacy to Sánchez's texts. At the same time that he deplores poverty and hunger as effects of the "*desmadrazgo*" (dispossession) suffered by Chicanos, Sánchez transforms these hardships into emblematic symbols of the struggle—not unlike the hunger strikes and modest lifestyle that are part of the legend of César Chávez, the late Chicano labor leader. The poverty and oppression suffered by migrant farm workers becomes a potent weapon and a unifying force in the struggle against an affluent and exploitative society. Ricardo Sánchez's poetics of liberation assimilates the lessons and contributions of César Chávez and the United Farm Workers, even as it gradually rejects the nationalist direction taken by Movement leaders such as Rodolfo "Corky" Gonzales.

As a critic of the Movement Sánchez uses the concept of *liberación* to recodify Chicano politics. Freedom was to be realized not by silencing persons like himself but by actualizing free expression in the present. In his poems and speaking engagements Sánchez did not make requests or recommendations; he made urgent (some would say unreasonable) demands. He courted the powerful by challenging them on behalf of the people: *la gente, pintos,* Chicanas, workers, the unemployed and their families. All the while, he denied that his ideas or actions were radical. To Ricardo Sánchez they were part of his politics of *humanización.*[25]

Sánchez continued to write and publish during the nearly twenty years that followed the publication of *Hechizospells* in 1976. From 1977 to 1980 he was an assistant professor in the Ethnic Studies Center at the University of Utah. In 1980 he left Salt Lake City for Texas to recover from surgery for diverticulitis. He worked as an orderly in a hospital for the mentally ill and helped to establish a halfway house for ex-convicts in Austin. He held teaching positions and was a poet-in-residence at a number of colleges, universities, and correctional institutions, from Juneau, Alaska, to El Paso, Texas, to Amherst, Massachusetts. He operated a bookstore in San Antonio and was a columnist for major daily newspapers in Austin, San Antonio, and El Paso, Texas. From 1989 until his death in 1995 he was a professor of creative writing and comparative American cultures at Washington State University. His writings, lectures, and readings in the United States, Mexico, and Europe brought him recognition as an outstanding Chicano author, despite the decline of critical interest in his work after the 1970s.[26] One reason for this decline was that Sánchez continued to write in a style that combined English, Spanish, and the vernacular *caló* dialect, even after the literary politics of the 1980s returned to the traditional demand for English-only writing.

In another study of Chicano literary criticism I argue that whereas the first generation of Chicano literary critics were specialists in the areas of Mexican and Latin American literature, the influential critics of the 1980s and 1990s were affiliated with English departments at major U.S. universities.[27] One outcome of this critical shift has been the de facto requirement that Chicano literature be safe and accessible for English monolingual students. Another is the argument by more recent critics of Chicano poetry that the multilingual production of the Movement period was necessarily inferior to the more recent, English-language poetry. Editors and awards committees in the publishing industry have, of course, promoted this trend.[28] On the other hand, Chicana poets such as Gloria Anzaldúa and Cherríe Moraga have worked to overcome this English-only bias by continuing to write in multilingual Chicano dialects. Anzaldúa's *Borderlands/La frontera: The New Mestiza* (1987) and Moraga and Anzaldúa's collaborative anthology, *This Bridge Called My Back: New Writings by Radical Women of Color* (1981), have been well received by feminist scholars and students despite the linguistic challenges that these texts present to Anglo readers.

In his book *My History, Not Yours: The Formation of Mexican American Autobiography* Genaro Padilla writes of a "nostalgia for the future [which] has played a central part in our survival in this country." Padilla cites autobiographer Cherríe Moraga's observation that "[e]very oppressed group needs to imagine with the help of history and mythology a world where our oppression did not seem the pre-ordained order."[29] Padilla notes that "[m]uch recent Chicano autobiographical narrative attempts to reconcile the dilemma between utopian desire for an 'ideal past or imagined future' and the startling realities of a present in which too many of our children are the victims of drugs and barrio warfare; a present in which most of us remain day laborers, maids, service workers subsiding [*sic*] on minimum wages and no health insurance; a present in which immigrants are commonly exploited by agricultural and industrial corporations as well as by small businesses and individuals looking for cheap labor and childcare; a present in which less than half of our young people ever finish high school and less than 30 percent of those high school graduates ever enroll in college, with fewer than 40 percent ever completing degrees."[30]

Ricardo Sánchez grew up in a barrio where such conditions, and worse, prevailed. He was a high school dropout due to educational neglect, and he spent nearly a decade in prison. Genaro Padilla does not refer to the many Chicanos and Chicanas incarcerated in state, local, and federal prison systems. However, he does mention that in the 1990s, more than twenty years after the "Chicano Renaissance," Chicanos remained subject to racial subordination and economic exploitation and that professors and researchers like himself find that these conditions have changed little in the last 150 years.[31]

Sánchez too was a university professor, and he wrote and taught that liberation from the social conditions that many Chicanas and Chicanos experience could be achieved only through unrelenting struggle against the racism and materialism of American life: "At this moment . . . in the 20th Century, Chicanos are still slaving and feeling the brunt and whip of this mad-dog society. Peonage is a reality in much of the migrant stream . . . we must prepare to fight our war here in the barrios, campos y valles—not in Asia" (*Canto y grito* 38). In addition to those moments when Sánchez's autobiography coincides with the agenda of the Chicano Movement, there are other times when he writes about personal experiences and emotions with the playfulness and distinctive sonority of his poetic languages. Thus, the poetic subject constantly surprises the reader as he moves from rage to serenity, from hostility to humor. His world can be a loving place of family, children, *carnales y carnalas,* or one in which rivalries and friendships are tested to the breaking point.

A Critical View

A quarter century after their publication, can we begin to overcome the obstacles that have prevented a better reading of Ricardo Sánchez's *Canto y grito mi liberación* and *Hechizospells?* Up to now, superficial readings have dismissed Sánchez as a poet "unfettered in his opinions, extreme in his views, and sometimes undisciplined in his form."[32] Other critics have failed to look beyond the scandalous aspects of the poet's life and language, his *vato loco* (gangster) demeanor learned on the streets of El Paso and Ciudad Juárez and reinforced in prison confrontations with guards and inmates. Chicano critics acquainted with the poet's work wrote favorable reviews of *Canto y grito mi liberación* and *Hechizospells,* but no one undertook the extended analysis needed to document the contributions of these texts to Chicano poetry. From the mid-1980s to this writing, it has fallen to European scholars of Chicano literature to question the marginalization of Ricardo Sánchez and other authors from the 1960s and 1970s.[33]

In order to sort out the reasons for Ricardo Sánchez's notoriety as *enfant terrible* and *poet maudit* we must carefully consider his work as the literary expression of his life and times.[34] As a number of critics have pointed out, Sánchez's poetry is an extended narrative that traces his life's itinerary from the harsh barrio schools of El Paso, to state prisons in California and Texas, to his travels in Mexico, Europe, and various regions of the United States.[35] According to Nicolás Kanellos, "[o]ne of the great achievements of Sánchez['s] poetry is, in fact, the power of his autobiography to convince us that his poetry is life, that the protagonist of his verse is the real-life, flesh-and-blood Ricardo Sánchez." Likewise, Juan Bruce-Novoa notes that "Sánchez is one of Chicano literature's most talented creators of poetic narrative. His apparent goal is to write the literary autobiography of Ricardo Sánchez, poet-militant, writer engagé."[36] Other critics, however, and particularly those trained in the Anglo American literary tradition, scarcely notice the autobiographical aspect of Sánchez's poetry. Yet, like entries in a personal diary, most of the poems in *Canto y grito mi liberación* are prefaced by a place and date of composition. The earliest are from the beginning of the 1960s when the author was in *la pinta,* California's Soledad Prison. Philip D. Ortego has called these poems "the best of Pinto poetry." According to Ortego, "Sánchez revels in that rogue spirit which characterizes a rich vein of his poetry."[37]

Without underestimating its importance as a poetic statement, we should view *Canto y grito mi liberación* (1971) as a prelude to the more ambitious and formidable *Hechizospells* (1976). At least one critic has commented on the close relationship between these two texts. Marvin A. Lewis wrote of *He-*

chizospells that "[i]n a sense this volume is an expansion of *Canto y grito mi liberación.*" The critic does not go on to explain the structural relationship that may exist between the two texts. He merely states that in *Hechizospells,* "Sánchez is given three hundred pages in which to expand his poetic horizons."[38] There can be little doubt that the success of *Canto y grito mi liberación* made possible this most complex and accomplished of Sánchez's works. The poet did not waste the opportunity (nor the three hundred pages), but given the innovative nature of the work it is not surprising that *Hechizospells* was misread, misunderstood, and in the end, neglected. Like *Canto y grito, Hechizospells* is the poet's critique of his own life, the Movement, and a racist "Amerika." It is true that Sánchez was not the first Chicano poet to address these themes. They had previously appeared in poetic form in *I Am Joaquín,* and *Canto y grito mi liberación* was, in large part, Sánchez's effort to establish his own poetic identity against this predecessor. But at the end of *Canto y grito* the momentum and development of the collection are abruptly truncated, as if the *cantogrito* had been cut off at full voice when the money ran out at Mictla Publications. Only later, in the lengthier *Hechizospells,* is Sánchez able to produce a fuller, more musical sense of development and resolution.

Hechizospells develops Sánchez's *entelequia* far beyond the historical thematics of *I Am Joaquín.* The collection presents the full range of the poet's powers up to that time, as well as his view of the future development of Chicano literature and culture. At the same time, Sánchez's autobiographical discourse scrutinizes his own actions, motivations, and mental states, which swing precariously from a paranoid dread of reincarceration to his schizophrenic search for Chicano identity. Both *Canto y grito* and *Hechizospells* blaze out a critique of pompous language, racist institutions, and petty individuals that may stun the reader with its ferocity. *Hechizospells* in particular challenges readers with its very size and appearance. But this controversial work did not elicit the response that its author intended.[39] Sánchez's friends praised it and wrote favorable reviews, but the work was generally ignored by the scholarly community. Whether on the plains and deserts of the Southwest, or the hills of Amherst, Massachusetts, the migrant poet and *raza* prophet of *liberación* was seen as a bearer of ill tidings and hard truths. "Pere grino soy!" he wrote in 1970:

> involved y embarcado   *and embarked*
> sonambulantly [*sic*] journeying,
> raza, to the core of being (*Hechizospells* 113).

According to Philip Ortego, "his voice, like the voice in the whirlwind, beseeches us all to redeem our humanity lest we perish by the ravages of the animal instinct confronting our spiritual essence." At Stanford University's Casa Zapata, a Chicano theme residence hall, Sánchez's image was literally erased from a mural depicting a pantheon of Chicano heroes. And although he continued to write, to celebrate *la raza* and attack his adversaries, Sánchez was never "given" another opportunity to publish on the scale of *Hechizo-spells*. Characterized by one reviewer as a throwback to the 1960s the book was met by a Chicano literary community unwilling to decode its difficult, uncompromising message.[40] Written in his characteristic blend of English, Spanish, and pachuco jive, *Hechizospells* was and remains inaccessible to most mainstream critics. Some commentators merely dismissed Sánchez's *grito* as a kind of childish plea or ploy for attention.

Cordelia Candelaria deals with Sánchez's work in her study, but by situating it within the context of the Chicano Movement, she is able to characterize it as an "early phase" in the development of "a genuine Chicano poetics." According to Candelaria's periodization, only the most recent phase exhibits "a sophistication of style and technique, an individuality in treatment of subject and theme, and a mature skill and control that signal an inevitably developed form."[41] Candelaria claims that after the Chicano Renaissance, the trajectory of Chicano poetry was characterized by progress and advancement toward a superior Chicano poetics of maturity and sophistication. However, another English professor, José Limón, believes that the opposite is true. Limón's book on Chicano poetry focuses on poems that adhere to the Chicano/Mexican corrido tradition. Following Harold Bloom's theory of poetic influence, Limón holds that the Mexican border corrido of the nineteenth and early twentieth centuries is the "master poem that, as key symbolic action, powerfully dominates and conditions the later written poetry." According to Limón, this "specific oral tradition, the Mexican corrido, takes a kind of primacy over written poetry."[42]

However, Limón incorporates a developmental teleology in his theory as well, so that "[e]ach succeeding poem manifests a more mature and sophisticated poetic relationship to the precursors and subsequently a richer political and cultural apprehension of the present." This allows a third English professor to claim that while Limón's book is concerned with historical continuity, his own study focuses on "historical rupture."[43]

While these critical models may be tipped in different directions with respect to the historical development of Chicano poetry, they avow a common admiration for "sophistication" and "maturity" in the genre. But are these values to be found in the past, the present, or the future of Chicano poetry? For the purpose of this discussion, I will stipulate that both the Candelaria/Pérez-Torres model and the Bloom/ Limón construct exclude important Chicano poets of the 1970s from the circle of sophisticated and mature poets. For just as José Limón believes that the poems of Ricardo Sánchez and Alurista fall outside the direct line of corrido influence which interests him, so Rafael Pérez-Torres excludes the work of Ricardo Sánchez from his notion of a "classic Chicano poetics."[44] Nor are Pérez-Torres or Candelaria willing to confront Ricardo Sánchez's poetic discourse on its own terms *as autobiography*. For these critics the testimonial meanings of the poetry seem to be a secondary consideration after the position that they assign to the work within their theory, which in the case of Sánchez's work they define as the "early phase" of Chicano poetry. And whether or not Sánchez portrays *himself* as *pinto* in "Reo eterno," as barrio dweller in "Out/parole," and as migrant worker in "migrant lament . . ." is not germane to their analysis of his texts.

Nor is careful analysis capable of altering the opinion of these critics with regard to what they have already designated as "early" Chicano poetry; rather than analyzing the poetry, they prejudged it using their own models. That is why, for example, Pérez-Torres's view of the correlation between the time-spaces of *la pinta* and the barrio in "Out/parole" is superficial. Furthermore, the critic fails to grasp the significance of *la pinta* and the migrant stream as scenes of human tragedy which possess their own moral and temporal integrity. While he notes a stereotypical machismo in the "testosterone-imbued view of the migrant's . . . struggle," he fails to explore the power of Sánchez's *entelequia,* seeing only a "vague vision of a world transformed," and "sweeping pronouncements about the overall conditions of humanity." Yet, Pérez-Torres makes some sweeping pronouncements of his own, calling Ricardo Sánchez "the grandest of the pinto poets," while placing the poet's figure of *la pinta* at the level of melodrama that allows no theoretical space for the tragic aspects of Sánchez's narrative to emerge.[45]

Pérez-Torres, like Limón, is entitled to propose his poetic criteria and tradition. But I would argue that his overview does not linger long enough on Ricardo Sánchez's work to offer more than a restatement of previous superficial and unsubstantiated judgments. Like other critics before him, Pérez-Torres seeks a shortcut through Sánchez's poetic universe by searching for a single poem ("migrant lament . . .") that is "typical of Sánchez's work."[46] But the critic fails to offer his readers a sense of how a single poem might function within the larger concept of a work like *Canto y grito mi liberación*. Finally, like José Limón, he merely points out why that particular poem is not successful according to his own theory of Chicano poetry. In fact, Pérez-Torres offers much less insight into the poetry of Ricardo Sánchez than does Marvin

Lewis, who at least was able to suggest a relationship between *Canto y grito mi liberación* and *Hechizospells*. Yet Rafael Pérez-Torres defends his project in the following terms: "I seek to avoid a discourse of progress or teleology. Chicano poetry has not been following a trajectory, an endless revolution against itself in order to modernize and advance. The ideology behind such assumptions of endless progress contradicts the engagement with tradition and history with which so many Chicano poems deal. This [Chicano] poetry does not turn away from its past. On the contrary . . . it retrenches itself in history, scrutinizes history, reenvisions, and—finally—rewrites history . . . Rather than excluding or denying, I argue, Chicano poetry incorporates and includes. This signals a movement toward mestizaje, toward a hybridization and crossbreeding on a cultural level that reflects the racial mestizaje which has produced the Chicano people."[47]

This statement is interesting because it would seem to repudiate Candelaria's periodization of Chicano poetry, which the critic praises two pages earlier, calling it "excellent" and "useful." Here Pérez-Torres is denying that Chicano poetry has left the past behind and is advancing on a rising path toward the values of modernity which, as we have seen, are maturity and sophistication. But this contradiction on the part of Pérez-Torres only mirrors the reversal which Candelaria herself performs as she executes a similarly belated effort to recover the past: "Looking back we can see that the progress of Chicano poetics was indeed forward, an advancement, but only because of the willingness of the poets to move both backwards in time and sensibility as well as to move diffusively as artists, eclectically picking up techniques from all quarters as long as they could be brought to bear on Mexican America."[48]

What criteria are these authors really proposing for their theory of a mature and sophisticated Chicano poetics? On the one hand is the notion of three chronological and rather arbitrary "phases" which Candelaria introduces in her table of contents and elaborates upon throughout her book. According to this scheme, brilliant poets who founded an original poetic movement can be labeled immature Phase I poets, while their epigones are celebrated in Phase III as the full flowering of Chicano poetry. In the passage cited above, Candelaria seems uncomfortable with her own proposition. She seems to recognize for an instant, as does Pérez-Torres, that a linear, chronological development is inadequate to an understanding of Chicano poetry and Chicano timespaces. She seems on the verge of an important breakthrough when she states that Chicano poets are willing to "move diffusively" and to advance by going backward. But in fact, her thinking remains predictably linear and chronological as she describes the "phases" of Chicano poetry, which Pérez-Torres would also adopt. Pérez-Torres reverts to a linear chronol-

ogy when he admits that the times and fashion have indeed changed, and
that the past is past: "The vision of politics and the voices used to express
relationships of power have, however, changed over the years. Gone is the
sense of didacticism or exhortation that marked the most forceful examples
of Movimiento poetry. In its place a quieter, more personal vision of the
political emerges."[49]

The charge of didacticism is one way that elites perpetuate the ignorance
that persists in this country with respect to Chicanos and other minority
communities that attempt to portray their experience. Pérez-Torres himself,
in yet another contradiction, concedes this point: "U.S. society has much to
learn from the discredited forms of knowledge Chicano culture exempli-
fies."[50] As for the character of contemporary politics, we may question
whether they are in fact more personal than in the past, or whether a quieter
politics is the best way to approach contemporary political reality.

When Pérez-Torres endorses Candelaria's neo-positivist periodization, he
collapses two "early phases" into one, thus further privileging the "recent and
contemporary poetry" that appeared in the decade after Candelaria's study
was published. Despite his promise not to do so, Pérez-Torres endorses a
teleology of progress and a discourse of linear development that ascends from
the "early" to the "recent," that celebrates the latter as "sophisticated" and
"mature," and that dismisses the former as unsophisticated and inferior, thus
almost completely discounting the possibility that "early" poems might be
found to exhibit as much or more literary value than later ones.

So where does the critic really stand? Pérez-Torres's argument, borrowed
from Candelaria, pretends to be "progressive" but is in fact consistent with
reactionary notions of linear historical development. The thesis thus offers
nothing new, but what most compromises the usefulness of Pérez-Torres's
study and the reliability of his conclusions are his many contradictions, his
inconsistencies, and his unwillingness to defend an argument. For he applies
his critical premises selectively, and only when it suits his political ends to do
so. One wonders if it is too much to ask of the postmodern critic that his
conclusions maintain some consistency with his premises. Or are such prin-
ciples of argument and intellectual honesty obsolete and bankrupt? Pérez-
Torres does not say it, but his method seems to demonstrate this very point.
Unfortunately, it is a method that displays more sophistry than sophistica-
tion, as well as a kind of disingenuous political expediency that compromises
its own findings. Having once defended Candelaria's reactionary principle
that temporal development determines literary quality, the critic might be
expected to live with that position. However, neither Pérez-Torres nor Can-
delaria finds it comfortable or necessary to do so. They simply execute a

strategic switch to a more complex, nonlinear approach, but only after appropriating the legacy of the Chicano poets of the 1970s with a linear model that places them in the underdeveloped past.

Gary Soto, another writer who was ambivalent about accepting the label "Chicano poet," states in an interview: "I'm thinking about Alurista, Abelardo Delgado, Sánchez, Corky González [*sic*]. I would never attack [their poetry]." Nevertheless, he proceeds to do just that, referring to the poets in the past tense: "[s]tylistically," he says, "they were archaic. I really didn't think they knew what they were doing. . . . Now, the poems, what can you say? They were not very well written."[51]

I would say that this sort of cool, self-serving dismissal of an important group of writers disguises an anxiety of influence that shaped the critical climate of the 1980s and 1990s. The mainstream perspectives of English department critics only served to postpone the day when critics as well as poets would come to terms with the achievements of Chicano poetry in the 1970s. It is useful, in these circumstances, to keep in mind something that the critic Genaro Padilla wrote: "[O]ur cultural production has been largely ignored, dismissed, and suppressed by a mean-spirited and ethnocentrically arrogant cultural elite. Our job is to restore the full genealogy of our cultural text—autobiographical narrative included—by recovering our literary production from obscurity and suppression."[52]

When Fredric Jameson wrote *The Seeds of Time* (1994) and suggested that postmodernism theory is future-telling with a faulty deck of tarot cards, he is rather belatedly comparing the soothsayer's well-worn tarot to postmodernist readings that, according to Ricardo Sánchez, distort and suppress Chicano culture:

> Like all literatures, the genesis of Chicano literature can be traced back to our poverty stricken barrios and oppressive pinta conditions. In the main, literature has always been born within the reality of the people—folklore—and not in academia, for the academic usually winds up being the critic, not the creator. Academia is too linear and sequentially logical to create, and art is a process of flux not to be contained or constricted, ever seeking spontaneity and multiavenues for its expression. Academia shrivels up flux, boxing it to meet scheduled criteria. Academia is serious and regulated, while art is new, spontaneous, and exhilarating; professors tend to take themselves and their studies seriously, stuffily, while artists/poets tend to laugh at themselves and their creations. Driven to write and paint, one seeks to enjoy the process and not become enslaved by it (*Hechizospells* xvi).

In the 1980s and 1990s this poet's name and vision were associated with
the failures of the Chicano Movement, no longer with the Renaissance of
Chicano culture celebrated by Philip D. Ortego.[53] The contemporary re-
reading of Ricardo Sánchez's poetic texts engages a cultural experience and a
literary sensibility that exist beyond the circumscribed notions of "Move-
ment literature." By re-presenting the poet's life, his writing attempts to me-
diate his claims to moral and literary authority, for in order to speak on behalf
of Chicanos the poet must place his life and experience before the reader. His
autobiographical discourse becomes an exploration of the social and individ-
ual self at whose center lies the assertion: "I AM CHICANO . . . confused no
longer. . . ." (*Canto y grito* 153). For Chicano audiences Ricardo Sánchez be-
comes a public figure, a recognizable voice that calls on them to imagine their
multiple selves, to challenge linear thinking and monolingual speech, to en-
ter multiple timespaces and hear the rich polyphony of Chicano voices. Sán-
chez's *cantogrito* is thus a cry of cultural pride and renewal in the form of
testimonial/autobiographical discourse. It is a caress offered to a child or
loved one, it is a lament and a critical, creative, deliberately political struggle
for Chicano/a liberation within the *entelequial* impulse for human liberation.

CHAPTER 2

The Languages of Ricardo Sánchez

An important feature of Ricardo Sánchez's "historical/cultural/linguistic experience" (*Hechizospells* 48), is the prominence of the Spanish language as an aspect of Chicano linguistic and literary expression, which according to the poet, "is now being written [by] countless other Chicano writers [who] are capturing the thought processes of a new people. We are a new people, but not in the sense that we just sprang up. We are a new people because we have just recently begun to define our humanity through our own art forms and social interpretations. By our own definitions shall we be known."[1]

The Spanish language has a prominent place in nearly all of Ricardo Sánchez's work.[2] Like the Movement poetry of the 1960s and 1970s and some Chicana poetry of the 1980s and 1990s, Sánchez's work placed Spanish and English in aesthetic proximity, with "español and English merging to create another apex of human expression."[3] This contact attempts to reproduce the everyday linguistic interactions of Chicanos and Chicanas, thus dramatizing the emergence of a literary/vernacular expression that exists beyond standard English and Spanish. In the poetry collections analyzed here Ricardo Sánchez develops a complex polyphony of Chicano idioms that include pachuco/*caló* dialect and the neologisms and creative wordplay (*cábula*) that were peculiar to the author's written and oral expression. One critic observes that "a constant in [Sánchez's] poetry is the experimental nature of language. *Canto y grito* more fully develops many of the techniques employed in *Los cuatro*."[4] The publication of *Canto y grito mi liberación* in paperback in 1973 offered mainstream audiences a unique view of contemporary Chicano thought and language. A reviewer wrote that "this book makes available to the dominant society prose and poetry written by a Chicano, in a vernacular far different from any presented in print up to this point. The language, a mixture of

English and barrio slang, will create difficulties for the average reader, but anyone who does understand some Spanish will find this an enthusiastic and powerfully written account of the Chicano's life in the barrios of the Southwest. . . . A first in the Chicano's struggle for recognition both of his unique culture and form of written expression."[5]

Cordelia Candelaria argues that Chicano speech is not "bilingual" but is characterized by "its *multi*lingualism, its polyphonic codes of sound and sense." She identifies six different language systems within Chicano speech:

1. Standard edited American English
2. English slang (regional vernaculars including Black English)
3. Standard Spanish
4. Dialectal Spanish (regional vernaculars including *caló*)
5. English/Spanish or Spanish/English bilingualism
6. An amalgam of pre-American indigenous languages, mostly noun forms in Nahua and Mayan.

She points out that "the phonological, morphological, syntactic, and semantic possibilities of Chicano poetry are astonishingly flexible and extensive."[6] By playfully composing a poem in eight languages Ricardo Sánchez demonstrates that these systems offer possibilities of expression that are virtually unlimited:

> miré la bella cihuatl
> y supe that
> deeshchíí, deeshchosh,
>
> de sus senos brotaron cauhuitl
> tetlxochitl,
>
> y los dahó 'aahii
> nos vieron como
> yá' ádaat' éehii, doo,
>
> resongué y nomás
> pensé
> en el yátashki' yé, iitsoh,
> hijo de los yé 'ii,
>
> en los entrañosos sueños
> nos vimos
> listos

para encedir conocimiento
con yá 'á 'ééh shouts of neon jubilation.[7]

Sánchez uses these languages as a tribute to specific neighboring cultures of his mestizo heritage. He opens his verse to a polyglot polyphony that can appear at any time. The interaction and flow of words and idioms as they become poetic language recalls Jacques Lacan's concept of "signifying chains." According to Gilles Deleuze and Félix Guattari,

> The chains are called "signifying chains" because they are made up of signs, but these signs are not themselves signifying. The code resembles not so much a language as jargon, an open-ended, polyvocal formation. . . . No chain is homogeneous; all of them resemble, rather, a succession of characters from different alphabets in which an ideogram, a pictogram . . . may suddenly make its appearance. In a chain that mixes together phonemes, morphemes, etc., without combining them . . . each chain captures fragments of other chains from which it "extracts" surplus value. . . . If this constitutes a system of writing, it is a writing inscribed on the very surface of the Real: a strangely polyvocal kind of writing, never a biunivocalized, linearized one . . . a writing that constitutes the entire domain of the "real inorganization" . . . writing that ceaselessly composes and decomposes the chains into signs that have nothing that impels them to become signifying. The one vocation of the sign is to produce desire, engineering it in every direction.[8]

Yet despite these chains of apparently hermetic nonsignification, in *Canto y grito mi liberación* Sánchez emphasizes, in Spanish, English, and *caló,* how important it is that Chicanos understand their poetry, and one another, in "our language." Indeed, he chastises the Chicanos of Denver for losing part of their linguistic heritage:

> denver, abject city of chicanos who no longer pueden hablar nuestro idioma (mestizaje), y les digo, carnales, que duele al oír mi raza periquiar en inglés o que ellos pidan poesía chicana escrita en el idioma del gringo . . . y no puedo traducir ciertas cosas, pues siento mi alma brotar cantos del espiritu chicano . . . y mi ser demanda la verdad de nuestro carnalismo escrita con sangre apasionada . . . [*Denver, abject city of Chicanos who no longer can speak our language and I tell them, brothers, it hurts when I hear my people rapping in English or ask for*

Chicano poetry written in the gringo's tongue . . . and there are certain things I can't translate, because I feel my soul creating songs of the Chicano spirit . . . and my being demands the truth of our brotherhood inscribed with passion blood] (*Canto y grito* 81–82).

This poetic stance may have influenced Gloria Anzaldúa, who writes in English of "Linguisitic Terrorism": "Until I am free to write bilingually and to switch codes without having always to translate . . . and as long as I have to accommodate the English speakers rather than having them accommodate me, my tongue will be illegitimate."[9] Tey Diana Rebolledo reports that "[w]hen I asked why they [two Chicana novelists] wrote these texts in Spanish, both authors said that it was the way it came out, that the text chooses what language it wants to be in. For Cota-Cárdenas as well as for Gonzales-Berry, it was the working out of internal conversations, conversations with their Chicana selves. Cota-Cárdenas said that for her there were many things she couldn't say in English, many things she would hear in her . . . memory. . . . It was also for her a resistance to what she felt was an annihilation, an aggression, an intrusion, a pushing and pulling."[10]

For these Chicana novelists, as for Ricardo Sánchez, writing in their own intimate languages rather than in a pure English becomes a transgression that is punishable. Sánchez, the *pinto* and barrio dweller, may, in turn, respond to aggression in a raucous flood of verbal blows: "Su *tour de force* es el empleo de un lenguaje agresivo, irreverente que procura producir una sensación de asco y repugnancia en el lector a través de un encadenamiento de palabras combinadas en forma sorprendente, que impresionan por su insistente semejanza al *graffiti*" [*His tour de force is the use of an aggressive, irreverent language that aims to produce a sense of nausea and revulsion in the reader by means of words linked together in surprising ways, that are impressive in their insistent similarity to graffiti*].[11]

Indeed, Sánchez's graffiti-like *placas,* or turf markers, suggest the terse, expressionistic markings of adolescent barrio dwellers, whose first *placa* begets another and another until entire walls are covered, and the *placas* of defiance are transformed into murals and statements of collective art. For the uninitiated, the *placa,* the mural, or the gallery installation may share a sense of being all but incomprehensible, beyond the mere fact of proclaiming their existence. To a certain extent, Sánchez's writing is directed at a core community of insiders who share an understanding of his world and its languages. These are languages of and for Chicanos, and for those non-Chicanos who are immersed in the culture and share the Chicano experience and the pachuco/*pinto* argot which the poet uses and reproduces. As we have seen above, it is a language that may exclude Chicanos who do not form a part of the linguistic community. It is not, however, Sánchez's intention to be obscure or hermetic, but merely authentic and real as he and his community define these terms. In general, poetry utilizes complex codes, languages, and techniques that can be interpreted on different levels. Chicano poetry is no different in this respect. According to Sánchez, the poet must be passionate and truthful, as though his words were written in blood. Furthermore, it is the audience and not the poet who must interpret the poem.

All of this suggests the stance of the artist, who will not pander to an audience or compromise his or her integrity. The artist's words will shock, disturb, and fascinate. Some members of the audience will stay to hear more, but many will not. So, we begin to understand the isolation that will result from Sánchez's poetic stance. To Philip D. Ortego this uncompromising attitude recalls former periods of literary history, which were notable for their passionate and grandiloquent expression. In his introduction to *Canto y grito* Ortego compares Sánchez to the Romantic poet William Blake: "No contemporary poet reminds me more of William Blake than Ricardo Sánchez. I do not mean in form or style, for Ricardo is a Chicano poet through and through. No. I mean in purpose. Like Blake in his time, Ricardo Sánchez is trying to tell us something."[12]

Ortego was no doubt correct in suggesting that the cataclysmic times of the two poets shaped their writing. And the critic's insight demonstrates the way in which Sánchez's poetic language became a kind of time machine that generates new and old realities, experiences, and timespaces that seem remote and alien to our own "postmodernity" yet are a part of it. The poet's role as "seer, prophet, and visionary," and also as "voice," allows his audience to participate in his vision.[13] If today Sánchez's poetic language identifies his work as belonging to a particular period or "phase" of Chicano poetry that has fallen out of favor among the leading-edge, postmodern critics, we again note the isolation that resulted from his poetic stance.

On the other hand, some critics celebrated the linguistic diversity of this type of Chicano poetry as its most distinctive feature. According to Tomás Ybarra-Frausto, "This renovation of language and the resulting aperture of fresh new vistas of reality is one of the most significant contributions of modern Chicano poetry. The invigorating investigations in the use of actual speech as poetic material is well demonstrated in many of the poems." Gary Keller writes of a "rich variety of literary strategies available to bilingual Chicano writers. Bilingual writers are able to depict characters, explore themes, express ideologies or messages, and fashion rhetorical devices in unique ways."[14]

These views were published in the late 1970s, in the belief that Chicano poetry in Spanish would continue to flourish. This was a time when discussions of bilingualism and multilingualism as aspects of Chicano literature were common in courses, critical anthologies, literary journals, and informal conversations. But this is no longer the case. Chicano literature is no longer meant to sound authentic to barrio *vatos*. Its ideal readers are now editors and English professors. The Chicano poetry of Ricardo Sánchez lives in exile, pushed out of the mainstream by an impostor, a pale imitation of the authentic, bronze, multilingual reality. Spanish and *caló* have been marginalized and Chicano literature is now written almost exclusively "en el idioma del gringo." How could this happen, and why?

In 1983 Rosaura Sánchez cited statistics indicating actual bilingualism among approximately three-fourths of the persons in households where Spanish is the usual language. She also noted that code switching was the most common mode of conversation among bilingual Chicanos of the Southwest. In the second edition of her study she wrote that despite the large number of Chicanos who use Spanish, economic pressures and predominantly Anglo control of political, economic, and cultural activities continued to diminish use of Spanish and promote a shift to English, especially among the second and third generation. The current predominance of English in cultural expression makes this trend abundantly clear.[15]

Tey Diana Rebolledo and other Chicana writers confirm Sánchez's findings. Rebolledo notes that "the reality is that most Chicano writers write in English, whether out of choice or out of necessity. They may nostalgically wish they could write in Spanish . . . [but] they feel unable to write in Spanish because of English-only policies that tend to erase alternative languages."[16]

Rebolledo cites the experiences of Margarita Cota-Cárdenas and Erlinda Gonzales-Berry. Because they wrote primarily in Spanish, they could not find a large Chicano press willing to publish their novels, so they turned to small private presses. Choosing to write in Spanish is, according to Rebolledo, a "political act and a declaration of loyalties." She goes on to mention that other Chicanas who initially wrote in Spanish ultimately switched to writing almost exclusively in English so as to gain access to a larger publisher and reading public.[17] The publishers' excuse that there is no market for Chicano literature in Spanish is refuted by the fact that Random House/Vintage Books, Anchor Doubleday, Warner Books, and other mainstream publishers are now publishing Spanish translations of classic Chicano texts such as *The House on Mango Street* by Sandra Cisneros, *Pocho* by José Antonio Villarreal, and *Bless Me, Ultima* by Rudolfo Anaya, all of which were originally written and published in English. The same houses are also publishing works in Spanish by Latin American authors, but they have yet to release a new Chicano text comparable to *Canto y grito mi liberación,* which Doubleday published in paperback in 1973.

Thus, despite the large number of Spanish-speaking Chicanos in the Southwest, the Chicano literature of the 1990s was written almost exclusively in English. As a result, it neglected the needs and interests of communities which ought to form its principal audience. Ricardo Sánchez knew that Chicano literature emerged to serve the needs of marginalized Chicano working-class and under-class communities in the migrant camps, the barrios, and *la pinta.* But, as a result of its institutionalization in the universities and among the major publishers, Chicano literature has become an English-only discourse. Of course, this need not be the case and would not be, if universities were the multicultural havens that they are accused of being and that many pretend to be. In fact, the schools remain subject to divisive political interests that exploit rather than promote cultural difference.

If Chicano literature emerged in the 1960s and 1970s primarily to serve the needs and defend the social interests of Chicano working-class communities, I would argue that its subsequent entry into the academy was an unintended side effect. This is especially true in the case of Chicano poetry, short narrative, and *teatro.* The early history of El Teatro Campesino and of works like *I Am Joaquín, Los cuatro,* and *Canto y grito mi liberación* supports this view. This literature was discovered by students of Mexican and Latin American literature, who soon included it in the university curriculum. Those Chicano poems and stories thus served to foster an exchange between social strata that had been isolated from one other. But Chicano literature could once again become the vital, multilingual, and multicultural expression that it was before its appropriation by so-called humanists and the English-only traditionalists who control university departments of English and the publishing industry in this country.

According to Rosaura Sánchez, "In the Southwest, all prestigious social roles and functions are the domain of the English language. Few formal domains call for the use of Spanish."[18] If this is so, then Chicano literature must be written in English in order that it be recognized as American literature and thus occupy a place in the prestigious halls of academia. The literature must shed as much as possible of its Spanish, *caló,* and native dialects. It must leave these authentic and essential characteristics at the door, to be duly objectified as vestigial remnants of an earlier, inferior phase of *pre-*Chicano literature, as Candelaria would have it. Cordelia Candelaria has argued that there is a progressive development in Chicano poetry.[19] But this "progress" is reproducing the English monolingual hegemony that blocks the contestatory potential of Chicano literature. This is how Ignacio Orlando Trujillo described the powers of the literature in 1979: "A literature that through its language radically scrutinizes the social reality from which it arises is bound to alter the consciousness of its readership. Contemporary Chicano literature's renovative ingenuity resides precisely in its language configurations, particularly in those of its poetry. Its inherent bilingualism and multidialectalism enable it to offer a dynamic confrontation of attitudes. Bilingual expression is not employed by the Chicano as a conceit or device but rather is part of the Chicano's normal language."[20]

The differences between the apologists for English-only censorship and those who write from a Mexicanist and Latin Americanist perspective are exemplified by these two critics. It seems clear, from their respective positions, that if Chicano literature is to serve the struggling communities in the barrios, camps, schools, and prisons of the Southwest and throughout the country, it should recover the linguistic and cultural diversity that it introduced three decades ago.

Precursors: *I Am Joaquín*, "El plan espiritual de Aztlán," *Los cuatro*

Rodolfo "Corky" Gonzales's poem *I Am Joaquín* (1967) and the anthology *Los cuatro* (1971), which includes the work of four Chicano poets, are considered among the founding texts of Chicano Movement poetry.[21] Another poet, Alurista, brought indigenous motifs, pre-Columbian symbology, and an array of linguistic variations and innovations to the movement. In this section I discuss some of these precursors of *Canto y grito mi liberación* and *Hechizospells* in order to follow the development of Sánchez's poetry beyond the limitations of Movement literature, as it attempts to proclaim a larger context and significance.[22]

Critics have read *I Am Joaquín* as a "rebellious self-styled epic" whose emotional fervor and themes of historical and national identity articulated the aspirations of an emerging Chicano literary and political movement.[23] The Chicano poetry of the late 1960s and early 1970s, including that of Alurista and in *Los cuatro*, continued the discussion begun by *Joaquín's* dream of a united, homogeneous Chicano collectivity. Joaquín, the poem's narrator, speaks for and symbolizes the Chicano community. Thus, the main characteristic of Movement poetry will be its adherence to the model established by *I Am Joaquín*. Movement poetry will gloss and comment upon what José Limón, following Harold Bloom, calls the "master poem."[24]

In his book *Mexican Ballads, Chicano Poems*, Limón analyzes Chicano poems that follow in the Mexican corrido tradition. He finds that *I Am Joa-quín* is part of this ballad tradition to the extent that the poem glosses the corrido of Joaquín Murrieta, a ballad about the legendary bandit who attacked Anglo American miners and settlers during the California gold rush. However, Limón concludes that "the corrido exists as a negative influence" in *I Am Joaquín* because it is "a poem largely in flight, in abstract historical counterexistence to the corrido with its penchant for historical particularity."[25]

Ricardo Sánchez was ambivalent about the poem as well, particularly with regard to Rodolfo "Corky" Gonzales, whom Sánchez claimed was not the author.[26] Nevertheless, *Canto y grito mi liberación* reveals, in poems such as "Reo eterno," "We Were Lost," "Flight," and others dedicated to Sánchez's activities in Denver, the intertextual presence of *I Am Joaquín*. Sánchez acknowledged this influence but would later try to overcome it. In *Hechizospells* Sánchez finally broke Gonzales's spell and the influence that the Crusade for Justice and *I Am Joaquín* had had on his work. Limón, following Harold Bloom's theory of poetic influence, describes a process in which "the ephebe's imagined achievement lies in the attempt to negate the precursor's primacy by replacing it with his own. . . . Yet by the very terms of this struggle, the precursor's influence marks the ephebe's poem even as the ephebe attempts to come to terms—his terms—with this influence."[27]

For Limón, "[t]he later poet's experience of the precursor's superior artistic power, together with the knowledge that the precursor has come *before,* is the origin of what Bloom calls 'the anxiety of influence.'"[28] According to this theory of influence, subsequent Chicano poems must either abandon or surpass the model established by *I Am Joaquín,* and in either case, this development will represent the decline of the project to build a politically unified Chicano Movement. With the crumbling of this political ideal, the term "Chicano" did, indeed, begin to lose currency and was substituted at times by "Latino" or "Hispanic" or broadened to include Chicanos/as. As a result of this diffusion of political focus, what remained of the Chicano Movement in the late 1970s and early 1980s was a site of much more contentious, ethnic, and political identities.

Published in 1986, Cordelia Candelaria's *Chicano Poetry: A Critical Introduction* reflected the further decline of Chicano Movement poetics. Her scheme was a periodization of Chicano poetry, but her view of the literature as a product of chronological "phases" neglected the creative development of individual authors. A prime example of this creative development can be seen in Ricardo Sánchez's poetic autobiography. It tells us that his contributions to *Los cuatro* represent one year (1970–71) that he spent in the Lower Rio

Grande Valley as codirector, with Abelardo Delgado, of the Itinerant Migrant Health Project. While still in prison at Huntsville, Texas, Sánchez had come under the tutelage of Delgado, a poet and Chicano Movement activist who kept Sánchez abreast of the activities of Movement leaders such as Rodolfo "Corky" Gonzales, César Chávez, and Reies López Tijerina. This personal and professional relationship between Delgado and Sánchez continued after the latter's parole in 1969 (*Los cuatro* 31). After his release from prison Sánchez was eager to join the Movement in Denver. However, his plans were delayed by difficulties with his parole, and this led to his year of study in Virginia and Massachusetts. From Amherst, Massachusetts, he wrote Delgado a "Misiva to a carnal" (*Hechizospells* 118), a poem/letter dated May 23, 1970, in which he describes "how . . . I feel, compa, knowing that I am returning to Aztlán, quitting this place and making it to Denver." The "Misiva" speaks of anguish and alienation: "being alone / within foreign multitudes / (who isolate you as they come in contact with your accented heritage) / plagues me / now / like yesteryear" (*Hechizospells* 118–19). The poet carries the painful memory of *la pinta* beyond the confining prison walls, all the way to New England's outposts of *chicanismo*:

> this soledad del alma [*solitude of the soul*]
> breeds
> aloneness
> covered with days and years gone by; horrendousness even
> in poesía [*poetry*] when mind runs amuck/berserk en medio del sol y
>   luna [*amidst the sun and moon*]

The *pinto* poet inhabits the half-light, "*penumbras poéticas*," of multiple, simultaneous, Chicano timespaces:

> all the madnesses
> universally embroiled
> in texas tragic valley
> echoing chamizalismo (*Hechizospells* 120).[29]

Notified by Abelardo Delgado about the political activity in Denver and the drafting of *El plan espiritual de Aztlán,* Sánchez prepares to join the Movement's ranks, knowing that he is not alone in his ferocity and rage:

> I read alurista
> con [*with*] sangría dripping

out his enraged mind and soul,
feeding social ravia y coraje [*rage and anger*] . . .

. . . .

cautivo siempre [*captive always*]
in the awesome awryness
soulful
awareness is.

. . . .

 frenzy personified,
 máscara de muchas caras muertas, *mask of many dead faces*
 grito de muchos duelos, *cry of many laments*
 . hambre de muchos ayeres, *hunger of many yesterdays*
 sensibilidez de muchos sentimientos *sensibility of many sentiments*
 (120).

Deeply embittered after nearly a decade in prison, an ex-convict with few prospects, the poet is nonetheless "ancioso pa' vivir más" [*anxious to live more*]. To Delgado, his friend and associate, he says, "yes, carnal, executive director / of migrant council hopes for change and love and revolution / and power to the people . . . [I] shall return to Aztlán . . . and lurch out with manic hope" (123).

 "Misiva to a carnal" makes palpable a time of exile prior to *Los cuatro* and Sánchez's work with the Movement in Denver. When he arrives in Denver with his family in 1970, Sánchez finds himself working in close proximity to the Crusade for Justice, a community organization that Rodolfo "Corky" Gonzales brought to the forefront of the Chicano Movement.[30] Thus, the influence of Gonzales and *I Am Joaquín* is evident in the highly political protest poems that Sánchez contributed to *Los cuatro*. Pieces such as "INDICT AMERIKA" and "L.A.P.D." were recited as part of the political theater that Sánchez, Abelardo Delgado, Reymundo "Tigre" Pérez, and other Movement activists staged in Denver on September 16, 1970 (*Los cuatro* 52). Candelaria notes that *Los cuatro,* edited by Sánchez and Delgado, is among the first anthologies of Chicano poetry to be published in this country. This distinction, along with the polemic nature of his work, established Sánchez's reputation as the voice or, as another critic called him, "the microcosm of the Chicano Movement."[31]

 This view became fossilized; years later the critics' consensus of opinion on Sánchez's subsequent work still had its basis in these poems written and performed during the brief period he spent in the Movement spotlight in Denver. He left Denver and returned to Texas, where he did more organizing.

In El Paso he founded Mictla Publications, through which he issued his first collection of poetry, *Canto y grito mi liberación*. With these projects, Sánchez was attempting to overcome the political influence of Gonzales's organization, the Crusade for Justice, as well as the literary influence of *I Am Joaquín*.

There is no doubt that some poems in *Canto y grito* continue to develop and elaborate the collective themes that were sketched in *I Am Joaquín* and *Los cuatro,* but many more address the author's personal experience, particularly the isolation of his prison years. As a whole, the collection stakes out new ground for Chicano poetry as an autobiographical aesthetic as well as the literary voice of an entire social group. Beginning with *Canto y grito,* Sánchez's work gives meaning to a collective Chicano identity through the experience of one individual—the writer. Further, it opposes the prescriptive demand that Chicano poetry represent the individual in terms of group needs and demands. Sánchez's first individual collection was, in a sense, quite literally a celebration of his *liberación* from prison but also a demand for personal and artistic freedom from undue coercion and censorship. Sánchez continued to be an activist in the service of *la causa,* but his determination not to subordinate his work to the demands of political programs or leaders was a defining aspect of his career. After spending more than nine years in prison, he refused to become a mouthpiece or to abdicate control of his artistic message. The founding of Mictla Publications was just one example of this determination.

In distinguishing Sánchez's message from that of the Movement, it is also important to note that *I Am Joaquín* and other Movement literatures tend to define the community in terms of the land. The heroes of the people are those who protect the land from outsiders and invaders:

> I am the Eagle and Serpent of
>   the Aztec civilization.
>
> I owned the land as far as the eye
> could see under the crown of Spain,
>
> . . . .
>   THE GROUND WAS MINE (*I Am Joaquín* 5).[32]

The nineteenth-century Mexican hero and president Benito Juárez is remembered as the "Guardian of the Constitution" and for safeguarding the archives of the Mexican nation, but he is revered for defending the land:

He held his Mexico
                    in his hand
                         on
          the most desolate
                    and remote ground
                    which was his country
And this Giant
                    Little Zapotec
                                        gave
     not one palm's breadth
of his country's land to
     Kings or Monarchs or Presidents
of foreign powers (8–9).

The revolutionary hero Emiliano Zapata enjoys the same distinction:

I am Emiliano Zapata.
          "This Land
                    This Earth
                         is
                              OURS"
The Villages
     The Mountains
          The Streams
               belong to Zapatistas.
                    Our life
                    Or yours
is the only trade for soft brown earth
and maize.
. . . .
"This land is ours . . .
          Father, I give it back to you.
          Mexico must be free" (9).

But Joaquín is a mestizo who is also willing to identify with the enemy and the invader, with Cortés and the Spaniards, the *rural*, the *hacendado*, the slavemaster, and even with the political *coyote* who sells out his brother. But the villain whose name Joaquín will not speak is the arch-traitor Antonio

López de Santa Anna, who sold an entire people and their land to Anglo America.

Thus, *I Am Joaquín* presents a list of grievances. It is a compendium of wrongs and charges that are to be substantiated with other evidence and addressed through other texts, as well as through political action. To right these wrongs, there must be texts that include a plan for a new social order which, in fact, will be a new nation predicated upon the recovery of the land. And just as the Mexican revolutionary tradition rallied the troops and the people around a *plan*—from Iturbide's Plan de Iguala, to Madero's Plan de San Luis Potosí, to Zapata's Plan de Ayala—so too the Chicano revolutionaries, with the help of the poet Alurista, drafted "El plan espiritual de Aztlán" at the First Chicano National Conference in Denver. The *plan* called upon a "new people" to liberate and reclaim their land, their sovereignty, and their ancient birthright, which they called Aztlán. "Brotherhood unites us," the document proclaimed, and the common enemy is the "gringo," the "foreign Europeans," the "gabacho."[33]

In response to this historic *plan* of the Chicano Movement, Ricardo Sánchez presents in *Los cuatro* a fictionalized *plan* and manifesto of Chicano independence (*Los cuatro* 33–34). Sánchez's mock-up of "El plan espiritual de Aztlán" is entitled "Libertad o muerte: Aztlán es nuestro . . ." [*Liberty or Death: Aztlán Is Ours*] and is embedded in a "story" titled "Mutations" and dated July 8, 1970. This fictional story begins one evening in South El Paso. Members of the Mexican American Youth Association (MAYA) are gathered to sign a document which demands the return of Aztlán, the territory that was stolen from Mexico by Anglo America. Sánchez's fictionalized manifesto reads, "we pledge ourselves to the reclamation of our lands at whatever the cost" and continues:

> Be it irrefutably known throughout the world that Aztlán is free, that revolution is here, and that if our blood must flow in order to secure our nation, we are fully prepared to fight in the barrios, cities, fields, and valleys that our people might live in harmony, love, and economic rectitude. . . . If war is the only avenue open to us, we here and now declare before all the peoples of the Americas, before all nations everywhere, that we have exhausted all other avenues in our struggle to regain our freedom from the oppression, exploitation, racism, and dehumanization foisted upon us by the new-oligarchical despotism of the gringoistic u. s. of a.;

We thus proclaim our freedom and separation from the United States of Amerika, and hereby give notice that we are Aztlán, a mestizo nation predicated on the principles of dignity, worth, freedom, humanness, and love. Viva el mestizage [*sic*], VIVA LA RAZA DE BRONCE! [*Long live the Bronze Race!*] (*Los cuatro* 33–34).

The first signatory of this pact is "R. Gurulé Chuco, Provisional President," who reads the document to the rest of the group. The date of the manifesto is "16 de Setiembre, el año del Chicano [*16th of September, year of the Chicano*]." After the members present sign the document, they place telephone calls to fellow revolutionaries in "Chicano barrios from Chicago, Los Angeles, Milwaukee, Kansas City, San Antonio, Albuquerque," and so on. Even a Chicano poet in New England is notified, and he "quickly hopped the first jet to El Paso." The rest of the vignette depicts scenes from a reign of terror, as the revolutionaries carry out their *plan:* "Within a couple of weeks, mayhem broke loose. Ammunition dumps were stormed; armories sacked; and the Alamo was burnt down. . . . Northern New Mexico became a battleground—the Alianza revived La Mano Negra, and every gringo there perished. . . . Meanwhile, blacks stood up in mass all over the South. There was an awesome bloodbath . . . in which the Klan was eradicated—irrefutably vanquished! Anger and reason stood side by side; turbulent forces which defined and constantly re-defined the revolution." There is no direct mention of Chicano casualties in the war, but in the end, a presumed orphan, "an almost shattered chicanito surveyed the carnage—his mind/soul flicked over past and present" (34).

"Mutations" reflects in part the horrors of the nightly news reports from Vietnam, and in this context, it allows Sánchez and his audience to peer into the future and speculate on the outcome of the violent revolution against the United States that some Chicanos are planning. It confronts the revolutionaries with the ultimate consequences of their rhetoric, and the abyss that may await. The story ends elliptically with "chicanito" looking "outwards at the people" as he is about to speak. In the story, the members of MAYA represent a microcosm of the Chicano Movement as they rally around a parody of "El plan espiritual de Aztlán." The members are empowered by the words as Chuco, their leader, reads the document. But finally, we see that this Movement is like no previous Mexican revolution. The participants are able to communicate instantaneously by telephone and to travel rapidly by jet to and from any part of the country. The author may be indicating that in this time, technology also threatens with its unspeakable power to destroy and thus, Chicanos cannot dream of engaging in an obsolete war for the land, because that would be a confrontation that they could not win.

How then are Chicanos to withstand the new threats to their survival brought about by the destructiveness of modern society and the racial hatreds that are rampant in America and the world? Sánchez believed that the people must take up new forms of struggle. Most importantly, they must develop new understandings of and new relationships to the land. These are the "mutations" that will be required. This apocalyptic story indicates that even before the Chicano Moratorium of 1970, the idea of a Chicano Movement proclaiming violent revolution was a fiction in the poet's mind. He would become even more convinced of this after police violence erupted at the anti–Vietnam War protests in Los Angeles, resulting in the deaths of three people, including Chicano journalist Rubén Salazar, a former resident of El Paso.

The Chicano Moratorium in Los Angeles was the first large-scale Chicano demonstration against the Vietnam War. In the course of the police riot that scattered peaceful demonstrators, the LAPD arrested Rodolfo "Corky" Gonzales and members of the Crusade for Justice, along with other organizers of the event.[34] In several poems from *Los cuatro* Sánchez comments on the police action at the Chicano Moratorium. For example, the poem "Methods of . . ." mentions "corky" twice by name: "corky's face / mirrored anger / against the injustice . . . and he manfully has asserted / his right to human dignity . . . / can we not listen now, after the deaths of two carnales / and the blinding of another?" The poet addresses "corky" and other "carnales," the leaders of the Movement: "y todos otros / que han marchado / heróicamente demandando / reparaciones y verdad" (*and all the others / who have marched / heroically demanding / reparations and truth*), and he offers them counsel:

> it seems not enough
> for our people to now die,
> to die at the whim of white amerika . . .
> it seems not enough
> to march and chant in hope of liberation,
> for Amerika keeps saying:
>> power must be taken,
>> revolution must be had . . .
> it is the amerikan-way
> to goad us to suicide . . .
> L.A. was but another gringo method of genocide (*Los cuatro* 36).

At this point, Ricardo Sánchez is already a dissenter from any *plan* of violent revolution, for the land or for any other cause. He believes that in following this course Chicanos will be playing into the hands of forces that wish to destroy not only the Movement but all Chicanos.

Although later poems by Sánchez and others would more effectively develop literary chronotopes and aesthetic representations of the land and the people of the Southwest, the ideology of the Movement set up *I Am Joaquín* as the epic statement that defined Chicano identity and proclaimed the dream of recovering the lost land. It has been stated more than once, however, that *I Am Joaquín* does little more than reproduce the clichés of schoolbook history.[35] Ricardo Sánchez demonstrated in *Los cuatro* that he was capable of overcoming this deficiency. Instead of reciting names and deeds from Mexican history books, *Los cuatro* calls attention to the history that Chicanos were living at that moment:

> well, we have marched
> in tune to the murder of our people;
> we have sung
> in harmony to clubs smashing our bodies;
> we have held out
> for that moment when our hope(s)
> would blossom into humanreality
>
> > > in this country . . .
>
> AND WE WERE SMASHED SADISTICALLY SMASHED
> and the sound of skull cracking   crashed
> crashed down so hard   our minds and souls still tremble
> and we must know MUST KNOW!!! that the gringo
> means to kill us off (38).

He reiterates the Movement's overwhelming concern for the land but suggests that now the stakes are higher:

> but our corazones [*hearts*] were hopeful
> that the gringo was a human,
> and all the time he plotted
> to deprive us of our land . . .
>
> > the gringo has our land,
> > now he wants our blood . . .

being that we mean to live,
being that we are tired of being whipped,
    we mean now to turn the tide (38).

But after the immediate crisis of the Moratorium has passed, Sánchez will address the problem of land tenancy in a very different way:

this land belongs
to all who wish to love it
and within it reside,
we'll be ourselves, ay, utah,
and celebrate our difference,
we'll look at you and smile
and continue on our way
to live within your valleys
while we project our name ("Letter to My Ex-Texas Sanity" 125–27).

In a 1985 interview we find the poet still expressing love for the land, but without the urgency to recover it. Rather, there is the certainty of having recovered it in a spiritual sense: "The land is one thing that I cherish. . . . My roots are in this land—roots that are cultural, ethnic, historical and linguistic. . . . My land—my sense of historical land—is that place we call Aztlán. . . . I know my land and feel its mountains, rivers, lakes, deserts, and panoramas pulsing in my being. I can appreciate other lands, even love their differences, but I can only truly understand my land—the land of my experiencing life in all its complexities."[36] We should note that Sánchez's sense of the land is accompanied by a sense of time, expressed in terms of the Chicano chronotope of Aztlán, and of a "historical land."

The critic Juan Bruce-Novoa notes that *I Am Joaquín* was "the first major literary work of the Chicano Movement, and for many it still expresses best what the Movement entails. Its wide and continued popularity and the many imitations the poem spawned make it, for many, the epitome of early Chicano poetry."[37] I would argue that even Ricardo Sánchez's rejection of Rodolfo "Corky" Gonzales as the *jefe* or leader of the Chicano Movement was expressed not as the repudiation of *I Am Joaquín* but in the denial of Gonzales's authorship. Nevertheless, Chicano poetry will move beyond the poem's influence. Through the production of Chicano chronotopes, poets such as Ricardo Sánchez, Gloria Anzaldúa, Alurista, and others develop a critical view of Chicano/a social history. Their work shows, more convincingly than does *I Am Joaquín,* how history is made present through the agency of collective and individual memory.

The Mexican influences on Chicano literature and history are evident in *I Am Joaquín.* According to Octavio Romano V., "the principal historical currents of thought" that have gone into the making of the *mexicano,* the *cholo,* the pachuco, the Chicano, the *pocho,* and the Mexican American flow from the ideological and military struggles of the Mexican Revolution of 1910. Romano cites two passages from Octavio Paz's *The Labyrinth of Solitude* that suggest some common elements between the Mexican conflict and the Chicano Movement: "The Revolution, without any doctrines (whether imported or its own) to guide it, was an explosion of reality and a groping search for the universal doctrine that would justify it and give it a place in the history of America and the world. . . . Our movement was distinguished by a lack of any previous ideological system and by a hunger for land."[38]

The Mexican philosophers of the revolutionary period embraced the ideas of French philosopher Henri Bergson in an effort to break the hold that the Díaz regime and its apostles of scientific positivism had on the life and politics of Mexico.[39] Once Mexicanized, however, those ideas do not remain in the country, but make their way across the border and into the minds of Mexican Americans and Chicanos in the United States. The principal transmitters of these ideas were José Vasconcelos in the first half of the twentieth century and Octavio Paz in the second.[40]

Although Vasconcelos's essay, *La raza cósmica* (1925), was often cited by Chicanos as a vindication of *mestizaje,* Paz's *El laberinto de la soledad* (*The Labyrinth of Solitude*) (1950) was also an important contemporary Mexican influence on the Chicano Movement. Jesse A. G. Contreras makes the analogy between "the post-revolutionary experiences of these Mexican intellectuals, their search for cultural and self-identity," and the situation of Chicanos in the 1960s.[41] Arturo Madrid-Barela notes that Paz was "perhaps the most famous and most widely read of the Pachuco's interpreters . . . who caught a glimpse of the conflictive existence of the *mexicanos de acá de este lado* [Mexicans from this side] when he lived in Los Angeles." According to Madrid-Barela, "Paz's thesis is worthy of serious consideration because he saw the Pachuco at close range and because, being a Mexican, he was free of the racial bigotry of some of the Pachuco's Anglo-American interpreters."[42] On the other hand, some Chicanos criticized Paz for his chapter "The Pachuco and Other Extremes" and for his views on machismo and Mexican women. Guillermo Hernández notes a class bias on the part of the Mexican author: "During the postrevolutionary and postwar years, an emerging Mexican middle class was in the process of consolidating an official version of Mexican culture, and the presence of Chicanos in the United States represented a 'shameful' reminder of a history (1848) and a class (*braceros*) that did not serve them well in their aspirations as a developing Western nation. Paz was a spokesman for this class."[43]

In an interview with Juan Bruce-Novoa, the poet, musician, and graphic artist José Montoya, known for his drawings of pachucos and for his poem, "El Louie," expressed dismay at Paz's description of the pachuco, "because he really didn't know what the hell he was talking about. But I still enjoy his work."[44] Paz's statement that Mexicans in the U.S. "feel ashamed of their origin" is echoed in *I Am Joaquín:* "I look at myself / and see part of me / who rejects my father and mother / and dissolves into the melting pot / to disappear in shame" (*I Am Joaquín* 13).[45]

Ricardo Sánchez takes up the problem and develops it in his characteristically emphatic voice. In the long poem, "EXISTIR ES . . . ," which appears at the end of *Canto y grito mi liberación,* he writes:

Yes, I now fully affirm the fact of my being—and especially of my being Chicano!— but not too long ago I labored under the illusion that I was AMERIKAN. . . . For a long time, my space-time dimensional frame of reference was askew—past merged into present and future and I could not tell the difference between illusion, allusion, confusion. . . . Why? I questioned did I have to daily portray myself as a neo-gringo cuando mi realidad tenía más sangre y pasión? . . . Mi conciencia protestaba las estupideces clandestinas que habían derrotado mi pensar y sentir tantas veces [*when my reality was more full of blood and passion? . . . My conscience protested the secret stupidities that had so often defeated my thoughts and feelings*]. . . . you taught me to hate myself. . . . I oftentimes get the same old urge to reach into my core and deracinate that smirking/gloating me in there. . . . My voice will lilt out self-acceptance, but my inner mind still fights me. . . . Sí, mi cobardía me enloqueció. . . . Todavía, sin darme cuenta, ¡pensaba como gringo, como déspota, como gachupín! [*Yes, my cowardice drove me mad. . . . Still, without knowing it, I thought like a gringo, like a despot, like a Spaniard!*] . . . I looked inwardly—but I really hated being me, for my eyes were brown, my hair black, and my voice modulated sing-song accents that did not meet the criteria set by gringo society. It was still a topsy-turvy world. Surrealism and gothic inscriptions ran holocaustically through me—yesterday was the only dynamics for today and tomorrow—for I was born into the cauldron of self-hate. . . . Brown . . . brown . . . brown . . . it is no joy being the sum and total of the Chicano experience . . . merged you are in the desmadrazgo of hispano father and indian mother, half-breed son-of-a-bitch whelping in your wilderness. . . . yo era dinámica de la pinta—bestia sin corazón en los llanos societales [*I was part of the dynamic of the prison—a heartless beast in the social wilderness*]. . . . i suffered the brunt of being a slave . . . of being powerless and stepped on, then i recovered part of my self—love and understanding and family. . . . it is no longer an equivocating i, but rather an adamant and affirmative I AM CHICANO . . . confused no longer (*Canto y grito* 145–53).

Ricardo Sánchez did not criticize Octavio Paz's representation of the pachuco. Rather, in confessing his own shame he helped to create an autobiographical Chicano poetry that told the pachuco's story and tried to explain the methods that were used to instill contempt, self-hatred, and a criminal pathology in his life.

In this section I have traced some of the literary and cultural influences that shaped Ricardo Sánchez's Chicano Movement poetry of the early 1970s. We will see how subsequent development took his work beyond and against the concerns of the Movement.

Ricardo Sánchez: Chicano Poet, American Poet, World Poet

The Mexican poet and essayist Octavio Paz wrote that the social unrest that the United States was experiencing in the late 1960s was "a rebellion against the idea of progress."[46] According to Paz, the protests of the 1960s revealed the discontent of racial, ethnic, and generational minorities of the post–World War II generation. At that time many young men who were not of voting age and who belonged to groups that had historically been denied suffrage and other civil rights were being drafted to serve in an unpopular war in Vietnam. The result was an intensification of the civil rights, the antiwar, environmental, feminist, black power, and Chicano movements that were demanding fundamental changes in a society and a government that were seen as immoral, corrupt, and anti-human. In the very year that Paz's remarks were published, *I Am Joaquín,* one of the most important poems of the Chicano Movement, also appeared. It too protested that

Yes,
I have come a long way to nowhere,

> Unwillingly dragged by that
>   monstrous, technical
>   industrial giant called Progress
> and Anglo success (*I Am Joaquín* 3).

The social movements of the 1960s were significant because they demonstrated the ability of disenfranchised sectors of society to confront entrenched elites who held power and defined knowledge in an advanced technological society. Paz's argument, however, conflates the political dispute over the ideology of progress with philosophical issues concerning the nature of time and temporal development. In order to draw a distinction between the two aspects of the problem, we need to first identify the critique of scientific rationality that Paz's statement suggests but does not enunciate. This critique views "progress" as the invention and project of rationalist orthodoxies that, in the process of promoting and defending "progress," have tended to marginalize other faculties of thought such as speculative metaphysics and aesthetic intuition. But underlying the critique of "progress" that Paz finds in the political turmoil of the 1960s is a basic question regarding the dominion which the notion of linear time enjoys as the technical and ideological instrument used to realize and measure progress.

In the 1960s and 1970s this dual critique of the ideology of progress and the notion of linear time that underlies it became a way to theorize a "politics of temporality" that might wrest the cognitive category of time (upon which modern scientific and economic development depends) from the exclusive control of an older generation of white male politicians, functionaries, specialists (scientists, sociologists, historians, economists), and special interests (business and industry) and place it in the public domain—in the streets, the arts, the schools—as part of a democratizing trend among the popular movements and advocacy groups already mentioned.

I will relate the critique of progress to two temporal issues that I address in this book: the identification of Chicano timespaces in the poetry of Ricardo Sánchez and the way in which Sánchez uses these Chicano timespaces to represent various communities, such as migrant farm workers, barrio dwellers, and *pintos* or Chicano convicts. But in order to do so, I will continue my discussion of Mexican notions of time and temporality and the influence which these have had on Chicano thought.

At the beginning of the twentieth century, intellectuals such as Henri Bergson in France and José Vasconcelos in Mexico tried to effect changes in the discursive value of time. Bergson was the author of treatises such as *Matter and Memory* (1896) and *Creative Evolution* (1907) in which he developed an intuitive method for critiquing scientific notions of space and time. Bergson's ideas reached Latin America early in the twentieth century and gained a following among the youthful intelligentsia.[47] Enrique Anderson Imbert notes that José Enrique Rodó, the Uruguayan *modernista*, "con o sin la influencia de Bergson, afirma la temporalidad de la vida psíquica. Participamos, dice, del proceso universal; pero, además, tenemos un tiempo propio" [*with or without Bergson's influence, affirms the temporality of psychic experience. "We participate," he says, "in the universal process; but in addition we have a time that is our own"*].[48]

Meanwhile, Mexico too had a youthful rebellion at the beginning of the twentieth century: "El positivismo mexicano tuvo sólida consistencia doctrinaria y prevaleció desde 1860 hasta principios del siglo XX, que es cuando el Ateneo de la Juventud se abandera con William James, Boutroux, Bergson y declara la guerra" [*Mexican positivism took on the solid aspect of doctrine and prevailed from 1860 until the beginning of the twentieth century, when the Ateneo de la Juventud adopts the ideas of William James, Boutroux, and Bergson and declares war*].[49]

The war of ideas launched by the young Mexican and Latin American thinkers was an intellectual prelude to the Mexican Revolution. Jesse A. G. Contreras notes that in their opposition to the scientific positivism of the Porfirio Díaz dictatorship, Vasconcelos and Antonio Caso "held that a deeper insight into reality could be obtained by intuitional or metaphysical understanding which goes beyond the limits of scientific knowledge. Both Vasconcelos and Caso contended that one had to understand the limitations of science and that metaphysics, grounded in aesthetic and ethical insights, had to be restored to philosophy."[50]

As noted at the beginning of this section, nearly fifty years after the Mexican Revolution, Octavio Paz, Mexico's most distinguished poet and man of letters, continued to argue against the scientific rationale of progress. Following the *ateneístas,* he too set out an aesthetic concept of time: "Poems and myths coincide in the transmutation of time into a special temporal category, a past that is always future and ever disposed to be present, *to present itself.*"[51]

Paz's countryman, the novelist Carlos Fuentes, concurs, noting that in the work of contemporary authors "the present is re-presenting and preserving itself in a myth that prevents it from being absolutely either past or future: [human motives] re-present themselves in spaces that may be shuffled, like those of a subterranean labyrinth that contains, within the present, all imaginable spaces and times."[52]

Indeed, in his 1950 book *The Labyrinth of Solitude* Octavio Paz had already written about Mexico's multiple timespaces: "Our territory is inhabited by a number of races speaking different languages and living in different historical levels. A few groups still live as they did in prehistoric times. Others, like the Otomies, who were displaced by successive invasions, exist on the outer margins of history. But it is not necessary to appeal to these extremes: a variety of epochs live side by side in the same areas or a few miles apart, ignoring or devouring one another. . . . Past eras never vanish completely, and blood still drips from all their wounds, even the most ancient. Sometimes the most remote or hostile beliefs and feelings are found together in one city or one soul."[53]

Mexicans have acknowledged, at an official level, the heterogeneity of their population and national experience to a much greater extent than the United States has. Mexico is "officially" a mestizo nation, while the United States has considered itself fundamentally a society of European heritage in which a "melting pot" theory sustains a Eurocentric world view. In Mexico City's Tlatelolco district the government has erected the Plaza of the Three Cultures, where the ruins of an ancient Aztec ceremonial site, a colonial church, and a modern high-rise structure symbolize the contemporaneity of past and present.

Unfortunately, symbolic gestures on the part of the political elite have failed to improve the lives of many Mexicans. For example, Paz writes of "the Indian-Spanish inertia" of the Mexican masses, and Carlos Monsiváis argues that ruling elites in Mexico have consistently promoted modernization while silently reproaching popular sectors that represent the past: "Sin que se diga abiertamente, lo campesino representa el México inmóvil para el criterio modernizador, es el país tristemente anacrónico. . . . los campesinos y los indígenas son el peso muerto de México: producen poco, se reproducen demasiado, no tienen modo de cambiar, son la esencia de la tradición porque sólo miran al pasado" [*While it is not stated openly, the peasantry is seen as a static Mexico by the standards of modernization(;) it is the sadly anachronic portion of the country. . . . the peasants and indigenous people are the dead weight of Mexico: they produce little and reproduce too much, they are unable to change, they are the essence of traditionalism because they only look to the past*].[54] In *The Labyrinth of Solitude* Paz admits: "My thoughts are not concerned with the total population of our country, but rather with a specific group made up of those who are conscious of themselves . . . as Mexicans. Despite the general opinion to the contrary, this group is quite small."[55]

In the era of postmodernity, according to Néstor García Canclini, this social reality "made it possible to think that it didn't make sense to be modern."[56] Theories of postmodernity only seemed to deepen the anachronistic quagmire in which the masses were trapped, subject to the political and market imperatives (time as money) that maintain regimes of linear temporality in both Mexico and the United States.

In this section, I cite a number of Mexican authors whose work provides a context for understanding Ricardo Sánchez's poetic timespaces as well as his critique of U.S. society. Sánchez's work was based on his personal experience and identity as a Chicano; however, we find that its message resonates in the work of contemporary authors from Mexico and other countries. Marcella Aguilar-Henson takes this view, pointing out that, "Ricardo Sánchez's work follows a line of social-political poetry that is found in such major Hispanic poets as Vallejo, Neruda, and Celaya." Américo Ferrari describes César Vallejo's search for poetic expression in a way that recalls Sánchez's search for his voice and freedom:

En la encrucijada de los años veinte-treinta, y entre la estridencia y los manifiestos de las vanguardias, es quizá Vallejo quien encarna de la manera más cabal la libertad del lenguaje poético: sin recetas, sin ideas preconcebidas sobre lo que debe ser la poesía, el poeta peruano bucea entre la angustia y la esperanza en busca de su lenguaje, y el fruto de esa búsqueda es un lenguaje nuevo, un acento inaudito [*In the transition years from the twenties to the thirties, and amid the uproar and manifestos of avant-garde movements, it may be Vallejo who represents most fully the freedom of poetic language: without formulas or prepackaged notions about the nature of poetry, the Peruvian poet dives deeply into the chasm between anguish and hope in search of his language, and the fruit of that search is a new language, an original accent*].[57]

An editor gives the following analysis of Sánchez's complex positioning from a U.S. perspective:

[I]t is impossible and would be foolhardy to try to consider either Dr. Sánchez or his poetry apart from a Chicano identity. On the other hand . . . we must be careful not to lose sight of the fact that Dr. Sánchez is a very accomplished *American* poet, writing in a specifically American idiom and out of a uniquely American experience.

In the case of Ricardo Sánchez that experience is hemispheric; his Americanness cannot be contained by either national borders or presumption's frontiers. . . . In the liveliness of his language, its spontaneity, its singing rhythms, its playfulness, its long sonorities, one observes the outlines of a Beat Sánchez. . . . In the way he appro-

priates personal detail as the envelope for his insights into the human
condition he resembles the confessional writers, Lowell or . . . Sex-
ton.[58]

Philip D. Ortego, who is reminded of William Blake when he reads Sán-
chez, also thinks of Sánchez as a part of the world of poets that includes
Walt Whitman, Rubén Darío, and José Martí. It seems that Ricardo Sánchez
adopted a Latin American as well as a North American literary tradition.
When asked about his relationship to Mexico, Sánchez claimed to live in
"occupied Mexico": "Agglutinated to *México* by culture and certain tradi-
tions, I am no longer *Mexicano*. Chicano is what I am now, for my world
view is different enough from the *Mexicano* . . . though I acknowledge those
traits which we did retain that come from *México*. . . . I think of myself as
being from the northernmost province of the Latin American Continent, a
member of that large community which includes Mexicans, Chicanos,
Puerto Ricans, Salvadorans, Colombians, Peruvians, etc. and can rejoice in
their culture, values, and customs. . . . The human condition is many diverse
conditions, a composite of all, the sum of all, it is not one linear definition
but many definitions—some spiral, some linear, and some fragmented con-
ceptualizations."[59]

Sánchez's eclecticism derives from his sense of *mestizaje*: "[M]y palate and
understanding also include elements which are not indigenous to the Ameri-
cas," he tells his interviewer. José Limón argues that as a Chicano poet, Ri-
cardo Sánchez is "engaged with a collage of influences, none really master
precursors, from pre-Hispanic, indigenous poetics to the 'beat' poetry of the
fifties, to African American culture. The result is an interesting but rhetori-
cally overextended and incoherent poetry in search of a sustaining tra-
dition."[60]

In this study I will show that it is not the case that Sánchez's poetry is
incoherent or overextended, but that the critical tools and efforts to under-
stand his work have been inadequate. I will also identify the tradition in
which Sánchez's poetry operates. A link in that tradition is *I Am Joaquín*,
which strongly influenced Chicano writers of that generation and provided
a nexus between Chicano and *mexicano* discourses. Luis Leal notes the influ-
ence that Mexican history had on *Joaquín*. According to Leal, the figure of
Joaquín "por primera vez en la literatura de su pueblo se identifica con el
hombre y la cultura de México y los realza exaltando su mérito y sus valores.
Directamente se identifica con varios héroes míticos mexicanos; desde el
punto de vista de la historia" [*For the first time in the literature of his (Chicano)
people he identifies with the Mexican and his culture, highlighting them and cele-*

brating their merit and values. He identifies directly with various mythical heroes of Mexico, from the point of view of history].[61]

As a Chicano, Joaquín claims Mexican culture as a universal humanistic legacy:

> The art of our great señores
>> Diego Rivera
>> Siqueiros
>> Orozco is but
> another act of revolution for
>> the salvation of mankind (*I Am Joaquín* 17).

In a later chapter I show how the multiple perspectives of Chicano time-space coincide with the efforts of twentieth-century modernism to subvert linear chronology in literature and art. However, these notions remained in the realm of elite culture and did not have a transforming impact on society until the 1960s.

What Is *Entelequia?*

Chicano writers of Sánchez's generation see their ethnic group as one that must overcome a number of stereotypes and masks. Arturo Madrid-Barela observes that the word *Chicano* "expresses the conflictive historical and cultural experience of a colonized people still politely and euphemistically referred to as Latins, Spanish, Latin Americans, Spanish Americans, Spanish-speaking Americans, Spanish-surnamed Americans, *never* Mexicans, and only recently Mexican Americans." Paz reminds us that at critical moments of their development, nations and peoples, like individual human beings, will reflect upon their situation.[62]

What does it mean to be Chicano rather than Mexican or American? What answers did Chicanos give to these fundamental questions of identity? According to Texas poet Tino Villanueva,

> En resumidas cuentas, se podría decir que, hoy por hoy, el término *chicano* abarca todo un universo ideológico que sugiere no sólo la audaz postura de autodefinición y desafío, sino también el empuje regenerativo de autovoluntad y autodeterminación, potenciado todo ello por el latido vital de una conciencia de crítica social; de orgullo étnico-cultural; de concientización de clase y de política. Ello, en conjunto, coincide con un decidido y sincero afán por cambiar estructuras sociopolíticas, y con una verdadera pasión humanística que

obran en aras de conseguir la justicia, la igualdad, la calidad de la vida, y devolver al individuo concreto la conciencia entera de la dignidad personal. Tal es el ideal genérico que impera en nuestro compromiso social y que enciende toda esperanza utópica por superar, finalmente, la marginación continua y la angustia prolongada [*Finally, the term Chicano nowadays encompasses an entire ideological universe that suggests not only an audacious stance of self-definition and confrontation, but a regenerative impulse of will and self-determination, all of which is made possible by the vital rhythms of social criticism and a growing awareness of ethnic and cultural pride. Together, these characteristics coincide with a firm and sincere effort to change social and political structures, and a truly humanistic passion that works to obtain justice, equality, and a higher level of life that returns to the individual a full sense of personal dignity. Such is the general principle that governs social commitment and that sparks utopian hopes for finally overcoming an ongoing marginalization and a prolonged anguish*].[63]

Villanueva's definition of the term *Chicano* suggests the scope of Ricardo Sánchez's concept of "entelechy" or *entelequia*. The word appears in Sánchez's work in 1978 in a screenplay titled "Entelequia III." Later, he plays with the term in a piece titled: "—ENTEQUILA, entelechy, hijola pero Entelequía: prose-poem dedicated to Carlos Rosas, muralist/artist/compadre/ & creator of *entelequía* apt mural at 6th & campbell—."

Carlos Rosas, who is the godfather of Jacinto-Temilotzín, Sánchez's youngest son, created a large mural in El Paso's Segundo Barrio. Unlike Sánchez, whose ancestors had lived for generations in the Indo-Hispano communities of northern New Mexico, Carlos Rosas, Alurista, Abelardo Delgado, Octavio Romano, and a number of other Chicano cultural figures of the period represented the large population of Mexican immigrants who had been transmitting Mexican cultural and intellectual values northward for half a century, ever since Mexico's revolutionary period (1910–1920). Like Sánchez, the majority of prominent Chicano writers, activists, and intellectuals were born in the United States, but as Jesse Contreras notes:

The central themes of Mexican philosophy were the revolt against positivist universalism in the sphere of culture and the search for the essence of the Mestizo culture (in contrast to European culture). These themes have obvious affinities to those of the Chicano Movement. The context of Mexican philosophy was a political struggle against a colonial heritage, and this context had an obvious appeal to activists who saw themselves as spokespersons for their own colonized peoples. The problems involved in becoming a "culture for itself" seemed identical in both cases. The Mexican philosophical tradition seemed to hold the key to defining the uniqueness of Chicanos in contrast both to mainstream American culture and to the culture of other minority groups in the United States. In the absence of an alternative Chicano Studies tradition, the appeal of the Mexican philosophical tradition proved to be irresistible.[64]

Thus, it comes as no surprise when, in the United Farm Workers' "Plan of Delano," César Chávez speaks for a budding Chicano Movement when he states that "we are sons of the Mexican Revolution, a revolution of the poor seeking bread and justice."[65]

In Sánchez's poem to Carlos Rosas, he mentions the artist's difficulties in creating the mural, then he praises the work and explores its meaning. The mural is dominated by three figures that represent the Chicano experience in terms of the spiritual development of a child. With this imagery Carlos Rosas is able to depict a struggle across timespace as tragic experience that makes possible a vital re-encounter with life and dignity. According to Sánchez, the work communicates the range of feelings and ideas associated with the concept of *entelequia:*

what matters now	
is the existence	
of entelequía, mural	
que cantagrita con pasión	*that sings and cries out passionately*
the exequies of being,	
la realización	*the realization*
of children becoming	
algo fortalizante . . .	*something fortifying*
el águila	*the eagle*
vigila	*keeps vigil*
cultura, y protége	*on our culture, and protects*
lo frágil del desarrollo,	*a fragile development,*
y en el proceso	*and in the process*
del juego social,	*of the social game,*
niños vitales	*lively children*
juegan bajo el sol	*play 'neath the sun*

en una distancia   *in a sun-bathed*
bañada   *distance*
y asoleada ("ENTEQUILA, entelechy" 119–22).

The word *entelequia* derives from a Greek term in Aristotle's philosophy which regained currency in the writings of modern philosophers. According to Spanish philosopher and novelist Miguel de Unamuno, "Aristotle considered the soul the substantial form of the body: the entelechy, but not a substance."[66] In his important essay on dynamics German philosopher G. W. Leibniz writes that

> primitive force (which is nothing but the first entelechy) corresponds to the *soul or substantial form.* But, for that reason, it pertains only to general causes, which are insufficient to explain the phenomena . . . once these [general] principles have been established, then afterwards, whenever we deal with the immediate and specific efficient causes of natural things, we should take no account of souls or entelechies, no more than we should drag in useless faculties or inexplicable sympathies. For that first and most general efficient cause should not enter into the treatment of particulars, except insofar as we contemplate the ends which divine wisdom had in thus ordering things, so that we might lose no opportunity for singing his praises and for singing most beautiful hymns.[67]

Leibniz's statement represents what Morton Bloomfield and Charles Dunn see as the transition from "wisdom, the world-view of most traditional societies [to] the fundamental world-view of science." According to these authors, "Poets in particular are regarded as the discoverers, preservers, and transmitters of wisdom."[68] More than modern science or even modern poetry Chicano poetry maintains a connection to the wisdom of its oral tradition. For example, Sánchez becomes a purveyor of sage advice when he writes, without a hint of irony, "Let us struggle together that we might all be worthier . . . for wisdom dictates this . . . if we fail to find meaningful areas of commonality, then we shall doom ourselves and turn to hate and total destruction. It shall be through sharing that we will create a moral world" ("ONE YEAR AFTER . . . ," preface to *Canto y grito mi liberación* 16). Bloomfield and Dunn note that modern literature and science are founded upon the rationality of wisdom, although modern poetics generally abhors the didactic and moralizing worldview of wisdom "considered to be dull and repetitious." According to Deleuze, with Nietzsche, modern philosophy "must begin by stringing up the moralists. . . . Let us face up to all these sages, illustrious for millennia; all of them old women." Nietzsche, in quest of an extreme vision, is determined to burn all bridges to the past as he marches relentlessly toward a brave new world. And if we are indeed condemned to the eternal return it is because the past returns of its own accord and not because the philosopher chooses to return. But on behalf of wisdom poetry Bloomfield and Dunn maintain that: "Teaching has always been recognized as an important function of poetry. Early poets were teachers, diviners, prophets, and preservers of tradition. Part of their sacred office was to admonish and warn rulers and subjects alike, and to hand on the accumulated wisdom of the past."[69]

Furthermore, we should not stereotype the wisdom of the past: "It must not be thought, however, that wisdom and tradition are necessarily conservative forces," write Bloomfield and Dunn. "They may be radical as well as conservative. The attainment of harmony between the rules of wisdom and the way of the world may lead to strong changes as well as to the maintenance of the *status quo*." Cordelia Candelaria relates these traditional practices to the "context of ritual" in which Chicano poets function. Such poets have not surrendered their license to scrutinize "the immediate and specific efficient causes of 'natural' things" and to also sing, praise, or lament the universal order.[70] Another such poet is Pablo Neruda, whose *Odas elementales* and *Canto general* elevate the everyday reality of common people and things to give them a cosmic significance that contravenes Leibniz's injunction against admixing the *entelequia* with mundane, natural phenomena.

A further sense of Ricardo Sánchez's *entelequia* is found in the following words from his collection *Hechizospells*: "I realize that there are many Chicano worlds—some of which gestated and gave birth to the Chicano Movement in the dire hope that others, with more mobility and access to resources, would take that explosive/implosive momentum racing hectically toward dignity, justice, opportunity, liberation, peace, and humanization and thus help catapult both La Raza and humankind into the 21st Century and therein see a human race conscious of its moral responsibility, acting humanistically, and affirming the edifying creativity of human diversity" (*Hechizospells* 8).

In *Canto y grito mi liberación* and *Hechizospells* we find states of desperation and self-hatred, as well as an awareness of Chicano pride and human dignity. But woven through the *cábula*, satire, and humor is this defining characteristic which Sánchez calls *entelequia* and which is, in part, a teleology that recognizes the historic struggle of Chicanos while expressing confidence in the community's future development.

In addition to the Rosas mural the term *entelequia* is associated with another project from the late 1970s. This was a short film entitled *Entelequia*

III that was produced in Utah while Sánchez was teaching at the University of Utah in Salt Lake City. Sánchez authored the script and had the lead acting role. In a draft of the script he offers the following definition of *entelequia* taken from *Webster's New World Dictionary:* "from the Greek entelecheia, the actualizing of potential in Aristotelian philosophy and/or the realization of true existence; and from a vitalist perspective, the immanent force which controls and directs life and its development."[71]

Sánchez specifically dedicates a number of poems and essays to this concept, and in them he brings together elements that are peculiarly Chicano and also broadly humanistic. The use of the Aristotelian term "entelechy" or *entelequia* suggests a connection to Aristotle's *Poetics,* which defines the theory and practice of tragic drama. Yet the poet's concerns in *Hechizospells* and *Canto y grito mi liberación* are painfully immediate and his means of expressing them characteristically Chicano. So it seems that Sánchez's utopian thought and his voice of *liberación* are offered as seeds from which a tragic sense of freedom can grow. In his poems liberation becomes a physical and metaphysical struggle, an experience of solitude and solidarity through which Chicano literature fosters the brotherhood and sisterhood of *carnalismo:* "[O]n a deeper level of compassion, i.e., the Chicano talks of *Carnalismo*[,] the process of human realization that we are all a *oneness* that goes beyond words, for we must ultimately accept human equitability on a flesh, blood, racial/ethnic, intellectual, mental, emotional and spiritual plane. Only then will we [be] able to deal with the humanistic/social needs crying out for resolution. The world is indeed too small and people must broaden their scopes if racism and other problems are ever to be resolved."[72] In verse he maintains that *carnalismo* must extend to *carnalas* as well, because it entails a common struggle for liberation:

ay, mujer libérate,	*oh woman, free yourself,*
cantagrita tu pasión humanizante	*singshout your humanizing passion*
y lánzate hacia tu liberación,	*and seek out your liberation,*
. . . .	
haz de tu vida	*make of your life*
un ritmo, un camino libre,	*a rhythm, an open road,*
cosecha la grandeza que aspira	*harvest the aspiring greatness*
en tu mentealmacuerpo,	*of your mindsoulbody*
lanzándote creativamente.	*as you launch out and create.*
No te dejes oprimir,	*Abolish oppression,*
pues tú también tienes derecho	*for you too have the right*
a fuertemente vivir	*to strongly live*

y reponsabilidades que cumplir . . .	*and responsibilities to fulfill . . .*
no odies, pero libérate, carnala,	*hate not, but free yourself, carnala,*
y date el valor que vibra dentro de tí	*and claim the valor that pulses within you*

(*Hechizospells* 311–12).

But in order to provide a still broader answer to the question that heads this section, we must consult additional authorities. *Webster's Third New International Dictionary* (1976) defines "entelechy" as a philosophical term, "something that contains or realizes an end or final cause." Or "a suppositious immanent but immaterial agency held by some vitalists to regulate or direct the vital processes of an organism especially toward the achievement of maturity—compare élan vital."

Webster's entries for "entelechy" offer a chain of related comparisons, terms, and concepts that revolve around the French philosopher Henri Bergson. The first of these, as noted above, is *élan vital,* which is defined as "the creative principle and fundamental reality held by Bergson to be immanent in all organisms and responsible for evolution." The dictionary then suggests a relationship between *élan vital* and the term "creative evolution," which is defined as "evolution conceived as creative rather than a mechanically explicable process—see Bergsonism; compare élan vital, emergent evolution." Turning to the entry for "bergsonism," we find: "the theories of the philosopher Bergson according to whom the world is a process of creative evolution in which the novelty of successive phenomena rather than the constancy of natural law is the significant fact, reality being regarded as time or duration that is the same as free motion and that is the expression of a vital impetus or creative force while the space world of science and common sense is taken to be the interpretation put upon sense images in the interest of practical activity and social cooperation and as a falsification of free-movement reality so that a true apprehension of reality is to be gained not by the analytical procedures of mathematics and science but by that intuition that can grasp wholes as such." Finally, we find "vitalism" defined first as "a doctrine that the functions of a living organism are due to a vital principle (as an élan vital or entelechy) distinct from physiochemical forces—compare mechanism, organicism" and secondly as "a doctrine that the processes of life are not explicable by the laws of physics and chemistry alone and that life is in some part self-determining instead of mechanistically determined—compare organicism, orthogenesis."

This chain of terms and meanings, which seems to expand indefinitely, took me from the dictionary to the French philosopher Gilles Deleuze, au-

thor of *Bergsonism* (1991). I consulted this text in search of Ricardo Sánchez
and detected an echo of the poet's *canto y grito* in the philosopher's discussion
of "freedom": "the *élan vital* was able to use matter to create an instrument
of freedom, 'to make a machine which should triumph over mechanism,' 'to
use the determinism of nature to pass through the meshes of the net which
this very determinism has spread.' Freedom has precisely this physical sense:
'to detonate' an explosive, to use it for more and more powerful move-
ments."[73] We need only substitute the *pinto* poet's image of prison bars for
Bergson's "meshes of the net" in order to hear the resonance of this philoso-
phy in terms of *pinto* poetics.

These examples of Bergsonist influence on Sánchez's work are evidence
of the impact of Mexican thinkers and artists on Chicano culture of the 1960s
and 1970s. The writings of Vasconcelos and Paz and the muralism of Rivera,
Siqueiros, and Orozco enabled Chicano literature and culture to reenact the
systemic clash of pre-modern and scientific world views that has been oc-
curring in Mexico and other parts of the world for the last two centuries.
Chicano literature documents a particular instance of this phenomenon by
means of a hybrid, folk-based poetics that uses pre-modern as well as modern
and postmodern timespaces to contest the authority exerted by linear tempo-
rality and the science-based ideology of progress.[74]

The emergence of Chicano cultural and temporal diversity can thus be
seen as a moment in a series of confrontations between "modern" and "ar-
chaic" world views. Without being the decisive or culminating moment, the
Chicano Renaissance was, nevertheless, part of the contemporary intellectual
climate that questioned the very concepts of modernity and progress. In
Bergson's system this sort of crisis is not necessarily the result of a fundamen-
tal contradiction or opposition between two world views but merely an error
or lack of insight in framing the issue. In Bergson's view, "False problems are
of two sorts, 'nonexistent problems,' defined as problems whose very terms
contain a confusion between the 'more' and the 'less'; and 'badly stated' ques-
tions, so defined because their terms represent badly analyzed composites."[75]
Bergson's method for differentiating between real and false problems relied
on intuition which, according to Deleuze, "is neither a feeling, an inspira-
tion, nor a disorderly sympathy, but a fully developed method, one of the
most fully developed methods in philosophy."[76]

Bergson's intuitive method provides a way to identify errors, failures, and
lacunae within the modern scientific method, which has become a privileged
and exclusive form of knowledge designed to exclude "archaic" forms such
as metaphysics and wisdom.

CHAPTER 3

The Recovery of Chicano Discursive Timespace

The poetry of Ricardo Sánchez develops a number of Chicano voices/languages/subjectivities/constituencies/audiences. Among these are the multilingual pachuco, the *pinto,* the mestizo/a, and the migrant. In the 1980s feminist writers and critics questioned the male-centered narratives and identities associated with Chicano literature and popular culture. They produced narratives of male dominance and oppression and theories of gender difference which focused on the role of neglected Chicana/o subjectivities. Some of the central figures of Chicano literature of the 1970s, including the pachuco, *la pinta,* and the migrant farm worker, were demythified by Chicana feminist critique even as they were being popularized by Hollywood and the media and appropriated for Anglocentric readings in disciplines such as cultural theory and popular culture studies.

But well before 1980 the incompatibility between the Chicano Movement's male leadership and the demands of Chicana feminism was quite evident. In the seminal anthology *This Bridge Called My Back: Writings by Radical Women of Color* (1981) editors Cherríe Moraga and Gloria Anzaldúa attempted to forge gender-based alliances between women of color who deplored the sexism and homophobia within their own ethnic communities as well as discrimination on the basis of class and race practiced by mainstream women's rights groups. Certainly, the emergence of a forceful Chicana literary and critical discourse in the 1980s broadened and enriched what had been a male-dominated field. But this development and the radical activism, particularly in California, of gay and lesbian communities confronting the specter of AIDS had a telling effect on heterosexual Chicano male representation in literature and the arts. In addition to the ideological and cultural challenges which feminists and gays posed to traditional Chicano world views, these groups were also extremely competitive in terms of gaining sympathy and support from mainstream audiences, critics, and donors in the wider cultural community.

In this environment, shaped by competition for scarce resources as well as by cultural difference, it became convenient to stereotype the literature, film, and theater of *pintos,* pachucos, and Movement Chicanos as "phallocentric" and retrograde, and thus relegate the material to a period of *early* (read *"inferior"*) Chicano cultural production in order to create space in the cultural vanguard for emerging Chicana/o voices. My effort to reopen and recirculate a discussion of Ricardo Sánchez and the Chicano poetry of the 1970s comes at a time when there are more poorly educated *pintos* in jails and prisons than ever before. And as Genaro Padilla reminds us, there are more multilingual mestizos, homegirls, and *vatos* in Chicano communities throughout the United States, suffering the effects of racism, drug addiction, gang warfare, and economic exploitation.[1] These communities remain an enigma to a social system that denies them cultural representation.

But on what basis can Chicanos establish the authority and authenticity of "our" cultural text and "our" literary production? Rafael Pérez-Torres claims that "anxiety about authenticity runs throughout a good deal of Chicano literary criticism."[2] But Pérez-Torres fails to contextualize this "anxiety" that may be the result of political factionalism, not just among literary critics but among Chicanos in general. For example, in *I Am Joaquín* we find a protest against

> Strangers
> Who
> changed our language
> and plagiarized our deeds
>
> > as feats of valor
> > of their own.
> They frowned upon our way of life
> and took what they could use.
> > Our Art
> > Our Literature
> > Our music, they ignored (17).

This passage presents anew an issue that was discussed and researched during the 1930s by scholars of the so-called "Mexican American generation."[3] These individuals documented the anti-Mexican bias of U.S. institutions, including the academic establishment. As Joaquín puts it, "They frowned upon our way of life." The work of George I. Sánchez, Arthur L.

Campa, and Carlos E. Castañeda, three scholars whom Mario T. García calls "the triumvirate of major Mexican-American intellectuals between the 1930s and the 1960s," provided an endogenous perspective on Chicano communities that were either ignored or maligned by Anglo American scholars.[4] More recently, Raymund Paredes discovered that "American responses to the Mexicans grew out of the attitudes deeply rooted in Anglo American tradition. Americans had strong feelings against Catholics and Spaniards and expected their evils to have been fully visited upon the Mexicans." According to Paredes, "The core of Anglo-American notions about Mexicans had always been an assumed depravity."[5] Historian Rodolfo Acuña (for whom the term "Mexican" is often synonymous with "Chicano") claimed that "the state institutionalized racism and justified discrimination toward Mexicans. Institutions such as the schools and churches and mythmakers such as historians reinforced and legitimated a multitiered society based on class and race. . . . Mexican nationalism, which flourished well into the twentieth century, was nurtured by their almost total exclusion from North American cultural and social institutions."[6] According to another commentator, Cecil Robinson, "the image of the American as aggressively hostile to the Mexican appears continually in modern American writing."[7] Prior to the Movement years, Américo Paredes cited the words of Walter Prescott Webb, "the most distinguished historian Texas has produced": "Without disparagement, it may be said that there is a cruel streak in the Mexican nature. . . . The Mexican warrior . . . was, on the whole, inferior to the Comanche and wholly unequal to the Texan. The whine of the leaden slugs stirred in him an irresistible impulse to travel with rather than against the music. He won more victories over the Texans by parley than by force of arms. For making promises—and for breaking them—he had no peer." Paredes wonders with a hint of sarcasm "what [Webb's] opinion might have been when he was in a less scholarly mood and not looking at the Mexican from the objective point of view of the historian."[8]

In the 1960s and 1970s Chicano scholars of the World War II and Korean War generations became part of a larger movement of cultural pride and revindication known as the Chicano Movement. The Movement provided Chicano scholars such as Américo Paredes, Luis Leal, and others a constituency for which they could develop a new literary history of the Southwest, one written from a different cultural perspective. In the 1970s Ricardo Romo and Raymund Paredes continued to assert the need for a new approach aimed at overcoming the biases of traditional American scholarship: "[S]uch studies of Chicanos have been marred frequently if not by antipathy, then by misunderstanding. Any scholar interested in the Chicano experience must begin by breaking through thick layers of stereotypes and misconceptions. . . . One of the most persistent stereotypes of Chicanos afloat in American culture holds them to be passive, inarticulate and virtually silent. Indeed, our ignorance of early Chicano literature derives largely from the assumption that a passive, silent people create none."[9] And as Francisco A. Lomelí has reminded us:

> Anglo settlers experienced shock and dismay at the degree of cultural hybridization among Mexicans, regarding Native American foods, customs, and racial makeup as mongoloid and therefore unacceptable. In their eyes, Mexicans were a race of "degenerated," "contaminated," or "colorized" Spaniards. In addition, they could not begin to conceptualize how Spaniards and Indians might have merged into a new social breed, lacking the proper genetic paradigms in their past to understand such intermingling. Anglo American settlers departed from premise of cultural essentialism whereas Mexicans have always defied it. . . . The Mexican background in American culture continues to be stigmatized as backward, racially inferior, religiously primitive, psychologically fatalistic, and socially deviant.[10]

The outpouring of Chicano artistic and political expression in the 1960s and 1970s was an unprecedented effort to lay some of these stereotypes to rest, and by the mid-1970s Luis Leal claimed that "in a relatively short time, Chicano literature has not only established itself as a significant part of minority literatures in the United States, and, at the same time, of literature in general, but has produced a criticism that has kept up with the rapid changes taking place."[11]

Although there were surely excesses during the Movement years, the "anxiety about authenticity" detected in certain critics was not gratuitous.[12] What I am suggesting is that this anxiety was the consequence of a long history of enmity and distrust between Anglos and Chicanos, gringos and *mexicanos,* which has left its mark not only on critics but on Chicano poets and on their audiences as well. For example, Ricardo Sánchez's answer to the question "What is Chicano literature?" was sometimes (but not always) a simple one: "What makes Chicano literature *Chicano* is the fact that it is created by Chicanos and expresses the way Chicanos see not only their lives, but the lives of other people" (*Hechizospells* xi).

But if Chicano literature was in part an ideological bulwark designed to counter the massive anti-Mexican propaganda originating in the larger society, it also had to confront internal differences among Chicanos and Chicanas. The dread of real and imagined enemies, of outsiders, spies, and *vendidos* led to turf battles and splinterings along class, gender, and other political divisions. While Ricardo Sánchez's ethnocentric definition of Chicano literature reflects these conditions, it nevertheless represents only one facet of his complex, multidimensional perspective. For an alternative definition of Chicano literature we can turn to an article by Luis Leal in which he defends a more open and confident understanding of Chicano literature. He argues that "the simplest but also the narrowest way of defining Chicano literature is to say that it is the literature written by Chicanos." In Leal's view, Chicano literature should be a way to encourage openness and breadth. He asks, "why should the Chicano experience be limited to the *campesino* struggle, the description of life in the barrio, or the social confrontation with the majority culture?" If it remained limited to the Movement's agenda, Chicano literature would stagnate and decline. Thus, Leal called for "new definitions of Chicano literature, which are not restricted only to social, realistic works . . . and can account not only for Chicano literature as it exists today, but for what is to be written in the future."[13]

There is no "anxiety about authenticity" here, and Leal, unlike Pérez-Torres, does not overlook the history of Chicanos but tries to persuade them to deal with the tragic aspects of their history by looking to the future. Leal's definition of Chicano literature is thus consistent with Sánchez's larger view: "Chicano literature is very encompassing—it is not only poetry and stories about life in the tenements nor is it only protest. It is such a panoramic state of flux that it has room for writings that deal with love, hope, aspirations, death, existence, etc. Because it merges all human experience, and also because Chicano writers are as diverse as the different bloods making up La Raza, Chicano literature also deals with existentialism on a transcendental level. . . . It seems, much of the time, that Chicano literature keeps time to the beat of many different drums. Sometimes, the drums which beat on pyramids join cathedral tintinnabulations, and the attunations leap historical chapters only to join with the chimes of Avon-Amerika-Calling."[14]

One way to grasp the Chicano critique of U.S. history and the discursive practices which that history entails is to confront as directly as possible the question of time. Ricardo Sánchez attempts to do this in his poetry, with narrative representations of his own lived experience and that of his community. This chapter engages Sánchez's figure of the *pinto* and the prison, the pachuco and the barrio, the journeys and toil of the migrant worker, not as themes or character types but as the inhabitants of particular Chicano timespaces. This strategy allows me first to show how notions of time determine culture, in the sense that differences in the way time is constructed and used in different cultures will produce variations in cultural comportment and expectations,[15] and, secondly, to argue that such culturally constructed notions of time, including the Western notion of linear time, be granted a circumscribed cultural validity rather than universality.

The Timespace of Chicano Poetry

As a poet who was encaged for nine years in state prisons in California and Texas, Ricardo Sánchez vividly recounts his experience of temporal oppression. Time is not an abstract concept for the *pinto* facing a second felony conviction, nor is its dynamic a linear one. The passage quoted in my introduction to this book demonstrates how time becomes a three-dimensional, ironic, and highly animated companion to the poet, who takes the opportunity to transfigure it into anything, anything at all except the linear burden that he already knows he must bear:

> time winks again at me,
> it clings to my fingers,
> strokes my mind and soul,
> its scabs laugh and mock me
> as it slides on bars
> and jiveass hops on my bunk
> and bounces off the walls and floors (*Selected Poems* 36).

In Sánchez's poem "Soledad," incarceration is a form of solitude akin to death, which must inevitably pass through the dark realm of madness. In Sánchez's poetry madness is a residue of the timespaces of *la pinta* and the barrio. It is a trait or condition common to those crazy *pintos* and pachucos who flow out of the barrio, into *la pinta* and back again, indefinitely, until they either die or are killed. These are the *vatos* that *la raza* appropriately calls *locos*. How do they get to be that way?

The *pinto* or convict serving a long prison sentence is oppressed by the linearity of time, which he can neither evade nor escape. The *pinto* poetry of Ricardo Sánchez depicts this sense of oppression as a madness that either stimulates the prisoner's imagination or provokes a sort of pathological frenzy, a loss of will and rational control that leads to withdrawal, drug addiction, and death. The convict's punishment, then, may take many forms. Although he is deprived of many things, including his freedom, dignity, privacy, and companionship, the burden of time is the most fundamental punishment that the *pinto's* mind must bear. But in Sánchez's poem

"Soledad," the *pinto* becomes aware of another kind of aesthetic temporality. In the throes of an intense and immediate pain, he realizes that humanity itself is an "eternal convict" under a sentence of death. All earthly souls, all entelechies are bound by the tragedy and mortality of the human condition. This awareness of an alternative temporality allows the *pinto* poet a respite from the everyday reality of linear time. Sánchez's *pinto* aesthetic of the human condition thus seeks consolation in an eternal, tragic sensibility that helps the convict to survive his sentence of silent, suffering solitude until he can shout his *cantogrito* of liberation.

Later, Sánchez will juxtapose conventional notions of linear time and spatialized thought with the chronotopes of Chicano literature in order to show that the dominant Western chronotope is a mere convention, a social myth that serves the existing political and economic order. In the pages that follow I argue that an oppositional model of temporal development is present in Chicano literature and that this model develops, in part, with help from outside influences such as Mexican literature and culture, which reinforce the long experience of Chicanos under the domination of an American capitalist economy that is fundamentally responsible for the ideological construction and regulation of time.

As an itinerant poet who participated in readings and speaking engagements across the United States and abroad, Sánchez exhibited a varied repertoire of performance styles, engaging audiences with his lyrical, theatrical, and comedic talents. Chicanos recognized in Sánchez's performances the *cábula* of the pachuco and ex-*pinto*, as well as the innovator in Chicano letters who was also a spokesman for *la causa*. In the 1970s Sánchez's name was routinely mentioned with those of Abelardo Delgado, Alurista, José Montoya, and Raúl Salinas on the short list of leading Chicano poets who cultivated a popular, nonacademic orality that spoke to the concerns of Chicano youth and working-class families, many of whom confronted the daily challenges of survival.

Cordelia Candelaria has seen this popular poetry as ritual: "Both in its overt replication of a communal rite through the poem/performance and in its recognition of an ethnopoetic tradition extending from the present to the primitive past, Chicano poetry is most fully comprehensible within a context of ritual." For Philip Ortego, Sánchez's poetry is part of an ancient, universal vocation, "a poet's way of knowledge."[16] Ortego's reading identifies the poet with the shaman or prophet and his verses, with the language of wisdom and the sacred. The poet's metaphors and imagery are part of the ritual that names the community, as in *I Am Joaquín*:

I am Joaquín

. . . .

La Raza!
Mejicano
  Español!
    Latino!
      Hispano!
        Chicano!
or whatever I call myself,
        I look the same
        I feel the same
        I cry
          and
       Sing the same

I am the masses of my people and
I refuse to be absorbed.
        I am Joaquín (*I Am Joaquín* 20).

Through the recitation of myth and legend, often sung in the sacred tongue of the ancestors, the community attempts to ward off external enemies, as well as the internal heterodoxies that threaten social cohesion.

In Europe as elsewhere, poetry traces its origins to tribal myths, legends, and epic songs that were composed and recited orally by anonymous bards. The principal functions of these poems were praise, blame, or lamentation.[17] Influenced by the Greek epics of Homer, the Roman poet Virgil produced an epic narrative, the *Aeneid,* which celebrated and mythologized the lineage of the Emperor Augustus.[18] In medieval Spain the distinction between popular and high poetry was constructed within a rigidly hierarchical and theocratic society. While educated monks, clerics, and nobles produced and copied texts for a literate elite, traveling minstrels, known as *juglares* in Spain, served both the educated aristocracy and the illiterate folk by proffering entertainment, news, and information to both groups.[19]

To the extent that they are participants in the cultural traditions of the West, Mexican Americans are heirs to this European legacy. However, in the 1960s Chicanos made it known that as mestizos they would not be limited by this European heritage. At that time the poet Alurista fulfilled the role of a postmodern Chicano *juglar,* bringing the people news and knowledge of Mesoamerican rather than European timespaces. Alurista was an exponent of *in xóchitl in cuicatl,* the Náhuatl/Aztecan term for poetry, rendered in

Spanish as *flor y canto* (flower and song). Alurista's poetry, influenced by the work of Mexican scholars such as Miguel de León Portilla, stirred much interest and discussion of the indigenous branch of the Chicano/mestizo cultural heritage. Its flowering as part of the Chicano Movement demonstrated that this branch, which had been forced underground by European conquest, had not completely lost its languages, cadences, myths, and customs. Luis Valdez, the founder and director of El Teatro Campesino, fostered interest in ancient Maya philosophy, just as Alurista's poetry recovered the timespace of Nahua culture and mythology.[20]

From this interest in their pre-Columbian legacy, Chicanos began looking to Aztlán as one of the most important of the Aztec myths for their resurgent culture. According to tradition Aztlán was the site of the ancient Aztec homeland in the far north, whence this tribe of warriors gradually migrated southward, to settle eventually in Anáhuac, the Valley of Mexico, and found their capital, Tenochtitlan.[21] In his poetry and in "El plan espiritual de Aztlán," which he helped to formulate at the Chicano Youth Conference in Denver in 1969, Alurista popularized the notion that northern Mexico and the American Southwest were, in fact, Aztlán. Alurista and other Chicanos appropriated the myth of Aztlán and extended its meaning to denote not only the ancient Aztec homeland but also the site of a new Chicano nation.[22] They stated that "[a] nation autonomously free, culturally, socially, economically, and politically will make its own decisions on the usage of our lands, the taxation of our goods, the utilization of our bodies for war, the determination of justice (reward and punishment), and the profit of our sweat. EL PLAN DE AZTLAN IS THE PLAN OF LIBERATION!"[23]

Chicano literature was part of the process of disseminating these ideas among Chicanos. While many, mostly small, Chicano publishing ventures were springing up in the Southwest and elsewhere, Alurista and other activists in California organized the Festival Flor y Canto poetry festivals. The first of these gatherings took place in 1973 at the University of Southern California and, thereafter, in a number of southwestern cities: Austin, San Antonio, Albuquerque, and Phoenix. The guiding principle of the organizers was as follows: "Oral presentation, *recitación* or *declamación,* is the established mode of literary expression at the *Flor y Canto* Festivals. Through this mode reverberates the spirit and the reality of Chicanos; and a national character, *chicanismo,* is the permeating refrain of each *recitación.* Originality and independence of expression are still within the realm of this national art as it is practiced and enjoyed by Chicanos throughout Aztlán, and as it is presented at the *Flor y Canto* Festivals."[24]

The published festival anthologies were "the subsequent reflection, in print" of literary symposia in which a "collective portrait of a creative community in action ensues, contributing to the vivid evolution of a mestizo aesthetic in the United States."[25] The original concept of national Flor y Canto festivals did not survive into the 1980s but was instead superseded by local events featuring Chicano poets, musicians, artists, and *teatro* troupes. These later gatherings tended to borrow the format and the generic title of the first *"floricantos."* Many were held on college campuses or in conjunction with scholarly conferences and became an occasion for Chicanos to celebrate and explore their cultural identity through art, music, poetry, and scholarship. The festivals provided an opportunity for both new and established writers to gather with friends and rivals to *comadrear* and trade barbs, *cábula,* and *carnalismo.* But they were also a way to demonstrate that Chicano/a literature was not a matter to be left in books, for the exclusive use of academics and critics. As Alurista stated in *Flor y Canto II,* the second festival anthology, one objective of the organizing committee was "to promote the appreciation of our literature by trying to take our works to people of the community not necessarily enrolled in university programs."[26]

Aztlán was the site, or more precisely, the timespace of this creative activity called the Festivales de Flor y Canto. However, some critics fail to make the necessary distinctions between Chicano timespace and the linear chronology of European tradition. For example, Rafael Pérez-Torres contends that "the deployment of pre-Cortesian symbology invokes a mythic 'memory.' . . . Chicano literature thus seems to 'reveal' connections between the troubled and unfulfilling present of Chicano disempowerment and a richer, fuller, more holistic but lost past."[27] This view would portray Chicanos as victims whose literature invokes a utopian, ahistorical, and illegitimate Golden Age. But I would argue that the opposite is true, that Chicano literature, as a product of mestizo values and history, represents a legitimate effort to recontextualize indigenous experience as part of Chicano identity in order to more fully recover those timespaces that have been unduly excluded by and from the linear notion of American history.

We have seen that in his effort to fuse postmodern theory and Chicano criticism, Rafael Pérez-Torres constructs a narrative of Chicano poetry that valorizes recent developments while minimizing the work of prior movements and authors. The critic does so by disguising residual notions of Comtean progress as postmodern theory. His ostensibly "progressive" argument harks back to a reactionary positivism that minimizes the recurring timespaces of Chicano literature that are marked by baroque styles and romantic sensibilities, as well as documentary realism. As Rosaura Sánchez notes,

"Chicano literature published since 1959 has, in fact, continued for the most part to lie within a heterogeneous literary space, as much modernist as pre-modernist, given its assimilation of older literary genres like sketches of manners and characters, folktales, chronicles, and other romantic and realist forms. . . . This is not to deny innovation in Chicano literature, evident in the case of writers like Alurista, for example, whose experimentation in poetry is now being matched in prose."[28]

What Rosaura Sánchez describes as a "heterogeneous literary space" is indeed a heterogeneous literary *temporality,* or an example of the multiple literary chronotopes theorized by Bakhtin. Unfortunately, her formulation reproduces the lamentable spatialization of thought that has been promoted by many, including Juan Bruce-Novoa, in the area of Chicano criticism. This spatialization of thought is a problem that Henri Bergson warned against decades ago but that continues to be one of our more damaging mental habits.[29] Rosaura Sánchez demonstrates a fine grasp of the concept of multiple Chicano timespaces, yet she seems to exemplify Ricardo Sánchez's observation, quoted near the end of chapter 1, that critics tend to be reactive, and lack the creative suppleness of the artist: "[C]ertain postmodernist strategies can be discerned in the literature, although these may be difficult to describe since critics often characterize postmodernist texts by a number of techniques and strategies already to be found in modernist literature or in the avant-garde strain of modernist literature, such as the fragmentation of time and space, shifts in narrative perspective, self-reflexivity, parody, emphasis on codes and language, intertextuality, ambiguity, multiplicity of narrative planes, cinematographic techniques, etc. Given this fluctuation, Chicano texts can be said to be both modernist and post-modernist, and even pre-modernist."[30]

Many Chicanos and Chicanas recreate and reenact history, legend, tragedy, and ritual in their own lives, on a daily basis. According to Rosaura Sánchez, these practices may appear in literary works that "reveal the group's historical memory, long neglected and overlooked by mainstream literature." She claims that this neglect explains why Chicano literature "does not rely on prior textualized pop images of the past, as is the case in postmodernist novels which seek to recreate history through stereotypical period images, for the Chicano experience has been absent, for the most part, from mainstream pop culture."[31]

Rosaura Sánchez proposes that Miguel Méndez's novel, *El sueño de Santa María de las Piedras* [The Dream of Santa María de las Piedras](1986), is a text in which "the passing of time is blurred so that events of one decade become indistinguishable from those of another." Santa María de las Piedras is a place "where time stands still: things happen, as the men's anecdotes confirm, but everything is still the same."[32] Social scientists have developed theories of an essentialist pathology on the basis of similar observations: the world moves on, but *la raza* refuses to change. Chicanos counter with a grim rejoinder: neither does it die out. Chicanos and Chicanas continue somehow to thrive in adversity. Ricardo Sánchez boasts that "the Chicano soul is so strong that it can even thrive in prisons and poverty" (*Canto y grito* 145). This boast echoes a theme in *I Am Joaquín,* in which the poet identifies with the hardiness and endurance of his people:

> I have endured in the rugged mountains
> of our country
> I have survived the toils and slavery
> of the fields.
> I have existed
> in the barrios of the city,
> . . . .
> in the prisons of dejection,
> in the muck of exploitation
> and
> in the fierce heat of racial hatred (*I Am Joaquín* 19).

According to Francisco A. Lomelí, "Chicanos are progressively undermining an Anglo sense of cultural essentialism which has been maintained through a long-standing monolithic iconography and its corresponding political plan of control." Lomelí finds temporal hybridity in the area of Chicano visual arts, as in "Gronk's gothic surrealism, Carmen Lomas Garza's quotidian primitiveness, Frank Romero's urban earthiness, and Amado Maurilio Peña's stylized neo-indigenism."[33] However, Yves-Charles Grandjeat has complained about the political consequences of a theory of multiple Chicano timespaces: "Chicano critics have to some extent used postmodernist terminology to voice a rather premodernist ideology of truth and identity." Grandjeat depicts Chicano discourse as one for which "decentering the subject was fine, as long as one left the ethnic subject intact. The center was then moved, not removed. 'Difference' seemed to be—wrongly—used as synonymous with 'opposition' or 'conflict' and 'dialogics' were—wrongly, again—seen as a form of the class struggle."[34]

In the first place, Grandjeat is, I think, unduly abrogating the right to determine that which is "rightly" or "wrongly" stated. The "difference" that he and other postmodern purists fail to grasp (or refuse to countenance) is not, in fact, the multiple subjectivities but the multiple timespaces that Chicanos inhabit. For Chicanos like Ricardo Sánchez, a linear, progressive, universalizing postmodernism is not that different from a linear, progressive, universalizing modernism; both are equally unacceptable. Grandjeat notes that Alvina Quintana, in her essay on Ana Castillo's *The Mixquiahuala Letters,* "takes us *back* to a petit-bourgeois representation of the individual as an ideal, sovereign, self-created entity."[35] Grandjeat seems indignant that Chicanos are going about flashing the verbal currency of postmodernist theory while exhibiting a crass disregard for the true meaning and value of this knowledge. To this purist, Chicano critics appear as inexpert interlopers and word smugglers who are scandalizing the well-bred arbiters of postmodernist theoretical discourse. And he may be right. Both Grandjeat and Rafael Pérez-Torres offer evidence that Chicano critics have been sneaking ideological contraband surreptitiously across the murky waters that divide their rhetorical borderlands from the mainstream. Those daring desperados have lately been detected wading in over their heads, stubbornly pushing and dragging their booty, against the current, to the *wrong side* of the stream where they scurry onto their primitive bank of the *río* and take flight "*back* to truth and authenticity, *back* to the center."[36]

While *faux*-postmodernist Chicano critics ferry their cultural contraband back and forth between the more accessible timespaces of the Chicano multiverse, the legitimate *europostmodernistas de raza* are in the vicinity as well, trying to police the bustling frontier zone like a tweedy *migra,* their one-way tickets in hand, demanding that the pesky and anarchic *chicanada* "fully embrace the theoretical implications of postmodernist thinking." I would agree with Francisco Lomelí when he states that "purist approaches, especially imported ones, don't quite stay apace with evolving social reality. The new dynamics defy neat formulas and high-brow rhetorical jargon filled with mental aerobics."[37]

Ricardo Sánchez and Chicano Timespace

In this section I focus my study of Chicano timespace on Ricardo Sánchez's first volume of poetry, *Canto y grito mi liberación.* I show how this autobiographical text interacts with the developing field of Chicano criticism, with poetic texts such as *I Am Joaquín,* and with Sánchez's second collection, *Hechizospells.* The complete title of Sánchez's first volume of poetry is *Canto y grito mi liberación (y lloro mis desmadrazgos . . .) pensamientos, gritos, angustias, orgullos, penumbras poeticas, ensayos, historietas, hechizos almales del son de mi existencia. . . .* This extended title, like other aspects of Sánchez's writing, suggests a revisiting of previous baroque and romantic styles, now tinged with parody, humor, pathos, and the rhythms and sonorous qualities of the Spanish language. For example, the visual and alliterative sound imagery of "*penumbras poéticas*" evokes the chiaroscuro sensibility of the *pinto* poet, whose moods oscillate between rage and hope, light and gloom. The author also re-presents the concept of "*hechizos*," which appeared in the *Los cuatro* anthology. A reviewer notes that "the Spanish word 'Hechizo' can mean 'bewitched,' which has a negative connotation, or 'enchanted,' a positive word."[38]

Indeed, the contrasting currents of meaning that weave, serpent-like, through the long title suggest a kind of madness. Both "*hechizos*" and madness evoke positive and negative nuances, as the *hechicero* or sorcerer can be an enchanter as well as the target of evil spells. In his introduction to *Canto y grito mi liberación* Abelardo Delgado mentions the poet's "yo-yo moods," which is a way of saying that *hechizos,* spells, and incantations are volatile forces that intersect within the poetic discourse as it declares "love for the valleys, mountains, cities, plazas, women, children, carnales, carnalas, gentes, and the entirety of the earth . . . also my anger at our failing to create a society of caring, our failing to attain humanness."[39] This sort of temperamental flux may be interpreted as an sign of insanity, but it is also attributed to poets, as we find in Erasmus's *The Praise of Folly* (1508), when the allegorical figure of Folly or Madness asserts that "the poets . . . by their own admission they are of my faction. . . . I myself am worshipped by no breed of men more devotedly or faithfully."[40]

Mindful of these considerations which are suggested by the book's title, let us proceed then to examine the first edition of *Canto y grito mi liberación*, which begins with a confessional piece titled "Opened letter to my conscience," dated in Spanish:

> 3 de Octubre, 1970
> el valle

In the second edition the dateline is as follows:

> el valle mágico/trágico
> Pharr-Tejas
> Aztlán

The occasion for the piece is the poet's sojourn in the Lower Rio Grande Valley of South Texas, where he is working with Abelardo Delgado's migrant health project. Of course, Sánchez himself is a migrant returning to Texas after a stay of more than a year in the eastern United States. He has been on parole from the Ramsey I prison farm in Huntsville, Texas, since March, 1969, and has spent a year completing a journalism fellowship in Virginia and working as a staff writer in Amherst, Massachusetts. For Sánchez, this has been a period of exile in a strange land, far from the people and culture of his native region. Yet his homecoming is not a joyful return to the state where he served long and painful years in prison. The reference in the marginal note to the "magic/tragic valley" signifies his ambivalence about returning to this "cauldron of chicanismo": "On every hand there is the dominant force of racism trying to oblivate [*sic*] la raza, while in every hovel there is the force of chicanismo . . . just driving thru McAllen, Pharr, Edinburg, etc., the soothing madness of need seeking the answer takes on a balming effect, and my soul soars high" (*Canto y grito* 1995, 25–26).

The poet speaks in praise of madness as if it were a familiar companion that can help him find answers to difficult problems. In *Borderlands/La frontera: The New Mestiza* (1987) poet Gloria Anzaldúa, a native of the Lower Rio Grande Valley, also writes of a return:

> I still feel the old despair when I look at the unpainted, dilapidated, scrap lumber houses consisting mostly of corrugated aluminum. Some of the poorest people in the U.S. live in the Lower Río Grande Valley, an arid and semi-arid land of irrigated farming, intense sunlight and heat, citrus groves next to chaparral and cactus. I walk through the elementary school I attended so long ago, that remained segregated until recently. I remember how the white teachers used to punish us for being Mexican.
>
> How I love this tragic valley of South Texas, as Ricardo Sánchez calls it; this borderland between the Nueces and the Río Grande. This land has survived possession and ill-use by five countries: Spain, Mexico, the Republic of Texas, the U.S., the Confederacy, and the U.S. again. It has survived Anglo-Mexican blood feuds, lynchings, burnings, rapes, pillage.[41]

Rafael Pérez-Torres notes that "Chicano poets in the 1980s affirm the influence of Mexican culture and history upon their articulation of Aztlán."[42] For her part, Anzaldúa reaffirms the multiple timespaces of *mestizaje* in the face of conquest:

> This land was Mexican once
> was Indian always
> and is.
> And will be again.[43]

Anzaldúa's gendered chronotope of the borderlands represents clear differences but also an interesting continuity of poetic sensibility between the 1970s and the 1980s. According to the critic Wolfgang Karrer, "[Anzaldúa's] dramatization of class conflict and exploitation is derived from Movement fiction and poetry of the 1960s and 1970s."[44] I would argue that Anzaldúa's concern with the land, and the dream of recovering it, is most reminiscent of *I Am Joaquín* and "El plan espiritual de Aztlán."

Again, the contextualizing chronotope of Sánchez's "Opened letter to my conscience" is the Lower Rio Grande Valley, a place that, like *la pinta*, is steeped in a tragic sense of time and the pain of *desmadrazgo*—Sánchez's term for Chicano dispossession. The poet's "Opened letter" appears at the "opening" of his autobiographical collection, in which he is at pains to impress upon the reader the candor and "openness" of his words. Apart from the title, which indicates that it is a literary composition, the "letter" has the appearance of a symmetrical, typewritten page of prose, with short paragraphs at the beginning and end and two longer paragraphs in between, separated by blank lines. The "salutation" of the letter is a simple "Conscience:" in the vocative case. In the Mictla edition the letter concludes with the author's name printed in lieu of a signature, with the date and place of composition repeated in English:

> Ricardo Sánchez
> the magic valley
> Pharr-Texas . . .
> Oct. 3, 1970

In this same edition, however, the author's signature appears several pages earlier, in bold script, at the bottom of the dedication page. It would seem then that the "Opened letter" is a postscript or continuation of the dedication page, but addressed to the poet's inner self, his "Conscience," where he finds the debt of gratitude owed to his wife, his family, and his friends for their support during his incarceration and parole. He also thanks his maecenas, Dr. Reymundo Gardea, who provided financial support to Mictla for the publication of *Canto y grito.*

The date of composition of the "Opened letter" is about eighteen months after the author's parole from the state prison in Huntsville. During that time he had been reporting to a parole officer, and in the letter he is preoccupied by the demands and the presence of that official. In the book's preface he refers to the circumstances of his parole: "[I]t became an ardurous [*sic*] set of experiences whereby it meant being told in word and adamant deed that in order to survive I WOULD HAVE TO CONFORM . . . conform to the wishes of a parole officer, who demanded utter capitulation, otherwise my parole would be revoked in no uncertain terms, and this because it was—and is—my contention that man must be a free agent and act for the good of humanity, and if this meant confrontation, so be it. It also meant that I might have to go back to a Tejas prison (for eight years), and I was naturally scared, but one's reality is that one must sometimes pay in order to play, and my wanting to serve La Causa was stronger than my fear of La Pinta" (*Canto y grito* 13).

Here Sánchez's ritualistic boasting and his admission of fear should be read within the conventions of a barrio vernacular which the *pinto* uses to vindicate his actions and command respect from a hostile world. Specifically, his intent is to state his motives to his immediate family, to the authorities that are monitoring his activities, and to the community that he knows and cares for. The last group includes the masses of dispossessed Chicanos, those "pent-up mad cabrones y desmadrados doing time . . . the migrant with all his cultural beauty and strength and his empty belly . . . the city chicano now plotting a return to dignity" (26).

Thus, Sánchez dedicates his autobiographical narrative to *la pinta,* to the "migrant stream," and to "the barrio" or rather, to the inhabitants of those Chicano timespaces with which he is well acquainted. The "Opened letter" concludes by addressing these folk in a final brief paragraph and offering them his poems: "Here, then, my compadres, carnales, y familia, is the residue and moment of truth and half-truth that I write" (26). By owning up to its half-truths in advance the text renews its autobiographical claim to the truthfulness and sincerity which was subverted in the equally brief first paragraph: "Lo, verily have I ever questioned my own development and sense of self; seldom have I taken myself to task when failing to follow-through on those aspects of my life that need redemption" (25).[45] The elliptical artificiality of this utterance combines the penitent's act of contrition with the inmate's performance before chaplains and rehabilitation counselors. Here the *pinto*'s "Conscience" is inhabited not by members of his family and community but by the officers and functionaries assigned to monitor the state of his psyche. In this way, the poet and student of Freud deflates the rhetoric of "rehabilitation" purveyed by the penal institution.[46]

The mock elevated tone and expressions of remorse place the speech

within the conventions of a picaresque first-person narrative. At the same
time, the text introduces the *pinto*'s problematic sense of identity, his pur-
ported knowledge and command of his faculties, and his ability to access and
analyze his own inner motivations. This discourse of self-analysis and self-
critique, appearing in a variety of forms and for a variety of purposes, will be
at the heart of Sánchez's autobiographical narrative. Here it is used to manip-
ulate and subvert the politics of prisoner reform and rehabilitation. If the
society that imprisoned him demands that he aspire to the status of a law-
abiding and productive citizen, the *pinto/pícaro* will pretend to accommodate
these expectations. As he states in the "Opened letter": "This then is my
redemption—the writing of this book in the hope of sharing it with family,
friends, and raza" (26). The text proclaims solidarity with Chicanos who are
"plotting a return to dignity" and seeking "a new social order [that] can begin
to mete out the justice that we not only need, but demand" (26). The ex-
pinto who remains on the receiving end of the Texas penal system is saying
that he is a conspirator with that Crusade for Justice that would turn the
tables on the system and begin to *mete out* justice. But unlike "Mutations,"
the "story" from *Los cuatro,* this call for justice does not involve war but rather
a commitment to a struggle of body and spirit.

Six years later, in *Hechizospells,* with less to fear from parole officers, Sán-
chez lays to waste the culture of confinement: "Meanwhile, you think in
terms of rehabilitation, and in your foolish trusting way, you ask La Burra
[the prison guard] about your being allowed to participate in rehab pro-
grams, and he laughs and says, 'Do it on your own time, meskin. Yo'all came
here to work in my fields, and Ah shore don't care nary a damn about sech
foolish thangs as reha-bi-li-tay-shun, hear?'" Moved by the will to survive,
the inmate persists: "You begin to enter into the pretentious world of livid
jive—alcoholics anonymous meetings, church attendance, school, group,
and psycho therapy, and anything that will look good on your jacket, for you
want the parole board to think that they have rehabilitated you. Inside you
seethe with anger and vengeance, and learn how to knock out safes, pull
robberies, assault, and rip off. Everything is a sham, so you've learned" (*He-
chizospells* 39).[47] Addressing the incarcerated self in the second person, this
text maintains the psychic split of the "Opened letter to my conscience," a
split between two moods that are really two opposing world views—a hope-
ful one and another that is full of hate.

The first two words in the title of the piece, "Opened letter" imply a
previous closure or enclosure of the writing and of the poet himself, which
were, until recently, enclosed within prison walls and bars. This "letter" thus
marks the beginning and partial opening of the poet's *cantogrito,* whose range

and power will not become apparent until time and distance have attenuated the poet's memory of incarceration and the censorship imposed directly and indirectly by the parole officer.

The poem "Soledad . . ." represents very different moments in the poet's life: first, the time of the poem's composition on November 29, 1961, in Soledad prison in California; and second, the year of its publication in *Canto y grito mi liberación,* ten years later. In terms of the autobiographical narrative the poem signifies the persistence of the chronotope of *la pinta,* the prison where the poet's body was locked away and where the poem was composed. The poem begins with a prose prelude: "Soledad means solitude in Spanish, to me it means differing levels of interminable deaths" (*Canto y grito* 27). It bears witness to a fragmented, paranoid consciousness in search of "meanings," which lie scattered across the Chicano timespaces of *la pinta,* "the barrio," and the "migrant stream":

> soledad
> inundated with turmoil,
> and my identity's lost . . .
> only instant coffee matters,
> tobacco, god, and tobacco.
>
>   o,
> mi barrio/chicano
> my other life
> show me,
> tell me
>   once more
> of my peasant origin;
> give me a happy, canorous
> grito . . . (28–29).

Entombed in a present of almost hopeless dread and loss ("soledad, / so dead") the prisoner accesses the outside world through memory. He recalls virtual timespaces that are no longer past, for memory re-presents them inside *la pinta.* As Gilles Deleuze describes this experience, "The whole of our past is played, restarts, repeats itself, *at the same time* on all the levels that it sketches out."[48] Memory becomes a means of survival, a link to an "other life" outside. But the poem's juxtaposition of "instant coffee," "tobacco," and "god" analyzes signifiers of value within *la pinta.* The prisoners' system of commodity exchange is linked to a devalued "god" who is a mocking witness:

"god must've laughed / (for) / nothing matters, / all is a shuck, lie, sham, / thoughtlessness!" (*Canto y grito* 30).

In the midst of this despair, how can the *pinto* find and maintain a vital connection, how can he *make present* other times and places that lie somewhere in the past or future? Henri Bergson insisted that subjectivity could not be understood in terms of spatialized language and concepts. Instead, he identifies the self with *duré* (duration). Bergson believed that our notions of time are contaminated by spatial components such as linearity and circularity. His efforts to separate extension (space) from duration (time) are central to his theory of difference and, indeed, to an entire philosophical project which holds that space and time are representative of fundamental "differences in kind" and not mere "differences of degree." When we merge time and space in our thinking, says Bergson, "we make differences in kind melt into the homogeneity of the space which subtends them." According to Deleuze, "What [Bergson] condemns from the start is the whole *combination* of space and time into a badly analyzed composite, where space is considered as ready-made, and time, in consequence, as a fourth dimension of space."[49]

Perhaps our answer to the question posed above is that the *pinto,* like the philosopher, is in a position to avoid the errors that Bergson deplores. It may be that the misfortune of his incarceration can help him to overturn ordinary notions of time and space and, if he is a writer, provide first-hand data with which to test Bergson's theories. For instance, it is obvious that as the *pinto's* movements in space have been drastically delimited and controlled, the empty time available to him has correspondingly increased. That, in effect, is his punishment. He has been isolated from society in such a way that he can no longer experience the categories of time and space as others do. In "Soledad," the space of the prison is "inundated with turmoil, / and my identity's lost." The convict's personal insecurity extends beyond the physical to the psychic:

soledad,
you lied!
        no solitude or serenity here,
just tormented souls . . . no,
not souls.
        o   please   unsanity   go   back!

only your mountains matter,
your name is wrong,
your keys clang at midnight,

your phantoms stalk, search,
and
haunt . . .

soledad,
land of retribution,
nation of rough guys,
       toughs and male whores,
owners of syphilitic brains
         shuffling by aimlessly (*Canto y grito* 30).

This predicament in which safety, dignity, and sanity are constantly in jeopardy signifies for the *pinto* a daily struggle for survival: the need to defend his personal integrity as *turf*. Where the turf marker lies is not always clear, and when the subject will suffer (or punish) a violation is not specified because a peculiarity of the *pinto* code is its latent bluff and violence, the negative face of *cábula*. In the course of his autobiographical narrative the subject portrays himself as having to choose between more or less violent responses to the dangers and frustrations that circumscribe his life. There follows a shifting ambivalence between the violent and peaceful aspects of his personality, which Abelardo Delgado has referred to as the poet's "moods." The *pinto*'s reactions often seem irrational, his responses unpredictable. To Nicolás Kanellos this recalls the mythological Minotaur's "looming threat of aggression."[50]

The *pinto*'s sense of time, like his sense of space, is distorted by confinement. The lack of space is accompanied by a glut of time that, unless he can put it to productive use, becomes a weight and a burden that the inmate must bear for the duration of his sentence. History records the experiences of thinkers and writers from Socrates and St. Paul to Miguel de Cervantes, Eldridge Cleaver, and Malcolm X, whose sense of the spatial deprivation and temporal disorientation of prison produced startling insights into the nature of time, the self, and their relationship to social composites.[51] We can attribute part of the *pinto* poets' impact on the Chicano Movement to the fact that, however unwillingly and unknowingly, they were part of a universal experience of persecution and incarceration that has been decisive in the emergence of many influential writers. For example Fyodor Dostoyevsky writes in his *Notes from a Dead House*:

I had meant to present a complete and vivid picture of our prison and all the years I spent there . . . sometimes I grow sick at heart from these memories. And I cannot remember everything, no matter how I try. . . . I only remember that one year, which was so like the other, dragged on sluggishly and bleakly. I remember that the long days were as monotonous as water dripping from the roof. And I also remember that only my longing for resurrection gave me the strength to hope and wait. Finally, I found the strength of resignation: I waited, counting the days, and though a thousand of them yet remained, it was with real delight that I ticked them off and saw them buried in the past. And when the new day dawned, I rejoiced at the thought that now there were not a thousand left, but only nine hundred and ninety-nine. . . . In my mental solitude, I reviewed every detail of my life, sternly judged my actions and even blessed my fate at some moments for having sent me such solitude, but for which I would have achieved neither self-judgment nor the stern scrutiny of my past experience. And what hopes filled my heart then! I reflected, resolved, I swore to myself that the mistakes and lapses of the past would never again occur. I mapped out a course for the future and decided to follow it faithfully. A blind faith was born in me that I could and would fulfill it all. How I longed for freedom and cried for it to come quickly. I wanted to try my strength in a new struggle. I was seized by feverish impatience at times. . . . I feel that everybody will understand it, since anyone would be sure to have the same experience if sent to prison in the prime of life.[52]

In Dostoyevsky's memoir there are moments of joy and hope combined with anguish and regret.

Biographer William Byron describes Miguel de Cervantes's time in prison in this way: "Any prisoner must make a mighty moral effort to push back the walls enclosing him, to encompass the injustice and violence of imprisonment. Either he will emerge from the struggle embittered, a hardened criminal, or he will be purified and enlarged. In prison, Cervantes was forced to face his grief, his past, like a dying soul reviewing its life, to examine his own sins and analyze his relationships with God and humanity. This is a perilous ordeal; only a hero can emerge from it sound and triumphant. Cervantes, we know, was a fighter. He would have made that moral effort, climbed that upward path." Scholars are generally in agreement that Cervantes began his masterpiece, *Don Quixote,* in prison. Byron notes further that "*Don Quixote,* the first of his works to appear in this new stage of his life, was indeed 'engendered in a prison'—and so were all the other plays, stories, poems, novels, that pressed so tumultuously against each other in the elation of those climactic decades to come. Those months in prison marked his own rebirth as well."[53]

St. Paul the Apostle also wrote on the subject of spiritual rebirth and liberation from his imprisonment in Rome: "I consider that the sufferings of this present time are not worth comparing with the glory that is to be revealed to us . . . for the creation was subjected to futility, not of its own will but by the will of him who subjected it in hope; because the creation will be set free from its bondage to decay and obtain the glorious liberty of the children of God. We know that the whole creation has been groaning in travail together until now; and not only the creation, but we ourselves, who have the first fruits of the Spirit, groan inwardly as we wait for adoption as sons, the redemption of our bodies."[54]

For Ricardo Sánchez too, the loss of freedom in space makes possible an intensified exploration of time and of his own conscience. In prison he must learn discipline in order to survive. He refines his responses and trains himself to see beyond the despair of the moment. And indeed, the anguish and tragedy of this *pinto* present is, in terms of the autobiographical text, now past; nevertheless, traces of the poverty, the insecurity, and the madness remain. A set of alternating perspectives persists in a text filled with personal and collective anguish and the hope that *liberación* is a reality.

A Critical Theory of Chicano Timespace

Like a prelude to *Hechizospells, Canto y grito mi liberación* suggests themes and traces episodes that will give shape to a narrative of dislocation. At the same time, it leaves gaps and silences to which the poet will return in *Hechizospells*. In June, 1969, Ricardo Sánchez accepted a journalism fellowship in Richmond, Virginia. He left El Paso to place distance between himself and his parole officer and to diminish the danger of reincarceration. A section of *Canto y grito mi liberación* titled "In Exile" is devoted to this period of wandering. It begins with the poem "Sojourns in Virginny," dated "June, 69 to January, 70." The poet reintroduces himself to the reader in a new setting: "a chicano, / lost in the wilderness of the deep south" (*Canto y grito* 55). The experience of cultural dislocation makes him yearn again for the El Paso barrio of his youth. With the uncertainty of a sojourner, the poet seeks reassurance in his *chicanismo*. He writes of "my people, LA RAZA! / with pride, love, and out of need . . . for / i am indelibly CHICANO" (56).

A poem from this section, "Flight: San Antonio, Houston, Atlanta, Richmond from El Paso . . . , " addresses issues of identity as the subject is drawn in different and conflicting directions. A sense of inauthenticity provokes a moral dilemma with regard to the benefits he receives under the protection of the Movement: "I question / self-motives," he writes, because "one-year journalistic fellowship / relegates La Raza, causa, etc., / to minor role . . . and / mi alma weeps out / its paradox; / pathos—theatrical soul / masks" (57). The poet confronts a recurring dilemma. In *I Am Joaquín*, the protagonist feels lost in a world of confusion. In this poem the exile is "lost in maelstroms" (58). The loss of integrity is very different from the turf battles in *la pinta*. On the outside he is, like Joaquín, a social misfit, wandering between the poverty of the *campesino* and the relative power of "the fat political coyote." Joaquín fears that he could become the betrayer who "rejects my father and my mother and dissolves into the melting pot / to disappear in shame. / I sometimes sell my brother out and reclaim him for my own when society gives me token leadership" (*I Am Joaquín* 13). At this point, Sánchez, too, is questioning the integrity of his actions and those of the Movement which he wants to represent.

In a longer piece titled "Stream . . . ," the poet creates patterns of interior monologue in which "i phantasmagorize about the stream of my life" (*Canto y grito* 76).[55] The monologue, composed mostly in English, is set off by irregular stanzas of short, energetic verses in Spanish. The poem breaks this pattern intermittently as it combines the two forms, the two languages, and the two moods in a rhyming lilt: "wending its way—como un duelo penumbroso y al mismo tiempo como canto ilustroso" (76). It shifts from first-person narrative to the second person as the poet addresses members of his family: his wife Teresa, son Rikard-Sergei, and his "new-born daughter, Libertad-Yvonne."

The poem's bilingual "stream of consciousness" depicts a moment of social awareness. It emerges from an inner, subjective temporality to speak of the "migrant stream" of agricultural labor in whose ebb and flow Chicanos "live, die, and somehow nothing is ever resolved in their lifetime" (*Canto y grito* 73). The migrant workers' unending oppression recalls that of the convict in the *pinto* poem "Reo eterno"; the poet is once again battling the despairing sense that "i still was imprisoned within the horrendousness of a social structure predicated on stricture and desecration" (78). Human suffering does not seem to matter to those who can make a difference: "somewhere, now, a child is dying for lack of certain things, *and no one seems to give a damn.*"[56] We read in *Hechizospells* (293–303) that this tragic form of death visited the poet's household a few years later, making his newborn son, Pedro-Cuauhtémoc, a victim of the unchanging reality.

Indeed, the first lines of "Stream . . ." outline the social reality: "Middle america . . . middle ameriKa . . . it all is the same / when hate becomes the calling card" (*Canto y grito* 73). The speaker's accusation against a compassionless society is not a testament of anti-Americanism, but of Amerika's anti-Chicanoism. In the essay "Desmadrazgo" the poet asserts that "hatred against Chicanos is one of the stronger forces running rampant from one point of Amerika to another" (33). Thus, it is not Chicanos who hate, but an essentialist "Amerika." Chicanos are not the aggressors but the defenders of their nonessentialist mestizo culture. This idea reappears in the brief manifesto, "the 70's . . . años chicanos," a piece that also elaborates on the concept of Chicano timespace. In the name of the Movement, the poet calls on "brothers everywhere to join in this struggle . . . understand, one and all that the movement is not any one single color . . . it is not of white skin and blond hair that we write against, but rather the gringoistic experience that we deplore" (143). According to the poet there is a gringo mentality that continues to essentialize skin color as "otherness," *otredad.*

This same piece repeatedly invokes "Chicano time," with reference to a kind of Chicano calendar or dating system. "Stream . . ." is dated in English and Spanish—"tenth month, / el año del chicano." The reference to 1970 as "the year of the Chicano" reappears at the conclusion of "Desmadrazgo," where it is emphasized in uppercase letters: "EL AÑO CHICANO!" Sánchez's first reference to "the year of the Chicano" appears in *Los cuatro,* the anthology that he prepared in collaboration with Reymundo "Tigre" Pérez, Abelardo Delgado, and Magdaleno Avila. His poem "We Have . . ." from that collection is dated "the 29th of Duelo, / the year of the chicano." This formulation calls to mind the reordering of the calendar and the renaming of the months carried out by leaders of the French Revolution at the end of the eighteenth century. Meanwhile, the naming rather than numbering of the annual cycles corresponds to the pre-Hispanic dating systems of the Aztecs and Maya.[57] "We Have . . ." was composed in the aftermath of the Chicano Moratorium debacle in Los Angeles:

for almost a year
we have talked and hoped
that this year
    EL AÑO DEL CHICANO [1970]
we would march forward
to change at least a part of the picture
(that cinemascopic picture of lugubrious racism
and horrid amerikanism . . .) (*Canto y grito* 38).

A chapbook by Reymundo "Tigre" Pérez, *Free, Free at Last,* concludes with the poem "Rebirth 1970." It celebrates "the Chicanos united after / the gringo aftermath."[58] And the next-to-last piece in the Mictla edition of *Canto y grito mi liberación* (third from the last in the Anchor edition) is the prose essay, "the 70's . . . años chicanos." This piece is a statement of Sánchez's early views and his commitment to the Movement. It begins by mentioning the poet's efforts to reconceptualize time as a specific project of the Movement: "El año del chicano, 1970, came and went. No one was aware of it, other than a few of us. 1971, designated as many things is here . . . no one is aware of it either" (*Canto y grito* 143).

Unlike the idea of Aztlán, which Alurista and others identified with the lost land and which the Movement enthusiastically embraced, Sánchez's proclamation of a cultural and political agenda organized around "the year of the Chicano" failed to win the recognition and support of the Movement. I would argue that this lost opportunity was an early indication of the Movement's decline after 1970, the year in which Los Angeles police aborted the Chicano Moratorium demonstration and arrested the organizers, among them Corky Gonzales and other members of the Crusade for Justice. However, Ricardo Sánchez was not discouraged by this lack of acceptance, and his response was to extend the idea further: "Let the world know that we are in the decade of the Chicano, that we, La Raza, have taken the entire decade to prove our case—whether in the courts or in the streets, but prove our case we shall . . . in the decade of the Chicano, we have started out with 1970, the Year of the Chicano; 1971, the year of carnalismo; 1972, the year of desmadrazgo; 1973, the year of retribution; 1974, the year of absolution; and so on, until we have taken our rights back, until we can walk these lands which are drenched with our blood, sweat, and labor" (143).

Sánchez invoked Chicano timespace in order to challenge, as in a court of justice, the prevailing systems of representation on which the political order rested. By promulgating "the year of the Chicano" and "the decade of the Chicano," the poet prioritized the category of time in order to argue against the power discourses of "progress" and "modernization" which have marginalized Chicanos in the United States. Thus, the passage quoted above makes the issue of the land and its recovery contingent upon the recovery of a cultural sense of time that will allow Chicanos to assert their right to tread with dignity upon lands marked by the labor and sacrifice of many generations. Sánchez admired César Chávez's United Farm Workers movement, which had struggled throughout the late 1960s and 1970s to gain legal rights for agricultural workers. He learned from Chávez that the battleground for these rights would be the agricultural fields, the courts, and the streets. But Sánchez's autobiographical poems reveal that it was in prison that he developed an acute sense of Chicano timespace and the ability to inscribe and critique it in his writing.

We thus see the migrant stream of farm laborers, the *pinta,* the barrio, and even Aztlán becoming literary chronotopes capable of representing the timespaces of these Chicano communities.[59] In the poem, "Stream . . . ," Chicano migrant laborers demonstrate an extraordinary dynamism and productivity along a spatial dimension. They move with the crops and the harvests across national and international boundaries. However, across time they suffer a social immobility which jeopardizes their health and welfare. Migrant farm workers do not benefit proportionately from technological progress and innovation in their industry, nor can they claim effective political representation and enforcement of government regulations that might protect their interests. One historian notes that "in spite of all the union and government activity throughout the twentieth century, by the 1960s the socioeconomic condition of farmworkers was still horrendous. Farmworkers historically have labored in the most hazardous, dehumanizing, and oppressive conditions, and farmwork has been the third most dangerous occupation in the United States because of accidents. While other workers have made gains, the situation for agricultural workers has remained the same."[60]

The *pintas,* the barrios, and the migrant camps are marginalized communities whose problems appear to be of a different order than those which the rest of U.S. society faces. Chicano barrios in the western and southwestern United States have existed as such since 1848, when they were annexed and cut off from Mexican national sovereignty with the signing of the Treaty of Guadalupe Hidalgo. Since then the welfare of the urban barrios and rural communities has historically been compromised by Anglo American expansion, neglect, and the unequal allocation of resources.[61]

In Chicano literature of the 1960s and 1970s the representation of these marginalized Chicano timespaces was often accompanied by the denunciation of the United States and a call for revolutionary action and Chicano nationalism. Ever since then the dream of Chicano unity has had a name: Aztlán. Unlike the chronotopes of the barrio, the migrant stream, and the *pinta,* Aztlán had no contemporary social correlative until Alurista and others reimagined it as the new Chicano homeland. As noted previously, "El plan espiritual de Aztlán" identified the mythical homeland of the Aztecs with a new Chicano nation that would be formed out of the barrios and territories annexed from Mexico in the first half of the nineteenth century. Aztlán, which had previously been a rather vague mythological toponym, became a vessel for the powerful chronotope of the *nation.* Of course, it was not long before social scientists brought a different perspective to the romantic dream of poets and revolutionaries. To become a reality, the Chicano nation would have to throw off its status as an "internal colony" of the United States.[62]

In any case, an embryonic national identity which presumably lay deep within the Chicano imagination suddenly emerged into the public arena.[63] And whereas the barrio, the migrant stream, and the *pinta* represented historical realities of Chicano existence that writers could project onto the pages of literary texts as chronotopes, the chronotope of Aztlán functioned differently, as a discursive teleology that gave impetus to a social movement which dared to question the territorial integrity of the most powerful nation on earth. Aztlán represented the affirmation of Native American and mestizo/a timespaces that were as diverse and strange to the European mind as the many languages of the continent: "[F]or a long time we have been denied a segment of our heritage. Our artistic roots go back thousands of years. The indigenous peoples in the Valley of Mexico, which is now Mexico City have ageless literary and artistic traditions. It is time Raza realizes this, because in essence, this country has striven mightily to destroy us in terms of culture. . . . Human beings are not bound by time or space. . . . We can utilize references through all kinds of life experiences. It is through the expression of art that we better understand the human process, the human condition. We wanted to get away from the linear anglo saxon ideal and project something that is ours."[64]

Ricardo Sánchez's work in general points out the failure of the Anglo American ideals of modernity and democracy. The ideology of progress and modern development has masked the greed and exploitation that have beset Mexico and Latin America, as well as Aztlán. In the essay "Desmadrazgo," the poet gives personal testimony of the unequal distribution of spiritual and material benefits on the basis of race, class, and nationality: "There is talk of a 3rd world coalition. Such a coalition is an important factor in the coming changes that shall transform Amerika's barbarity-and-people-chewing into a just society built on love, trust, freedom, justice, and truth—all of which must be weighed humanistically. . . . We, los mestizos del mundo tercero [the Third World mestizos], are aware that we are not alone in our struggle against the desmadrazgo [dispossession by] the Useless States of Amerika" (*Canto y grito* 37–38). Sánchez's message is full of rage that violates the academic and commercial standards of literary expression but that, nevertheless, discourages physical violence. The poet consistently urges Chicanos to find humane alternatives to "Amerika" within their culture.

As we saw in "Stream . . ." the construction of multiple timespaces occurs through the parallel hybrid nature of the poet's languages. This hybridization of time and language is a strategy that attempts to overwhelm and finally overcome residual "American" notions of linear time and monolingual purity. The literary representation of *mestizaje* and Chicano speech produces "a desiring machine" of multiple languages and cultural forms that dodges and defies notions of purity and primacy, particularly those which have hindered the participation of Chicanos in the affairs of their own country. According to the authors of *Anti-Oedipus,* "the work of art is itself a desiring-machine. The artist stores up his treasures so as to create an immediate explosion, and that is why, to his way of thinking, destructions can never take place as rapidly as they ought to."[65]

In this chapter I have been mindful of Genaro Padilla's admonitions with regard to Chicano autobiography as I considered how the writings of Ricardo Sánchez represent Chicano timespace as a living genealogy and as an emblem of cultural survival. Another example that I would cite is the title page of the Mictla edition of *Canto y grito mi liberación,* whose design may be read as a collage of the cultural, linguistic, and temporal elements with which the poet constructs Chicano mestizo identity. The title page includes the author's name, with the place and date of publication in Spanish:

> por Ricardo Sánchez,
>> east el paso, tejas
>> barrio del diablo,
>
>> AZTLÁN . . . 1970
>> el año del chicano.
>>> 1971
>> el año del carnalismo (*Canto y grito* 1971, n.p.)

Also on the title page (as well as the book's cover) is Manuel Acosta's design of the plumed serpent, Quetzalcóatl, the principal deity of the ancient tribes of central Mexico. "Mictla," the publisher's name, is a Nahuatl term for the underworld. Thus, the title page announces the book's strategy of representing Chicano timespace as a *stream,* not of linear time but of temporal systems and contexts, including the indigenous American multiverse which, despite centuries of immigration from other continents, has not been erased from the present reality of the continent.

The poet's understanding of the American experience of conquest, colonization, slavery, and economic integration is not constructed on a time line of fossilized archaeological remnants and discrete chronological strata. What he proposes is something like a high-volume *mestizaje* machine that reproduces itself and multiplies, rather than annuls, the chains of its constituent elements. Sánchez's poetic *entelequia* begins with this science of Chicano and *mexicano* cultural continuity, whose larger implications address the global interdependence and welfare of nature/humanity. In no sense is Sánchez the poet of a minimalist generation or movement. As Philip Ortego suggests in his introduction to *Canto y grito mi liberación,* Sánchez's revolutionary, globe-embracing vision could be compared to that of the nineteenth-century European Romantics, except that Sánchez's language, urgency, rage, and hope can only be understood as products of a Chicano life experience.

In contrast to the Chicano Movement's call for the immediate recovery of lands and territory—the concrete *spatial* component of the nation—as expressed by Reies López Tijerina's takeover of "government lands," Sánchez felt that claims to the land could be fairly addressed after Chicanos recovered their dignity as human beings.[66] After all, the practice of the native ancestors was to hold the land in common; no one could claim definitive *ownership* of the land because any attempt to do so would only result in strife and warfare. Therefore, rather than evoking "the barrio" and Aztlán primarily within their *spatial* dimensions, Sánchez's elaboration of Chicano timespace emphasizes the second term—time or duration. The poet called attention to this vital category whose effect he compared to that of a powerful mechanical force: "The 70's thus mean much to us. . . . they mean the fulcrum, the lever by which the world can change or be changed. The 70's are the signal for the impetus of the self-affirmation existential process to begin for La Raza" (*Canto y grito* 143).[67] According to Deleuze, we can find support for this view in Bergson's system: "Duration seemed to [Bergson] to be less and less reducible to a psychological experience and became instead the variable essence of things, providing the theme of a complex ontology."[68]

Einstein's theory of relativity proposes that concepts of space and time stand in relation to one another as "a four-dimensional *space/time* manifold."[69] Modern scientists have embraced Einstein's theory and praised its contribution to the understanding of the physical universe. Bergson, however, in his book *Duration and Simultaneity* (1922), finds Einstein's system incomplete. According to Deleuze, "This book led to so much misunderstanding because it was thought that Bergson was seeking to refute or correct Einstein, while in fact he wanted, by means of the new feature of duration, to give the theory of Relativity the metaphysics it lacked. . . . For Bergson, science is never 'reductionist' but, on the contrary, demands a metaphysics—without which it would remain abstract, deprived of meaning or intuition."[70]

Bergson's critique challenged three centuries of scientific and philosophical thought. Ever since Leibniz, scientific methodology had progressively abandoned entelechy and forms of metaphysical speculation. Bergson's view was that Einstein perpetuated this error with his "numerical and discontinuous" concept of time which "revived the confusion between space and time." This confusion overlooked the Bergsonian notion of duration as a "virtual or continuous multiplicity. . . . By confusing the two types—actual spatial multiplicity and virtual temporal multiplicity—Einstein has merely invented a new way of spatializing time."[71]

But even Einstein's supposedly modern and scientific view of time was absent from the marketplace, where modernity continued to operate on the basis of an ancient calendar that was used by the Romans to measure an uninterrupted stream of time, without consideration of differences in space, location, matter, and so on.

Bergson, on the other hand, claimed that his intuitive methodology allowed him to "seek experience at its source . . . where . . . it becomes properly *human* experience" and also to go "beyond our own experience . . . which forces us to think a pure perception."[72] According to Deleuze, "It is in this sense that Bergson on several occasions compares the approach of philosophy to the procedure of infinitesimal calculus: When we have benefitted in experience from a little light which shows us a line of articulation, all that remains is to extend it beyond experience—just as mathematicians reconstitute, with the infinitely small elements that they perceive of the real curve, 'the curve itself stretching out into the darkness behind them.'"[73]

On the popular level, of course, Western culture has hardly understood either Bergson's philosophy of temporal multiplicity or Einstein's relativity, which theorizes time as a function of space. There is general agreement among scientists and philosophers that Isaac Newton's belief that "absolute, true and mathematical time, of itself and from its own nature, flows equably without relation to anything external," is obsolete.[74] Kant's transcendental philosophy proposed an inverse relationship between space and time, but employing the same principles of simultaneity and succession. According to Kant, "Time has one dimension only; different times are not simultaneous, but successive, while different spaces are never successive but simultaneous."[75]

As a culture, we continue to live by these outdated ideas. Time is still understood as a continuous stream of events which flows from the immediate but unknown future, through the fleeting present, and into the reservoir of the past. This is basically the same system for understanding and measuring

time that was employed by the Roman moneylenders when they devised the
kalendae, an antecedent of the modern calendar, in order to maintain their
accounts. This linear concept of time was useful to the Europeans during the
Industrial Revolution when market capitalism was in its infancy, and it re-
mains in effect today, in the era of so-called postmodernity and "late capital-
ism." Thus, European notions of time, like European languages, manners,
and science, have accompanied the expansion of colonial power around the
globe, displacing in the process the human diversity in this area as well. Berg-
son attempted to get beyond this imposed cultural limitation, yet finally con-
ceded that "our condition condemns us to live among badly analyzed com-
posites, and to be badly analyzed composites ourselves."[76]

But why should we be so condemned? What is the condition or condi-
tions that condemn us? Perhaps we should not expect highly developed, tech-
nologically sophisticated economies to abandon an obsolete concept of time
as long as that concept operates to the benefit and satisfaction of its owner
classes. Linear time provided the capitalist class with a profitable solution to
a complex philosophical problem. Like the Roman money changers before
them, the mercantilist bankers of the sixteenth and seventeenth centuries
concentrated ever more wealth, converting it to universal commodity value
as money. Absolute linear time became a pillar of modern capitalist econom-
ics, inherited, virtually unquestioned, from the ancient Mediterraneans.
There seems to be little doubt that after centuries this arbitrary, unscientific,
but useful method of measuring time has acquired a naturalness and inevita-
bility which the human condition is obliged to respect. The idea of linear
time (expressed as "spirit" by Hegel, as "history" by Marx), makes possible
the emergence of capital as the materialist entelechy of the ancient world,
whose potential can be fully realized only recently, at the beginning of the
nineteenth century.[77]

The ideological force of linear time, like Darwinian evolution, prevailed
over other, more pluralistic and less oppressive alternatives that tended to
undermine the "inevitability" and "manifest destiny" of European civiliza-
tion to reproduce wealth and increase its dominance over a degraded *space*
(the natural environment) and an alienated *time* (human labor).[78] If, for the
writer, "Time, as it were, thickens, takes on flesh, becomes artistically vis-
ible," for the capitalist, the flesh of the laborer is time incarnate, which be-
comes commercially visible as the world of commodities produced by la-
bor/time.[79]

Any notion of postmodernity as rupture will therefore address the subver-
sion of modernity's fundamental law of linear time by discourses like the
Chicano poetry of Ricardo Sánchez that depict *space/time* as multiple, plural-

istic, and nonlinear. While spatial representations serve as arenas of political action and conflict with respect to property and civil rights, the work of Sánchez and other Chicano and Chicana authors has shown that it is a function of culture to bring specific attention to the virtual multiplicity of time through the production of chronotopes.[80]

CHAPTER 4

In the Movement and Beyond

After 1970 Ricardo Sánchez's polemical literature made him a controversial figure in the community of Chicano leaders and writers. One critic asserted that Sánchez was a poet "shouting loudly for attention." Another placed Sánchez in the category of Chicano "social poets," describing him as "a trumpeter blasting loud, strident notes as he noisily calls our attention to the mostly grim side of social reality." A third claimed that "Sánchez's poetry is not the polished poetry which has seen countless revisions" but is "to a large degree 'protest poetry' which has given strength and spirit to the Chicano movement."[1] Such views are indicative of a critical consensus that has hindered the study of Sánchez's development. For even before he was paroled from prison in 1969, Ricardo Sánchez and the Chicano Movement began a difficult relationship that has been misunderstood by critics.

In the poem "Three days to go," dated March 10, 1969, Sánchez celebrates the Movement and Chicano power, yet he is already expressing concerns about the leadership of the Movement (*Hechizospells* 83). Later, Sánchez became an outright dissident who refused to moderate his attacks on particular strategies and individuals. He was disciplined repeatedly by the leadership of the Movement, but this only resulted in a reenactment of his prison experience in which punishment led to more rebellion and then to his marginalization. Sánchez seems to be reflecting on his own experience when he writes: "A plethora of situational/circumstantial/existential ills subvert the hope(s) and struggle(s) of a people to re-humanize the social process, to imbue it with cultural/linguistic diversity; activists pursuing change, only to find themselves bandied about and blacklisted—further alienated because they dare(d) speak out" (*Hechizospells* 6–7).

In the 1980s and 1990s, from the bitter timespace of isolation and exile, Sánchez looked back upon his role as a dissident: "During the heyday of the

Chicano Movement, it was considered sacrilege to openly criticize leaders or fellow Chicanos. We were supposed to turn away from the graft and corruption afflicting our movement and pretend that we were truly the only honorable people in the world. Such foolishness merely crippled the movement and retarded its growth" (*Eagle Visioned/Feathered Adobes* 10).

My analysis of Ricardo Sánchez's major works and their reception sheds light on the relationship between the Chicano Movement and one of its most vocal critics. Ironically, literary scholars have usually identified Sánchez with the Movement, going so far as to describe him as "the microcosm of the Chicano Movement." But I would propose a different view and say that Ricardo Sánchez's work marks the boundary between the political praxis of the Chicano Movement and the political aesthetic of Chicano literature. Luis Valdez also straddled that boundary in 1967 when he chose to distance his Teatro Campesino from its original role as the agit-prop arm of César Chávez's United Farm Workers Union.[2]

In those years the Movement consisted of a number of local and regional efforts to develop social and economic alternatives for Chicanos. The agenda became one of economic justice, cultural pride, and national self-determination, goals that were shared by a number of politicized Chicano students, intellectuals, and workers, both urban and rural. According to Carlos Muñoz, the participants in the 1969 Chicano Youth Conference "developed a series of resolutions outlining the goals of Chicano liberation within the context of the nationalist ideology. . . . The resolutions exhorted students to take up a struggle to unite all Mexican Americans regardless of social class. The basis for unity would be their pride in Mexican ethnicity and culture. . . . Nationalism, therefore, was to be the common denominator for uniting all Mexican Americans and making possible effective political mobilization. . . . The resolutions also called for a struggle to win political and economic control of Mexican American communities."[3]

Juan Gómez-Quiñones notes that "[t]he emphasis of *Chicanismo* was upon community autonomy, individual self-worth, cultural pride, and political and economic equity."[4] However, the planned consensus came apart (or failed to develop) in the process of selecting means and methods. For example, Chicano literature may have been a socially committed praxis for writers like Ricardo Sánchez who considered artists and poets to be participants in the political arena and political dialogue. But for Movement ideologues literature represented a propaganda outlet, a *means* of communicating an agenda to a given constituency. Marxist critics, cultural nationalists, feminists, and others demanded that authors adhere to a prescribed agenda or

formula of literary representation which often had little regard for the exigen-
cies of the creative process. Sánchez stated his position in "Some thoughts:
on writing," his preface to *Hechizospells:* "Most artists create ways of life that
they later capture in words or on canvas, as if to say that life is to be lived
and enjoyed, even though it's a hurting bitch of a life. Just as the most effec-
tive activists have been the ones to laugh and enjoy the movement, not the
ones who have become diehard fanatics driving the people to truebeliever-
ism" (*Hechizospells* xvi).

Sánchez did not deny the role of politics in art and vice versa, but he
made a distinction between politics and what he considered improper ideo-
logical intrusions into the domain of art and the prerogatives of artists: "Ul-
timately, I believe that art exists as a political statement—a statement that
speaks of the human condition and the will to create beyond the constric-
tions of social norms, an affirmation of soulmind, a tearing down of barri-
ers. . . . Art as an ideological form becomes a trite, clichéd, passionless out-
burst that is akin to a politician's mouthings, but art as a political statement
becomes the expression of peoples' living/loving/suffering/creating/struggl-
ing within their world of hurt, retribution and awareness. . . . Our sense of a
spiritual universe—one that is not to be found neatly packaged in cathedrals,
temples, or gideon bibles—is a linkage to earth, cloud, river, and our human
materialism" (*Hechizospells* xv).

In *Canto y grito* as well, Sánchez declared his independence from any kind
of ideological control, from whatever quarter: "We do not propose to be
masters, nor shall allow anyone else, irrespective of race and/or skin color-
ation, to be our masters. I shall just as soon struggle against a Chicano Cau-
dillo as I will against wallaces, rockwells, and other despots who in effect rule
the world at this point" (*Canto y grito* 143–44). The reference to a "Chicano
Caudillo" may well be an allusion to Rodolfo "Corky" Gonzales, which
would indicate a falling out with the leader of the Crusade for Justice.

As much as he denounced the rule of capitalists and their apologists, Sán-
chez also rejected the Marxist dogma that was growing within the leadership
of the Movement in the early 1970s:

A world without cábula is linear and hierarchical—and just as I fear
living in a Nixonian world that is sardonical and serious, with a con-
stant scowl cresting my mind, so do I fear a strict soviet world that
would make crime of the picaresqueness of life. Art liberates us from
taking ourselves so damn seriously that we wind up serving the state
and not living. I have no quarrel with Marxist ideas, but I do reject

the imposing of structure on the spirit; I also view capitalism as a horror that deracinates humanity. . . . To demand that the people capitulate and lose their sense of culture, that they become malleable and fit themselves into a marxist world is also to oppress the people. Those who have pretensions of leading the people should participate with the people in real life. . . . [T]hey should live with the people, suffer with them, walk/talk among the people, and break bread with them spontaneously (*Hechizospells* xvi–xvii).

Sánchez declares a popular *liberación* and not a *subordination* of the kind demanded by parties and politicians: "[T]here are those who embrace marxist/leninist/maoist extrapolations and as strict constructionists regidify [*sic*] their minds, demand utter capitulation of/by the people they allegedly lead. . . . Totalitarian methods that force the people to accept any singular/ linear direction(s) are not what leadership should be. Such authoritarianism is but the usurpation of the people's historical right to create their own destiny out of their own experiential process through reflection and action within their own historical/cultural/ linguistic milieu" (*Hechizospells* 17).

By 1976, when *Hechizospells* was published, the viability of the Movement's nation-building strategy was past. The cultural nationalists' dream of a united Aztlán as set forth in "El plan espiritual de Aztlán" had collapsed. This failure was not the result of an unfortunate "fragmentation" within the Movement; it happened because the leadership never attained a workable consensus among the diverse regional and ideological interests that it pretended to pull together.[5] Undoubtedly, the Movement was under attack from a number of quarters. Federal, state, and local authorities were targeting political actions organized by Chicano activists, from the marches and demonstrations of striking farm workers, to the school walkouts and moratoriums against the Vietnam War, to Reies López Tijerina's occupation of federal and state property in New Mexico. For a time the Movement, with its revolutionary activity and separatist ideology, seemed to pose a real threat to established authority. One scholar, Carlos Muñoz, Jr., states that the Brown Berets, a Chicano youth paramilitary organization, "adopted as their prime responsibility the defense of the Mexican American community against police harassment and brutality. They were therefore heavily infiltrated by police intelligence agencies and COINTELPRO."[6] Muñoz describes COINTELPRO as "the FBI's counter-intelligence program . . . [which] attempted to destroy the civil rights movement and undermine the positions of Martin Luther King and other leaders."[7]

In the meantime, Mexican American middle-class reformers, the members of the League of United Latin American Citizens (LULAC), local members of the Republican and Democratic Parties, the GI Forum, and other politically moderate organizations saw Chicano militancy as a threat to their hard-won prerogatives. Some older and more established Mexican Americans rejected the "Chicano" label and the brashness of the young people's methods.[8] Mario T. García observes that "clearly, reform and not revolution characterized the Mexican-American Generation . . . it, unlike European ethnic groups, failed to capture first-class citizenship for its people. Mexican-American reforms and a new consciousness did not, in the end, affect the structurally deep-seated class and racial limitations on mobility imposed on people of color. . . . The Mexican-American Generation influenced and pressured this stratified system but could not fundamentally dent it."[9]

García notes that "for the Chicano Generation, reforms were not enough. National liberation—Chicano Power—or some form of it [was] now demanded."[10] But he concludes that this strategy, too, failed to satisfy the aspirations of young Chicanas who staked claims to leadership and rejected the subservient role that many of them had played within the history of these generational movements. Cordelia Candelaria acknowledges that "one of the difficulties faced in the feminist project undertaken by women of color in the United States has been to avoid privileging gender over race because Chicanos and other men of color are themselves members of politically and economically subordinated classes. Yet, to recognize the compound oppression referred to as 'double' or 'triple' jeopardy of Chicanas, Latinas, and other women of color demands recognition of the additional burden of gender for women as it is interpreted within political hierarchies in all patriarchal societies."[11]

Tey Diana Rebolledo describes the way in which a number of Chicana poets have confronted this issue: "Many of the writers have not considered themselves feminists because they have remained ideologically devoted to traditional values of caring for family and sticking with their men. This has been generally viewed as necessary to the cause. A criticism of the Mexican-American system or of sexism itself by women is, in effect, a breaking of the ranks of ethnic solidarity and an abandonment of 'the culture.' Thus, the system creates tremendous pressure and feelings of ambivalence for the writer, feelings which she sometimes expresses directly and sometimes indirectly through humor and irony. For example, movement women felt relegated to the kitchen to fix the beans while the men talked revolution; there are many comments in writing to this effect."[12] Rebolledo cites Lorna Dee Cervantes's poem "Para un revolucionario" as an example:

you speak of the new way,
a new life . . .
Pero [*But*] your voice is lost to me carnal,
in the wail of tus hijos [*your children*],
in the clatter of dishes,
and the pucker of beans upon the stove.
Your conversations come to me
de la sala [*from the living room*] where you sit,
spreading your dream to brothers.[13]

Ricardo Sánchez saw early on that the militant bluster of the Movement was a fraud, and this is particularly evident in *Hechizospells,* where he warns that Chicanos "can no longer dream of government sponsored freedom nor of funded revolutionary movements" (*Hechizospells* 194). When the Movement proved ineffective in aiding the poor, Sánchez blamed a self-serving leadership for cynically selling out the dream that he and others had nurtured. In the preface to the second edition of *Canto y grito mi liberación* Sánchez recalls the opposition he faced when he tried to publish his first book in El Paso: "Though there were concern and enthusiasm on the part of a lot of carnales, there was also the feeling that I would fail—and sometimes that I *should* fail" (*Canto y grito* 11). In the same "Update on the Movement" he writes of his return to El Paso: "I became aware that I should have stayed away; for many quasi-movement types felt uneasy and challenged by my presence. . . . [A] fellow who was supposedly one of THE LEADERS, smiled politely, and then walked away to call me names behind my back" (12).

Although Sánchez maintained a nucleus of friends and colleagues, including Abelardo Delgado, Nephtalí de León, Reymundo Gardea, Raúl Salinas, and others whom he credits in his poems, he nevertheless refers to this period as a "diaspora" which few leaders survived unscathed. César Chávez, Reies López Tijerina, José Angel Gutiérrez, and the Raza Unida Party all suffered setbacks during this time. Sánchez's particular admiration for Chávez's struggle is restated in a collection published after Chávez's death in 1994, in which Sánchez dedicates several poems to the fallen labor leader.[14]

Sánchez believed that his role was to support the cause of the poor and working classes that were denied access to political representation, cultural expression, better schools, jobs, and public services. He understood the term Chicano as designating these historically marginalized groups of migrants and immigrants.[15]

In some respects the Chicano cause moved forward with new vigor, new ideas, and new leadership provided by Chicanas and a younger generation of activists. The charismatic machismo of the Movement years was checked to some extent by a new feminist assertiveness that challenged assumptions about Chicana passivity and domesticity. For his part, Ricardo Sánchez had been sensitive since his early poems to the representation of Chicanas, mesti-zas, and *mujeres indígenas.* He recognized their struggle as part of the history and vision of the people, *el pueblo chicano.* For example, recalling the time-space of the Conquest, Sánchez defends *la Malinche,* the Indian princess who was given to the *conquistador* Cortés as a slave and who served him as an interpreter and bore him a son. Sánchez defends her against those who accuse her of betraying her people: "no, no fuiste [no, you were not], / Malinche, una traidora [a traitor]," says the poet.

solo fuistes [*sic*]   you were only
una mujer esclavisada,   a woman enslaved
and like all slaves
you sought but the way
to liberate
yourself
from the entrails
of an oppressive people. . . .

no te odio carnala Malinche,   I do not hate you
al contrario   on the contrary
te respeto   I respect you
porque peleastes   because you struggled
para defenderte. . . .   to defend yourself

let others hate or mock you,
those who have not looked
their oppression in the face

. . . .
es un mundo aplastante   it's a crushing world
es cual vivimos todavía,   in which we still live
carnala   sister
y se tiene que reconocer   and we must recognize
que mientras   that as long
la mujer no sea libre   as women are not free
                    pues   well
tampoco el hombre   neither can men
no será libre   be free
("No, no fuistes" 24–25).

The struggle of Chicanas appears in Sánchez's poetry as an historical/transcendental process of liberation, a central feature of his *entelequia*. As early as 1971, in the poem "A veces la luz es oscura" [Sometimes the light is dark], we see the feminine figure as a sensual body and as a person conscious of her dignity and equality vis-à-vis men. A number of critics noted this in their reviews. Charles Tatum wrote, "Sánchez also takes on a number of sacred cows within his own culture, debunking, for example, the myth that drugs are a positive part of the Chicano tradition or that the superiority of the male is a desirable aspect of Chicanismo." In his review of *Hechizospells* Abelardo Delgado observes that "the sacredness of the Chicano movement, too, gets desecrated almost in every page."[16]

Nevertheless, by the 1980s Sánchez was identified by academic critics as a *movimentista,* a *veterano* of a lost cause. He was seen as part of the Movement's failure and not as someone who was pointing in a new direction. Although the Movement punished Sánchez for his critique of its philosophy, academics did not recognize his critique as an attempt to redefine Chicano literature. Instead, many scholars focused on Sánchez's critique of Anglo American society. For example, Enid Zimmerman wrote that "[the] tension between Chicano values and longing for basic human dignity and Anglo-America's 'hydra-headed racism,' exploitation, and disenfranchisement of its Chicano people is both a clearly articulated and subtle theme infusing all of Sánchez's works." No explanation is offered by this critic for the fact that "although he has published four books, earned a Ph.D., received numerous awards and honors, and held the titles of professor, lecturer, and writer-in-residence, Ricardo Sánchez still characterizes his survival as 'hand-to-mouth.'"[17] In fact, one reason for this hardship was the poet's isolation. He suffered exclusion and pariah status in a number of Chicano communities (including El Paso) whose leadership he had alienated. In a poem written for former Raza Unida Party leader Juan José Peña, Sánchez seems to be referring to his own experience:

> . . . you have fought
> until tiredness, envy,
> bickering, police threats,
> economic isolation, and
> so many other problematic
> 　　　quand[a]ries
> have stripped you
> of will, strength (*Eagle-Visioned/Feathered Adobes* 77).

In a dramatic dialogue Sánchez presents the opposing arguments of the *movimentistas:* "I recall, Toño, the day you first came here. You acted truly docile and domesticated. You spoke about the need for organization and carnalismo. Now you berate those who made it possible for you to become a successful and leading Chicano intellectual. Those who most paved the way for you are the very same ones you continually deprecate and lambaste. Por que? Do you resent them for having helped you out of your morass and inadequacy?"[18]

Massed against the poet was the old guard of the Movement, his former allies situated along the north-south axis of the upper Rio Grande, from Rodolfo "Corky" Gonzales and the Crusade for Justice in Colorado, to the Academia de la Nueva Raza in northern New Mexico, to the Chicano leaders and academics of El Paso. No wonder, then, that accusations of betrayal are a recurring theme in Sánchez's writing: "It was depressing, such as any discordant note can be jarringly depressing. Searching for faces which once peopled the 'Chicano Movement' in manitoland [New Mexico], I found complacency and indolence. A deep fear of repercussions was pervasive. La Academia de la Nueva Raza had become but a flimsy shell of its former, robust declarations of activism. Its leaders had succumbed and joined those whom they had once protested. Pogo's admonition had arrived in full uniform—feathers and beads, hash pipes, tired jokes and a depressing wish for entrance into mainstream America. Railing against former compañeros was an exercise in futility" (*Eagle Visioned/Feathered Adobes* 10).

While living in San Antonio from 1983 to 1988, Sánchez added the leaders of the city's Guadalupe Cultural Arts Center to his list of targets: "Returning to Texas, the same conditions prevailed, and where the Academia had faltered and lost its meaning, the Guadalupe Cultural Arts Center was likewise beginning to exhibit a voracious appetite for joining the American mainstream. It did so by becoming a showcase theater in the barrio catering to the well-heeled who so often enjoy moseying down to barrios and ghettos and slumming with the peasants" (10).

In the 1980s, as a columnist for the *San Antonio Express-News* and the *El Paso Herald-Post,* Sánchez brought to his cultural reporting the flair for controversy that had marked his confrontations with Movement chieftains during the previous decade. The feud between Sánchez and Rodolfo "Corky" Gonzales had produced serious threats and allegations by both parties.[19] As founder and leader of the Denver-based Crusade for Justice, Gonzales also claimed credit for writing the landmark poem *I Am Joaquín*. Gonzales was in the first echelon of Movement leaders, which included César Chávez, the founder of the United Farm Workers Union, Reies López Tijerina, leader of the land grant revolt in New Mexico, and José Angel Gutiérrez, leader and founder of La Raza Unida Party. Of this group, César Chávez, who according to some historians declined the political leadership of the Movement in order to devote his energies to the farm workers' struggle, never faded in Sánchez's estimation.[20] By contrast, he dedicated a rather critical poem titled "Confe de Brotherhood Awareness" to Reies López Tijerina:

Reies, I love you as a carnal,   *brother*
I respect Tierra Amarilla and the past,
but I question now your words;
josé angel is a fiction
which never materialized, but you
once acted—¿qué pues hoy? chingao   *what about now? damn,*
bato, you were one of the heroic ones
who pulled this chavo   *fellow*
out of the lethargy of prison grey,
gave me reason and hope,

. . . .

we can never stop
poniendo la vida en la línea   *putting our life on the line*
for you taught us to militate,
to stand up strong for our beliefs,
you spoke of righteousness,
and we willfully believed you
in barrios/campos/pintas/colleges . . . (*Hechizospells* 262).

In another poem, "Crítica for an arse poeticus," also from *Hechizospells*, Sánchez openly attacks the author of *I Am Joaquín* ("I AM/we are/they are/all are/ JOKING/YOLKING"), as well as the alleged abuses of the Crusade for Justice, ridiculing the organization's "true believerism" and the personality cult around the leader(s):

bastardos dastardly resigning mindsouls
to northern mandated catacombs,
generales, capataces, caudillos   *generals, bosses, chieftains,*
jefes, patrones, cabrones   *overseers, masters, bastards.*
    líderes, chingones, chingonas   *leaders, fuckers,*
    casi dioses   *demi-gods . . .*
    (313).

In his "Notes" on the screenplay for the film *Entelequia III* Sánchez states that "*Entelequia III* was written to express autocriticism and a strong statement on the state of what is known as the Chicano Movement, especially within its arts." Sánchez also states his suspicions with respect to the origins and authorship of *I Am Joaquín:* "Rumors have come and gone, some remain, i.e., the rumor that rebounds in Colorado is that the Jewish wife (now divorced) of a prominent Chicano lawyer would write *I Am Joaquín* and that Abelardo 'Lalo' Delgado or Alurista would translate it into *Yo Soy Joaquín,* and that Rudolpho 'Corkee' Gonzales was to be credited with the work in order to promote him as an authentic leader of our pueblo."[21]

In the same year, after the first Canto al Pueblo festival in Milwaukee, Sánchez laments in Spanish the decline of the Movement:

la belleza	*the beauty*
que ayer fué	*that yesterday*
proyectada	*we projected*
hoy se viste	*today is dressed*
de luto,	*in mourning,*
la envidia	*envy*
y el oportunismo	*and opportunism*
sepultaron	*buried*
lo bueno	*all the good*
no hemos aprendido	*we haven't learned*
mucho	*much*
y hemos comprendido	*and we've understood*
menos—seguimos	*less—we continue*
siendo	*to be*
nuestros	*our most*
enemigos	*ferocious*
más feroces . . .	*enemies . . .*
raza enjaula raza,	*Chicanos imprison Chicanos,*
muchos judas	*many Judases*
y muy pocos	*and very few*
cosechadores	*harvesters*
de la justicia,	*of justice,*
muy pocos	*very few left*
cultivadores	*to cultivate*
de lo humanizante	*humanity*
(*Milhuas Blues* 20–21).	

In *Canto y grito mi liberación* Sánchez is also concerned with existential issues that affect the Chicano intellectual but transcend the parochial politics of the Movement. Certainly the anomie and rage of the poet-activists who joined the Movement present a very different cultural context from the personal turmoil that drove a number of American modernist poets to the point of madness and suicide. But on the other hand, contemporary Anglo American poetry also speaks to a loss of community that affects all participants in contemporary society.[22] Like the *pinto* locked away in an institution, tortured spirits such as Lowell, Plath, and the Beat poets felt a spiritual isolation, an entrapment and longing for liberation from American middle-class values and the strictures of the Cold War mentality. There is no doubt that European poets, like their American counterparts, were deeply affected by World War II, the Holocaust, and the response of existentialist philosophy to those events. Mary Ann Frese Witt, a critic of contemporary European literature, finds that modern French literature is the best example of a literature whose preoccupation with confinement has some of its roots in the prisons and concentration camps of the period. Witt theorizes "literary prisons" in light of "a tendency in modern literature to favor representations of enclosure and, more generally, spatiality over temporality."[23]

The existential issues in the poetry of Ricardo Sánchez are founded upon a history of persecution: "Amerika's" efforts to destroy the cultural dignity of immigrant Mexicans and Chicanos. But the threats to Chicano survival are somehow linked to a Cold War scenario that grips not only the West but all nations that endured two world wars and confront the specter of a third:

> out in the streets
> z movie announces the loss;
> it is a variation
> of the same thematic desmadre
>
> all humanity
> but an eternal convict
> suffering the binding of its soul;
>
> and the gavels come down hard,
> hard nosed justices mete out
> measured eternities
>
> from capitol hill to wall street jungle
> and humanity doesn't have a chance . . .
> and no one seems to give a damn (*Canto y grito* 45).

In contrast to the modern European tendency cited by Witt, Sánchez employs temporality as an aesthetic response to the prevailing sense of entrapment and loss of freedom. In *Canto y grito*'s "Evening in Prison: Theme & Variated Vibrations—Beethoven's Quartet in C Sharp Minor," the *pinto* seeks solace in memories of love and music. Dated "12/7/68," this poem in English expresses hopes of freedom and renewal. Composed as a series of nine unrhymed quatrains, the poem draws inspiration from Beethoven's passionate music and creative freedom:

> Dearest, someday
> >   we shall again hear
> >   Beethoven and
> we shall be enraptured (*Canto y grito* 49).

The musical theme awakens desire, leaving the inmate "en-webbed cocoon / like / in the caressing wool music / love is . . . tonight soft sounds will emanate / and flood my thought world / again I shall behold you / in the furtiveness of hope" (49). Music enables the prisoner to endure the present in hope of the long awaited reunion with his loved one.

The prose piece "We were lost . . . ," also in English, offers a bitter counterpoint to the *pinto*'s dream of a romantic reunion. Here the dream shared by two people becomes a surreal nightmare and their freedom is merely another form of captivity. The title of the piece again recalls the opening lament of *I Am Joaquín:* "I am Joaquín, / Lost in a world of confusion, / Caught up in a whirl of a / gringo society, / Confused by the rules, / Scorned by the attitudes" (*I Am Joaquín* 3). "We were lost . . ." presents a devastating variation on this theme as it teeters on the verge of a hopeless "I" and an equally forbidding "we." The piece is one of the few in *Canto y grito* that appear without a date of composition or other marginal notes. It is composed in a hard, spare American English totally devoid of the sensuous musicality of "Evening in Prison" and lacking the characteristic rhythms and vowels of Sánchez's *caló* and Spanish dialect. Unlike "Evening in Prison" there are no prison bars or walls dividing the plural subject "we." On the contrary, the couple is driving along the open road, modern America's metaphor for freedom. But they are lost, and after stopping on the highway for gasoline and a map, they "decided to drop out." With a new car and enough money to go wherever they wish, they nevertheless feel trapped: "so pervasive is the societal way of life, that there is no place for anyone to drop out to" (*Canto y grito* 41). The fact that the system has beaten them will mark a turning point in the migrant's journey: "Meanwhile my mind traversed other moments when she had asked other pleading questions, and I seriously entertained the thought of . . ." This half-stated notion suggests that the speaker has considered abandoning his partner; however, he will remain with her as their dilemma forces him to question the meaning of his liberation. This poem generates a feeling of isolation in which the speaker faces a harsh reality: "I . . . resigned myself to being lost for the rest of my life" (42). The reality of the wanderer's release from *la pinta* does not measure up to the dream of *liberación,* for a world of hate, fear, and materialistic sterility awaits outside, offering him little chance of escape. Even beyond *la pinta,* the Chicano subject's existence continues to be a precarious one, faltering between the danger and stagnation of the barrio and the wandering uncertainty of the migrant's life.

The playful improvisation of poetic languages that characterizes Sánchez's writing is absent in this somber piece. Yet alongside the despair and hopelessness there is, in the poet's very will to write, a fundamental *activism* which he does not surrender. It is at this crossroads of failure and spiritual renewal that Chicano poetry becomes the conjunction of postmodern and premodern poetic practice, because it is here that the harrowing experience of a modernity bereft of community is recorded and the poetic word, through its connection to ritual, finds a way to subvert modernity's seemingly implacable linear progress to self-destruction. Through the agency of memory and imagination, Chicano poetry shares events and experiences and provides a poetic awareness of humanity's place in/as nature. Luis Valdez identifies a particular sense of time in this process:

> Chicano time por ejemplo   *for example*
> has never been gabacho [*gringo*] time
> because the Chicano exists
> in time with the temporadas   *seasons*
> and the movement of the planets
> and the stars.
>   . . . .
> The wristwatch is a game
> an arbitrary improvisation
> invented in Europe (*Luis Valdez—Early Works* 185).

In Ricardo Sánchez's *entelequia* as in Valdez's *pensamiento serpentino,* poetic language continues to play a vital role with respect to identity and difference. At times the authors draw circular demarcations indicating insiders and outsiders, or a Manichean line that distinguishes the correct from the unacceptable; but there is also a flexible, curving path of inclusiveness:

To be CHICANO is not (NOT)
to hate the gabacho [*gringo*] or the
gachupín [*Spaniard*] or even the pobre
vendido [*sellout*] . . .

To be CHICANO is to love yourself
your culture, your
skin, your language

And once you become CHICANO
that way
you begin to love other people
otras razas del mundo   *other races of the world*
los vietnamitas   *the Vietnamese*
los argentinos   *the Argentinians*
los colombianos   *the Colombians*
and, yes, even los europeos   *the Europeans*
(*Luis Valdez—Early Works* 175).

For Sánchez liberation from prejudice and fear is a global struggle and a promise "that no longer will there be masters and slaves, for both live in a world lacking dignity and human validity . . . one for oppressing, the other for not defending himself" (*Canto y grito* 16). As the *pinto* poet strives for personal liberation, he longs to also participate in a collective movement that will work for the liberation of Chicanos and all people.

Desmadrazgo: A Pachuco Self-Portrait

The title of the essay "Desmadrazgo" in *Canto y grito mi liberación* appears in the book's subtitle: (*y lloro mis desmadrazgos*). The first three words in the subtitle translate easily into English: "and I cry my." However, the noun *desmadrazgos* is an expression that Sánchez has improvised and expanded. It appears in no dictionary but derives from the verb *desmadrar,* meaning to separate young animals from their mother. The authoritative *Diccionario de la Real Academia* gives the colloquial sense of a "loss of reason and dignity" and "of conducting oneself, producing [something] with a lack of respect or measure [decorum]." The noun *desmadre* is defined as the action or effect of abandoning norms or exceeding oneself or as a disproportionate excess in words or actions.

But without reference to the madness and rage that prevails in the timespace of *la pinta* and that spills over into the barrio, the above definitions provide little more than a polite, bloodless perspective on the *pinto's* response to his personal and cultural dispossession. In "Desmadrazgo" and "Existir es . . . ," the final poem of the Mictla edition, Sánchez conveys his personal narrative and his critique of American society from the sociohistorical context of Chicanos. The two pieces function together to develop the theme of dispossession. In "Desmadrazgo" the critique begins with an individual, Stan Steiner, the author of a study on Chicanos entitled *La Raza* (1970).[24] In the Mictla edition of *Canto y grito mi liberación* Sánchez describes Steiner's book as "myopic . . . more farcical than factual; more projection than observation, and more in keeping with the faggoty image of the gringo of himself than with the recording of the virile machismo and hembra-ismo of La Raza" (*Canto y grito* 1971, n.p.). In the Anchor edition, in which epithets and other offensive remarks were expurgated, the attack is only slightly less virulent: Anglo "would-be ideologists and sociologically oriented saviours" are insensitive and incapable of studying Chicano culture with understanding. They "should go and study the weird habits of the gringo . . . therein lie the fertile fields of fermented racism . . . for them to study!" (*Canto y grito* 31–32).

Sánchez wanted to discredit the latest Anglo depictions of Chicanos and the barrio in order to replace them with his own more authentic and informed view. As we saw in chapter 3, this has been a strategy used by Chicano studies scholars to document the Chicano history of dispossession. In "Existir es . . ." Sánchez restates the problem: "Alli . . . por aquella calle, en aquel barrio existiamos . . . y nosotros [*There . . . along that street, in that neighborhood is where we lived . . . and we*], well, we did love it—but not in the sense that carey mcwilliams and stan steiner write that we loved it" (*Canto y grito* 141).

The attack against Steiner and his book also appeared in the testimonials that Sánchez and Abelardo Delgado wrote and which appeared in *Publishers' Weekly.* Abelardo opened the harangue by stating that "among the institutions in this country that have either purposely or unintentionally damaged and obliterated our culture is book publishing. . . . Because of you," he tells publishers, "the Anglo knows us not." Delgado then offers a remedy: "We suggest that now the Chicanos be counted as competent writers at all levels and in all fields—and that the efforts to scout out Chicano writing talent fall upon the publishing establishment. . . . We do resent having to read about our own Raza from the Steiners of the book world." Sánchez follows with his tirade: "Those who publish the mendacious accounts and histories that rip off our own sense of self must give more than an accounting for the racist onslaughts on Chicanos, Indians and Blacks. . . . We do not need your Stan Steiners to define us or exploit us; we do not want our history written by a monolingual academician. We want to be the exponents of our own human experience."[25]

Sánchez's critique of *desmadrazgo* abandons Anglo American norms of proper conduct and literariness in order to create an opening for his own historical, autobiographical, and literary discourse. He asks, from the point of view of the gringo, "What is this mass of brown people? Who are they? Where do they come from? What are their goals, objectives, and reasons for seeking a change in the status quo they have been forced into?" (*Canto y grito* 32). *I Am Joaquín* and "El plan espiritual de Aztlán" had addressed these questions, but unlike *Canto y grito mi liberación* those texts advocated the recovery of the land. Sánchez's work recovers instead the multiple timespaces that can properly represent the culture and hopes of Chicanos. *Desmadrazgo* is Sánchez's term for the dislocation and disconnection that persist in the Chicano soul, not only because of the lost land but also because Chicano history has been forgotten.

The essay "Desmadrazgo" removes the reader from the timespace of *la pinta* that we find in the poem "Soledad. . . ." In the essay the conflict between Chicanos and Anglos is played out not in the isolation of the *pinto's* cell *cum* conscience, but in a broader historical timespace: "The desolate Southwest, with its sage, cacti, and serene beauty" (*Canto y grito* 32). The 160-year U.S. occupation of this land has meant "neo-colonialism and slavery" for the dark-skinned, mestizo population, and the essay recites a bill of twentieth-century grievances, including the discrimination, dispossession, and disenfranchisement endured by Chicanos who have created the country's wealth and served loyally in its wars.[26]

The piece then returns to the timespace of the barrio and the autobiographical narrative. It recalls the recent past and the emergence of the essay's central figure, the pachuco, who appears among the soldiers, veterans, and younger brothers of the World War II generation. According to Sánchez, "the Pachuco became a movement . . . that had its genesis in El Paso, Texas."[27] The poet guides us to the city's old barrio near the Rio Grande where the dangers of drugs and police lurk. The account of the poet's youth is woven into the story of the pachuco and his barrio: "Lack of organizational skills forced the Pachuco to go underground during the late 50's. Submerged, he lay—thinking, plotting, and soaking up organizational skills. The plight of La Raza had to be alleviated, somehow . . . and soon!" (*Canto y grito* 35–36). In this essay it appears that the Chicano Movement is the result of conscious planning: "Thinking has jelled [*sic*]. Now there is structure and organization" (37). The poet picks up the pachuco's *caló* vernacular and *cábula* improvisations in order to record and promote the emergence of new possibilities. Giving his energies over to *la causa,* he encourages his readers to do the same.

In his study of the pachuco Arturo Madrid-Barela notes a development of this figure from the "zoot-suiter" of the forties and fifties to the *vato loco* of the Movement years. He asserts that "for many young Chicanos . . . the Pachuco represents a spiritual ancestor."[28]

In his article on the pachuco in Chicano poetry, Rafael Grajeda concedes that "if one . . . recalls the 1943 riots between pachucos and U.S. sailors, during which the pachuco suffered violence and harassment at the hands of law enforcement, legal and political agents, as well as grossly unfair treatment by the journalists, then it becomes clear how in the 1960's and 1970's the pachuco emerges as a hero."[29] However, Grajeda does not focus on pachucos as a group or class of marginalized youth within a particular social environment. For him the pachuco is a discursive archetype invented by other Chicanos for hero worship but "treated otherwise by most of the poets."[30]

Grajeda does not mention Sánchez's work directly, but by referring to "most" Chicano poets, he actually argues against the view of the pachuco held by certain other poets, including Ricardo Sánchez.[31] For example, Grajeda presents a critical reading of Tino Villanueva's "Pachuco Remembered," which he describes as "a poem that glorifies the pachuco as an early antecedent of the 1960's Chicano activists."[32] On the other hand, the critic praises poems by J. L. Navarro, José Montoya, and Raúl Salinas because "they represent the pachuco *realistically* by placing him in the midst of a political and psychological world that he fails to understand." At this we hear echoes of Joaquín in the sixties, "lost in a world of confusion," and, given his standard for the construction of pachuco "reality," it becomes apparent why Grajeda omits the work of poets like Alurista and Ricardo Sánchez from his analysis. The critic claims that he does so because their "concern is not the pachuco himself."[33] That is, these poets are dealing with a socially contextualized figure rather than with the isolated archetype that Grajeda describes. Yet the critic violates his own criteria by including in his study Raúl Salinas's "Un Trip through the Mind Jail," which he admits "is not a poem about the pachuco experience, but rather about [the] barrio." Clearly, the critic's intention is to detach the pachuco from any kind of social context or process, but Grajeda seems to overstate his case: "Poets believe that to glorify the pachuco, to recast this figure of the angry and hip street dude into that of a revolutionary Chicano who consciously and violently opposes a social order that denies him a rightful place, at this time would be counterproductive; and as literature would be dishonest."[34]

Published in 1980, almost a decade after the appearance of *Canto y grito mi liberación*, Grajeda's article begins with the argument that "realism" in Chicano poetry is inconsistent with the glorification of the pachuco. However, in the passage quoted above he is not denying the "reality" of the pachuco as a revolutionary hero; rather, he claims to be reporting what "poets believe . . . at this time." The validity of even this claim is weakened, however, by the fact that Tino Villanueva's poem and Ricardo Sánchez's "Desmadrazgo" contradict it: "Discontent, lethargy, hate, turbulent twinges of revenge, a driving energy to fire at the world, a million drives and furies: these make up the new zoot suit of the revolutionary. . . . The Brown Berets, MAYO, MAYA, MAPA, CRUSADE FOR JUSTICE, and other organizations have started on the road to taking reparations and following through with planned out strategies" (*Canto y grito* 37).

Written under the sign of the Movement, Sánchez's essay is neither a glorification nor a sympathetic treatment of the pachuco as a revolutionary figure. Rather, it is a portent of a social upheaval in process and a warning that it should not be ignored. But when the revolution fails to burst forth according to "planned out strategies" and almost everything about the Movement—its rhetoric, organization, and funding through "reparations"—is subjected to reevaluation, it will appear as a confused and chaotic experience simply because the leaders failed to understand it. *Hechizospells* and Sánchez's subsequent works describe the painful aftermath of the Movement. But in *Canto y grito mi liberación* the poet is still engaged in the process of inciting revolution through the subversion of "ordinary" time.

A final example is the poem "and it. . . ." At the beginning of this piece, where the poet usually dates his poems, letters, and essays, we read in Spanish, "-sintiempo-," meaning "without time" or "timeless." In this case, the text does not insist on the annihilation of time itself but on the destruction of the notion of linear time that is imposed on everyday experience. The destruction of linear time does not eliminate the whole concept of time. On the contrary, the disappearance of linear time is but the necessary precondition for adopting *alternative* timespaces, in this case, the timespace of the barrio. Like "Opened letter to my conscience," this poem begins with a salutation. Here again, the poet's voice addresses the *carnales* of the barrio who are both the audience and the subject of his writing. Upon entering into the timespace of the barrio, the first verse of the poem is an improvisation and paraphrase of the call to national identity found in the first line of the U.S. Declaration of Independence:

> cuando en el curso   del desafío y desmadre
> [*When in the course   of the struggle and dispossession*]
> (*Canto y grito* 39).

This poem is both a political manifesto and an emotional lament that advances the argument of "Desmadrazgo" by calling upon *carnales* (brothers and sisters) to rise up and take the necessary action to relieve the hurt and hunger of "chicanitos born only to die / swollen eyes and bellies / in the land of plenty / and it hurts, and it hurts" (40).

In these poems the figure of the pachuco and the *vato loco* do not stand in isolation—they are denizens and products of the barrio and the poet's figure of *desmadrazgo,* a condition which affects the entire Chicano community and also the dispossessed communities of Native Americans and African Americans in the United States. Spurred by the need for "dignity / and human-ness / and love," the poet puts forth this direct apprehension of reality, this truth, which must serve in the process of liberating himself and his community.

The Emergence of the Migrant

If Aztlán represents the timespace of the *nation* for the Chicano Movement, the barrio is emblematic of historical struggle and continuity. I've tried to demonstrate the importance of *la pinta* and "the migrant stream" as chronotopes in Ricardo Sánchez's work, but at no time does the poet abandon the important chronotopes of the barrio or Aztlán, although he deplores the abuses committed in their name.

Canto y grito mi liberación is the powerful, anguished voice of the Movement in its heyday, and the second half of the collection presents El Paso's Barrio del Diablo through the vivid images of the poet and his friend, the artist Manuel Acosta. These scenes dramatize the particular importance of the barrio in the poet's autobiographical narrative. The barrio is his birthplace, the place where he first attended school, grew to adolescence and, in a hostile environment, struggled to define his manhood through codes of *chicanismo* and *machismo*.[35] Throughout his years in prison and later, on the intellectual migrant stream of lectures, conferences, and readings, the poet's ties to El Paso (El Chuco) are a defining characteristic, despite (or because of) the poverty of its Chicano population, its proximity to Mexico, its blazing sun and arid landscape—the very things that might make it an inhospitable place to outsiders.

But much of the time El Paso functions as an absence in Sánchez's work. He spends long years in prison or in a kind of exile, and when he is home, it is often a disappointment because it cannot match the dreams and expectations which repeatedly drive the poet and his family back to the migrant stream. Thus, the dynamic *between* chronotopes, particularly *between la pinta* as a solidified, stagnant timespace and the migrant stream as a fluid and unstable one, permits a complex, *deterritorialized* reading of a Chicano subject who must endure exile in places like California, Massachusetts, Wisconsin, Utah, Alaska, and Washington State.

According to Mikhail Bakhtin, for the writer, "Time . . . thickens, takes on flesh, becomes . . . visible."[36] For the *pinto* as well, the immobility of prison produces a dense mass of time. No longer a stream, it becomes like a solid weight that pulls the convict down and can eventually kill him. In his preface to the poem "Soledad" Sánchez writes: "When a man goes to prison, he might become an integral part of it; and it, in turn, is unto that man like a big protective womb. He might try to rebel against the security afforded him by being good and getting out soon because he knows deep down that the more he accepts and adjusts, the more of a robot he will become. . . . If he fails, he will shortly give up his garrulous rebellion and become institutionalized and will eventually die in prison" (*Canto y grito* 27).

When he was released from Soledad prison in California, Sánchez returned to an El Paso of the mid-1960s where the weight of congealed time continued to oppress the inhabitants of the barrio. There had been little change. There was no Chicano Movement at that time, and there were few jobs or opportunities that would permit an improvement of the "normal life" of the barrio. In "Out/parole," a poem published in *Hechizospells* but composed shortly after his release from Soledad, Sánchez makes an explicit comparison *between* the two realities/timespaces of the barrio and *la pinta:*

> tasting freedom,
> a freedom
> that even now hides;
> people here
> in this hideous factory,
> This Farah nightmare,
> hate themselves
> just as much as pintos do;
>
> . . . .
>
> even soledad
> was understandable,
> after all convicts commit crimes,
> but what crimes do the poor commit
> to be sentenced by fate
> to toil out empty lives
> in cavernous factories

that demean
what should have meaning?
pura raza
dies in these monstrous
caverns of destitution;
would hate
to work forever
like all these salivating
people (*Hechizospells* 80).

Sánchez abhorred the strictures and conformity that he identified with both his prison experience and mere survival in the barrio. A common oppression connects these two realities and draws many Chicanos back and forth *between* them, which Sánchez himself experienced.[37] Unable to find work to support his family, he was arrested again, this time for armed robbery, and sentenced to another term, in Texas' state prison in Huntsville. Upon his parole in 1969 the poet feared that yet another return to prison might be his last: "I was back in El Paso. It was a perilous moment, for my parole officer wanted arbitrarily to revoke my parole. He disagreed violently with my coming back home—and more so with my involvement in the Movement and with my writings. I bobbed and weaved, and for sketches of time saw prison just around the corner."[38]

The parolee was thus forced to make a quick transition *between* two time-spaces, from the stagnation and confinement of *la pinta* to its opposite extreme, a life of constant movement on the "migrant stream." The middle course, the barrio, had to be avoided because it afforded him no security. This time, however, Sánchez was able to accomplish the transition, in part because the Chicano Movement provided a context for his development as a writer and activist.[39] In a poem dated March 10, 1969, just a few days before his final release from prison, Sánchez issued a characteristically audacious warning:

. . . and I mean it
when I say
that serving raza
is my answer
for the reason to my being;

if we have to burn
or shout or sing

or act or whatever
we have to do
to make our freedom real,
i am ready,
and so are other pintos,
but if the movement is a game
and hucksters are hustling
all our people
just to make themselves look big
or get more money
by pimping off the people,
then i'm also ready
to just go back to criming,
to looting and conniving,
for a pinto has no future
in this gringo/sordid world (*Hechizospells* 83).

There is no hope or expectation of security and a "normal life" for the *pinto* and his family. Comfort and complacency represent dangers for those who must remain ever wary. In *I Am Joaquín* they represent corruption and accommodation to a gringo middle-class mentality, and the dedicated Chicano activist must choose

Between
the paradox of
Victory of the spirit,
despite physical hunger
Or
to exist in the grasp
of American social neurosis,
sterilization of the soul
and a full stomach (*I Am Joaquín* 3).

The ex-*pinto*, however, has little choice except to commit himself and his family to *la causa* and to a life on the migrant stream in order to stay out of prison: "and my stream elongated and expanded . . . from the mired-up madness of amerika's hateful south (virginny) to washington, d. c., baltimore, new york, and massachusetts . . . then on to chicago, harvard, yale, northwestern, columbia, etc., all for rapping and more and more awareness . . .

then to denver, oregon, michigan, the mid-west . . . the stream wends on and on and on . . . never a surcease, tal es la vida [*that is life*]" (*Canto y grito* 81–83).

Ricardo Sánchez became a sojourner in various cities and universities throughout the country, a migrant intellectual who kept a solemn/joyful vow of poverty. He served as director of the Itinerant Migrant Health Project in the Lower Rio Grande Valley and wrote about the life of migrant workers from the perspective of a barrio dweller who had returned to "stream con- sciousness" (*Canto y grito* 73).

Hechizospells as Tragedy

With *Hechizospells* Ricardo Sánchez's poetic life achieves its full and tragic maturity. In this final chapter I argue that Ricardo Sánchez is the first great tragic figure of contemporary Chicano literature, a writer/protagonist who represents the conflicts of an individual within himself, with his people, and with the values of the larger world beyond his community. *Hechizospells* reveals a Ricardo Sánchez of gargantuan appetites and energy, a man with an epic vision who seems larger than life, but who acknowledges personal defects and failings that he strives to overcome.

In this chapter I also show that the three sections of *Hechizospells* ("Notes on the Human Condition," "Poetry," and "Estos poemas los dedico" [I Dedicate These Poems]) develop three statements or expressions of the poet's tragic theme and his tragic life. I also demonstrate how this three-part organization distinguishes *Hechizospells'* perspective on time from that of *Canto y grito mi liberación,* which was more concerned with the subject's past and present experience than with the philosophical problems of maturity and death that we find in *Hechizospells.* Indeed, the poet's sensibility now reveals a contemplative side, and the concept of *entelequia* will become Sánchez's way of representing his particular view of the human condition as it was shaped by the Chicano timespaces of the barrio, the *pinta,* and the migrant stream, which I described in the preceding chapters.

I must emphasize, however, that the mature phase of Sánchez's writing does not displace his poetry of social protest. In fact, *Hechizospells* provides a more solid philosophical basis for many of the same concerns and many of the actual poems of his earlier period. The poet's perspective arises from the ongoing personal and political travails which continue to affect him, his family, and friends. By the mid-1970s economic insecurity, paternal responsibility, the illness and death of loved ones, the death of barrios that are razed in the name of progress, and the failure of the Chicano Movement have all chastened the *vato loco* of *Canto y grito mi liberación.*

The poet is now more a *pinto viejo* and a *veterano* who in the span of a few years has redirected his poetic expression from immediate and urgent concerns of here and now, to the enigma of the future and what it may portend for himself and *la raza chicana.* The essays in the section "Notes on the Human Condition" give the first indication of the reflective turn Sánchez's writing has taken, while the poetry sections reveal a thoughtful response to the changes in the author's personal and political environment.

The third and final section of *Hechizospells* is dedicated to the poet's infant son, Pedro-Cuauhtémoc, "a su valentía infante, y al reconocimiento que el vivir es una lucha constante hacia la liberación" [*to an infant's courage, and to the recognition that life is a constant struggle toward liberation*] (*Hechizospells* 293). But the dedication goes out to others as well: "a todo pueblo que lucha por sus derechos humanos y sociales, al espíritu que nos encomienda a batallar contra la opresión . . . a los pueblos de Aztlán luchando y toda gente del mundo haciendo por fraternizarse con la humanidad al compartir la lucha hacia la liberación popular humanizante" [*to all the people who fight for their social and human rights, to the spirit that moves us in the battle against oppression . . . to the struggling people of Aztlán and all the people of the world who do their part for human understanding, and who share the struggle toward a humanizing, popular liberation*] (293).

I first show how a discussion of tragic genres becomes pertinent to the study of this Chicano poet and his autobiographical narrative. Tragedy, the most venerable of literary discourses in the Western tradition, continues to exert a powerful influence on the literature of the twentieth century. Yet to my knowledge, no work of Chicano literature has entered into the modern canon of tragic literature. I believe that in addition to Sánchez's *Hechizospells* there are a number of works by authors such as Gloria Anzaldúa, José Montoya, Raúl Salinas, Tomás Rivera, Miguel Méndez, and Aristeo Brito which may be read as Chicano tragic literature. Inasmuch as it continues to redefine the tragic condition, the work of these Chicano authors may be compared to that of Sophocles, Shakespeare, Faulkner, and others who wrote for their time and their people.

To begin an analysis of Sánchez's work as tragedy, I turn to Aristotle. According to his definition in the *Poetics,* tragedy is "[t]he imitation of an action that is serious and also, as having magnitude, complete in itself; in language with pleasurable accessories, each kind brought in separately in the parts of the work; in a dramatic, not a narrative form; with incidents arousing pity and fear, wherewith to accomplish its catharsis of such emotions."[1]

Many authorities believe that tragedy "in the first place almost certainly denoted a form of ritual sacrifice accompanied by a choral song in honor of Dionysus, the god of the fields and the vineyards. Out of this ritual developed Greek dramatic tragedy."[2] The dramatic form was further developed in the early modern era and was used to represent, among other things, an absence of hope: "There is hope, perhaps, *after* tragedy, but not *during* it." Tragedy was also seen as a kind of protest: "a cry of terror or complaint or rage or anguish to and against whoever or whatever is responsible for 'this harsh rack,' for suffering, for death. Be it God, Nature, Fate, circumstance, chance or just something nameless. It is a 'cry' about the tragic situation in which the tragic hero or heroine find themselves."[3]

Critical studies of Chicano literature have tended to avoid tragic interpretations or associations, concerning themselves instead with the cultural vindication of the Chicano community through representations of racial, class, and gender issues. Nevertheless, some tentative discussions of Chicano literature as tragic discourse do exist. For example, the critic Charles Tatum affirms that, "considering Chicano fiction as a whole, it offers us a chronicle of a half-century of misery. Its effect is cathartic, providing a release for the accumulated suffering and frustration so that a new consciousness of *La Raza* might be formed from the experience."[4]

More recently, Francisco A. Lomelí has seen in Miguel Méndez's *Peregrinos de Aztlán* "un trasfondo ya trágico que acompaña a los trashumantes peregrinos. Sobre todo, consigue ubicar la mayor parte de la acción en un espacio indefinido, la frontera—que parece purgatorio—, donde los personajes están en proceso de integrarse a un mundo de desilusiones" [*a now tragic background that accompanies the migrating pilgrims. Above all, he is able to situate the main part of the action in an indefinite space, the border—which seems like purgatory—, where the characters are in the process of incorporating themselves into a world of disappointment*].[5]

In her study of *Peregrinos de Aztlán* Cecilia Ubilla-Arenas questions the novel's resolution of historical oppression by means of a fantastic dream-reality: "Así, toda la indignación acumulada, el hambre 'de siglos,' las quejas, la humillación y las lágrimas; toda la lucidez que permitió ver quién es oprimido y quién es opresor, se subliman en el sueño de un futuro que parece recreación de un pasado" [*Thus, all the accumulated indignation and the hunger 'of centuries,' the plaints, the humiliation and the tears; all the lucidity that permitted one to see who is oppressed and who is the oppressor, are sublimated in the dream of a future that appears to be a re-creation of the past*].[6]

Ubilla-Arenas asks, "¿Cómo explicar y cómo entender este desenlace? La explicación debemos buscarla en parte en la concepción que Méndez mismo tiene de la literatura y su función" [*How can we explain and understand this outcome? We must seek at least part of the explanation in Méndez's concept of literature and its function*].[7] She quotes the following passage in which Miguel Méndez outlines his Chicano aesthetic:

El hecho de que el ánimo de nuestra gente se haya encendido para luchar bajo metas comunes, ha predispuesto un ámbito donde resuenen las voces y donde la literatura sea como un aliento que anime los anhelos del Chicano, exponiendo el reflejo de su vivir, dando a nuestro pueblo conciencia histórica, y algo muy importante: su verdadera identidad, el conocimiento de sus grandes valores humanos y el factor impostergable que constituye la necesidad de una literatura que nos enlace bajo su comunicación para celebrar nuestros triunfos o para gritar la indignación que provocan las injusticias, para exponer las cualidades de nuestro espíritu y también para documentar a las generaciones venideras, que en nuestras experiencias habrán de basar sus decisiones [*The fact that the enthusiasm of our people was ignited in a common struggle has prepared an environment in which voices ring out, and where literature becomes like a breath that revives the yearnings of Chicanos and reveals their way of life, thus giving our people a historical consciousness and something that is very important: their true identity, a knowledge of their tremendous human values, and an urgent factor which is their need for a literature that will bind us through communication, so that we may celebrate our triumphs or shout our indignation when provoked by injustice, thus making apparent the qualities of our spirit and also documenting for future generations that will be obliged to base their decisions upon our experience*].[8]

It is worth noting that Méndez's formulation resembles Ricardo Sánchez's *entelequia* in this respect: both writers embrace the pain and joy of the Chicano experience and both take responsibility for providing a literary foundation for *"generaciones venideras,"* future generations of Chicanas and Chicanos (*Hechizospells* xviii). Méndez uses phrases such as *gritar la indignación* (shout of indignation), and *grandes valores humanos* (tremendous human values), which are strongly reminiscent of phrases used by the *pinto* poet. The similarity of their ideas regarding literature are perhaps not surprising given that both Méndez and Sánchez are natives of the border region and have endured a common isolation and exile from the literary mainstream. According to Lomelí, "A pesar de ser reconocido como una de las máximas voces chicanas, sobre todo en México, Miguel Méndez sigue siendo relativamente postergado como escritor de primera fila" [*Despite being recognized, especially in Mexico, as a major voice among Chicano authors, Miguel Méndez continues to be largely excluded from the first rank of important writers*].⁹

Lomelí attributes this relative obscurity to Méndez's narrative style, which demands considerable effort on the part of the reader. Of course, we can say the same about Sánchez, even though (or precisely because) he does not write exclusively in Spanish, as Méndez does. Another important difference between these two authors is that the concept and technique of Chicano timespaces is not well developed in the work of Méndez. Indeed, this seems to be a technique which so far only Sánchez has mastered. His depiction of time as multiple and simultaneous rather than linear is the crucial innovation of an intertextual *mestizaje* that binds his *entelequia* to the tragic traditions of both Greece and America, to Sophocles and to Nezahualcóyotl.¹⁰

According to this view, Chicanos, as the mestizo offspring of Mexico, Spain, and the United States, are heirs to a tragic history and literature. From the Spanish Conquest and Inquisition to colonial dispossession, peonage, and revolution, to modern economic and political dislocations, Mexican mestizos have a profound cultural memory of death, ruin, and oppression. It is little wonder that in the face of this history many have expressed admiration for the Anglo American values of progress, democracy, and optimism.¹¹ In the case of Chicanos, ignorance of their own history and literature is part of the long struggle against oppression and exclusion in the United States. But this does not mean that they have forgotten their tragic legacy or have failed to produce a written record of it.

La raza claims literary and cultural roots that reach back to Spain and New Spain, to Mexico and early New Mexico, Texas, and California. The baroque poetry and drama of Spanish and Mexican writers such as Pedro Calderón de la Barca, Tirso de Molina, and Sor Juana Inés de la Cruz exhibit tragic qualities that were to some extent mitigated by their Catholicism. This is also true of the Spanish writers of the Generation of 1898 who were younger contemporaries of Nietzsche and Bergson. One of the leading members of this group, Miguel de Unamuno, was the author of a book-length essay titled *The Tragic Sense of Life in Men and Nations* (1912), in which he elaborates a Kierkegaardian form of religious existentialism.¹² But the Spanish writer who, after Cervantes, had the strongest influence on Ricardo Sánchez was the poet and playwright Federico García Lorca. Lorca wrote about his visit to the United States in his collection *Poeta en Nueva York,* which Sánchez read in prison. Sánchez later dedicated to the Spanish poet a poem which consists of seven parts, five in Spanish and two in English. The fourth and fifth parts read as follows:

IV.

te encontré, Lorca,	*I found you, Lorca,*
a la orilla	*on the edge*
de un barranco de acero,	*of a steel ravine*
en una celda	*in a cell*
donde se moldeaban	*where they molded*
almas de azufre y cobre,	*souls of sulphur and copper,*
vi tu sonrisa gitana	*I saw your gypsy smile*
culebrear por una fila de rejas,	*snake along a row of bars*
las sombras bailaban	*the shadows danced*
enloquecientes rimas	*their maddening rhymes*
en lo infinito de un mundo sin sueños,	*in an endless world without dreams,*

abrí tus páginas, Lorca,	*I opened your pages, Lorca,*
con la locura de un duende,	*with the madness of a ghost,*
buscando en tu canto a Whitman	*searching in your song for Whitman*
una cáscara de vida-frutal,	*a scrap of fruitful life,*
la noria daba aguas	*the well gave forth water*
y mi sed brindaba	*and my thirst offered a toast*
al océano de imagen y canto	*to an ocean of image and song*
inundando lo solitario	*that inundated the loneliness*
del cimento [*sic*] y acero	*of the cement and steel*
de mis ensueños . . .	*of my dreams*

V.

ante los fusiles	*facing the guns*
un poema lloró	*a poem cried*
lo grande de su expresión,	*the greatness of that expression,*
el plomo voló	*the lead flew*
con fuerza torquemeante,	*with Torquemadean force,*
los crédulos festejaron	*the believers celebrated*
lo vacío de sus antojos	*the emptiness of their whims*

("Notas a Federico García Lorca [con festejos y disculpas]" 42–43).

Sánchez's poem laments the destruction of Lorca, who was a homosexual and a victim of fascism during the Spanish civil war of 1936. Fascism was the latest incarnation of Spanish state tyranny which historically had had millions of victims in America as well. The Catholic church's role in the tragic history of both Spain and Mexico was the result of the Spanish monarchy's theocratic system of government. Both church and state endorsed and carried out the Inquisition, the forced conversion and/or expulsion of Jewish and Islamic populations from the Iberian Peninsula, as well as the conquest and destruction of native Mexican cultures and the persecution and enslavement of native peoples in North, South, and Central America. In return, the Church offered a culture of faith and religious practice that would help the Mexicans—indigenous, mestizos, and *criollos*—and later Chicanos as well, to survive the genocide, terror and dispossession that was perpetrated against them.[13]

Although Sánchez deplored this tragic legacy many times and did not speak or write as a Christian himself, he nevertheless respected the religious beliefs of others, including members of his own family. He frequently collaborated with Christians who were involved in projects to aid the poor, the *pintos,* the mentally ill, and migrant families. Sánchez tended to reject conventional religious beliefs that threatened his own freedom of thought and cultural expression, yet his poetic sensibility emerged from a deep spirituality, and he particularly admired the spiritual practices of North American Indian cultures.

When comparing Sánchez's Chicano existentialism and his sense of tragedy with other tragic authors such as Nietzsche, Faulkner, and Malraux, I find some interesting similarities. For example, both Sánchez and Nietzsche question and ultimately reject dialectical thinking. Sánchez's *entelequia* and Nietzsche's Dionysian tragedy are both joyous celebrations of the survival of human life in the face of anguish, pain, and loss.[14] Not surprisingly, however, there are important differences between the Chicano poet and the German philosopher. Sánchez's thought rejects the intolerance and uncompromising individualism of Nietzschean doctrines like the Will to Power, which becomes a one-dimensional quest for philosophic truth. As Gilles Deleuze observes, "Nietzsche insists on the fundamentally Christian character of the dialectic and of German philosophy and on the congenital incapacity of Christianity and the dialectic to live, understand or think the tragic."[15] While *Canto y grito mi liberación* narrates an individual's reckless and desperate quest for freedom, in *Hechizospells* the poet has survived to elaborate a hybrid, mestizo sense of tragedy that places limits on individualism and defends Indohispanic norms of respect for family and community, particularly the poor and the oppressed.

For both Nietzsche and Sánchez, art is "the highest task and the authentically metaphysical activity." In Nietzsche's philosophy, artistic creation becomes "the great stimulus of life," which "drives the creator on to overcome himself: art enlarges the world by returning it to its originally explosive and chaotic character. Art is drunkenness, celebration, orgy, break with identity—whereas science contents itself with ordering that which is basically already acquired. If art intensifies the feeling of power, it is because art reaffirms all reality in and through its power of establishing as real any 'appearance' simply by confirming it *as* an appearance. The appearance is selected, corrected, and magnified; but this procedure entails an adherence to what has always been regarded merely as illusory: it entails a glorification of illusion as illusion."[16]

Ricardo Sánchez, on the other hand, never seeks a level of abstraction that might erase the concreteness of his own experience or the social circumstances that he is projecting through his art. When he achieves a tragic identification with the universality of the human condition, this is not an individual achievement. Rather, his philosophic and aesthetic insights are determined by the particular circumstances of his identity as a Chicano. It is this "being Chicano" which unifies the themes of freedom that we find in *Canto y grito* and the tragic insights of *Hechizospells*. As a poet, Sánchez wishes to make apparent those circumstances which historically have been invisible or forgotten. Juan Bruce-Novoa has observed that Sánchez "is the epitome of the artist: a person incapable of living anything without raising it into an aesthetic experience, expressed in whatever media are immediately available, and eventually transposed into the written word. In other words, Sánchez makes living an art. And he lives to the extreme."[17]

"Extreme" is an adjective that may be imputed to both Sánchez and Nietzsche, but in very different ways. According to Alphonso Lingis, for both the poet and the philosopher, "the horrible and the absurd are neither negated nor dissimulated in art—which ultimately is tragic art: the horrible is sublimated, rendered sublime; the absurd is rendered comic."[18] As in the tortured, baroque sensibility of Francisco Quevedo, for whom the work of art bears the grotesque, graffiti-like mark of the *pícaro* who offends and amuses at the same time, the poetry of Ricardo Sánchez elevates Chicano folk *rascuachismo, pachuquismo,* and *chafismo* to the level of tragedy. In doing so, he initiates the *rascuachización, chicanización,* and re-*humanización* of high art and high criticism—all of which constitute a process that is inevitable because high art and high culture are not eternal forms—they are nourished and transformed by folk art and by popular forms of speech and expression that have achieved an acceptability which was previously denied.[19]

Deleuze's account of Nietzschean philosophy describes the dialectical opposition between Dionysus and Apollo in *The Birth of Tragedy* (1871), which later becomes an opposition between Dionysus and Socrates and finally an opposition between Dionysus and Christ. *Canto y grito mi liberación,* like Nietzsche's early formulation in *The Birth of Tragedy,* seeks the dialectic, "the movement of contradiction and its resolution."[20] For Sánchez and for Chicanos the adversaries are clear and concrete: technological, economic, and political systems they cannot control. Their powerlessness in society is confirmed by their absence from canonical discourses of any kind, which means that their concerns and interests will be denied by Nietzsche's construction of the tragic: "The tragic is not to be found in . . . anguish or disgust, nor in a nostalgia for lost unity. The tragic is only to be found in multiplicity, in the diversity of affirmation *as such.* What defines the tragic is the joy of multiplicity, plural joy. Nietzsche can attack all theories of the tragic for failing to recognise tragedy as an aesthetic phenomenon. *The tragic* is the aesthetic form of joy, not a medical phrase or a moral solution to pain, fear or pity. It is joy that is tragic."[21]

But if Nietzsche's Will to Power remains an expression of philosophic purity—a theory for elite minorities only—*los de abajo,* the colored masses of America, Asia, and Africa, are the negative aspect in Nietzsche's definition of the tragic. And today it is precisely their tragedy to be the negative side of the Overman's joy of affirmation. They are what a powerful America ignores when Nietzsche's theory fails, in practice, to affirm multiplicity and temporal diversity.

The evils of Native American genocide and African American slavery may be difficult to redress, but their existence has not been forgotten. Chicanos, on the other hand, face a situation in which their historical experience is little understood and easily ignored. Despite the continuous presence of Chicanos in America, they were long ignored as part of the silent landscape. The emergence of Chicano studies and Chicano discourse seems to be part of a relatively recent, postmodern phenomenon in which America struggles to find its identity. In the early 1970s, Ricardo Sánchez asks the same questions America is struggling to answer. He asks in "Desmadrazgo," "What is this mass of brown people? Who are they? Where do they come from?" According to Luis Leal, the seeming invisibility of Chicanos was due to the fact that for years their literature had been ignored because much of it was written in Spanish.[22]

During the period of antiwar protests, civil rights activism, and political turmoil in the 1960s and 1970s, Chicano literature, some of which was written in Spanish, tended to reflect the political militancy of a Movement that defined itself as separate from American society. Chicano authors denounced the social exclusion suffered by Mexican Americans for more than a hundred years. More recently, however, Chicano critics have tried to redefine Chicano literature *within* the context of American literature and have deplored its (and their own) continued exclusion from the national critical scene.[23] I would argue that the question of tragic genres lies at the heart of this debate over the place of Chicano literature, and the question may be posed in this way: When will Chicano critics and, after them, the critical mainstream recognize Chicano tragic discourse on its own terms and in its own languages? This has yet to happen because Chicano literature is still regarded by many critics as a form of ethnography rather than an aesthetic practice, as more polemical and didactic than artistic.

Leal insists that it is on the question of language that "the traditional definition of American literature breaks down, as these works in Spanish are not considered as properly belonging to the Anglo-American literary tradition." Leal's recommendation is that "literary historians should re-write the history of American literature incorporating that literature written by Hispanics living in the former Spanish colonies, then a part of Mexico and later a part of the United States, together with the literature written by Mexican Americans and Chicanos."[24] If Leal's recommendations were carried out, it might become commonplace for critics to compare, for example, the works of Ricardo Sánchez with those of other tragic authors and to study them with the seriousness and rigor that is devoted to literature written in French, English, Russian, or other languages. Francisco Lomelí suggests that critics who defend universal standards of literary excellence may not be capable of reading and understanding Chicano literature: "Our literature needs to be judged according to universal literary criteria, but its own particular modes of expression and motifs should not be sacrificed in the process. Its origin already implies distinctive features, such as the motif of the barrio, codes of meaning through interlingualism, and the relationship between Anglo and Mexican histories."[25]

Setting aside language differences and the problem of understanding, Ricardo Sánchez views the question of universality as a thematic given. In his preface to *Hechizospells* he states: "That [any work of literature] might touch universal themes is not the question, for all creations by human beings will touch universal themes, for the human condition is basically the same all over the world" (*Hechizospells* xi).

Here Sánchez, who rarely used the word "tragedy," expressed a fundamental postulate of tragic literature: that tragedy is inherent to the human condition, regardless of time, place, or circumstance. That is to say, tragedy is not determined by nationality, nor is it limited by accidents of birth, and no human being can be certain of escaping its ravages. Tragedy touches everyone, high or low, rich or poor, male or female, in different ways. According to the American novelist William Faulkner, the concept of tragedy "as Aristotle saw it, is the same conception of tragedy that all writers have." The author of *La condition humaine*, André Malraux, believed that "[a]ll suffer, misery is ubiquitous and classless."[26]

Nevertheless, the catastrophes and joys of the mighty are famous while the lowly are forgotten, and for Ricardo Sánchez this is the particular anguish of the poor in the prisons, the barrios, and the migrant camps—the reduction of their tragedy to silence. America has embraced the doomed Willie Loman and Blanche DuBois, the Estragons and Vladimirs, and other middle- and lower-class figures who are confounded by the absurdity and cruelty of modern life. According to critic Haskell M. Block, in the celebrated novels of William Faulkner "both the guilty and the innocent are doomed, sometimes as the result of blind chance, sometimes through their violations of established order." Faulkner believed there existed a "blind tragedy of human events," which "entails both aspiration and catastrophe." Although Faulkner's view of tragedy was not always consistent, in some contexts he wrote of human life as "rooted in tragedy and all human beings are condemned to struggle and defeat."[27] Faulkner's tragic novels attempt to recreate the emotional impact of the Greek and Renaissance forms in a modern genre. Block notes the influence of the classical forms on Faulkner and on André Malraux: "In commenting on *Absalom, Absalom!* at the University of Virginia in 1957, Faulkner described Sutpen as a victim of the Greeks, 'the old Greek concept of tragedy . . . Man's free will functions against a Greek background of fate. . . .' Like Malraux, Faulkner embraces the Greek example."[28]

Ricardo Sánchez was familiar with this modern tragic tradition that I am tracing.[29] He chose to give autobiographical form to his tragic themes and was thus able to depict a way of life that is uniquely Chicano. An early example of this appears in *Canto y grito mi liberación* where the "magic/tragic valley" of South Texas becomes, for Sánchez, "this very cauldron of chicanismo" (*Canto y grito* 25). At this point, we must turn away from the universality of tragic experience and recognize once again the real differences, particularly the cultural and linguistic differences, inherent in our topic. Liberal critics may be glad to see a formerly Spanish-speaking (or formerly silenced) minority assimilating and depicting its cultural life in English. Merely on that basis, they may regard Chicano literature of today as an improvement over what was available just a few years ago. But in doing so, they continue to minimize the real impact of Chicano culture on America. According to Luis Leal, "So conditioned are critics of American literature that when they review books of minority authors the only values they find are ethnological. . . . As early as 1919, when Louis Untermeyer reviewed a collection of translations from [American] Indian oral poetry, he said that the book was a document valuable chiefly for its ethnological interest, adding that the collection, for the man of letters, was 'a crude and topheavy monument with a few and even lively decorations.'"[30] Bloomfield and Dunn argue that "poetry in the West, especially popular or folk art, still teaches and enables humanity to face destiny and existence. This is a role which many poets, often looked down upon by their more exclusive colleagues, still fill. . . . Yet even here most of the educated pay little attention to such activities, and usually the name of artist is withheld from such a creator."[31]

We have seen that Sánchez stands at a distance from Nietzsche's elitist interpretations of the tragic, but at the same time the Chicano poet's *entelequial* and mestizo sense of tragedy coincides with some aspects of the Nietzschean system. Critic Michel Haar, for example, argues that Nietzsche's concept is "not at all sad or pessimistic: it is a state in which, thanks to an affirmation of the highest degree, we are able to include within ourselves, and to vindicate, even the deepest suffering."[32] The implied conflict and resolution between the tragic "high" and "low" might be seen here in terms of Abelardo Delgado's folksy metaphor of the poet's "yo-yo moods." For Sánchez's autobiography is a story of conflict and suffering and of strength in overcoming suffering. It is a battle between the forces of life and death, beauty and horror, which is told over many pages, that seems to repeat itself, manically and obsessively, as it re-experiences the past from different perspectives and different timespaces. Death and tragedy have taught the protagonist that he must be strong enough to fight: in the barrio, in *la pinta,* and in his poetry. Death and tragedy are a constant presence that he cannot escape, and to which he is reconciled only with his passing. In the meantime, he states in typically belligerent fashion that "in the face of moral cowards, I staunchly proclaim my right to my own humanity—and it is beautiful—gratifyingly beautiful—to sense how much of a threat a man can be only because he wants to realize as much of his humanity as possible" (*Canto y grito* 15).

In taking a stand against what he calls moral cowardice, Sánchez identifies his sense of tragedy with a social activism that refuses to fatalistically endorse the status quo and that struggles and advocates tirelessly for change. In *Canto y grito mi liberación* he contrasts the concept of humanity to that of "man": "[W]e must . . . realize how morally irresponsible *man* has been. . . . we must declare our humanity in unequivocal terms" (*Canto y grito* 15, emphasis in original).

Sánchez avoids the overused terms "tragedy" and "the tragic." In his writings he employs other words, such as *locura,* madness, *desmadrazgo,* death, and the "human condition" to convey the various meanings of "tragedy." Part of the difficulty with the signifier is precisely the universality of the experiences which it suggests. Since "the tragic" by definition can afflict all human beings, of all social strata, the signifier will carry different connotations depending on its use in everyday speech, in the press, in the social sciences, or as a technical term in literature and philosophy. Chicanos do not often use the term since they have a rich lexicon in this semantic area, which Sánchez also happens to prefer. Nevertheless, "tragedy" has a powerful political and emotional impact in the sciences, the social sciences, and the humanities. In *Hechizospells* Sánchez writes that social scientists, politicians, and other experts control the meaning of tragedy in America. Specialists study it as a phenomenon, as an effect of poverty, ignorance, hunger, and other social ills. Sánchez is skeptical of their motives and he denounces their cynicism: "These new priests—cobol-fortran-scientific-formuli-and-social-science-fantasizers—have been uncaring, callous, wanton, and egotistically arbitrary in their hocus-pocus villainy to help the powerful, through deceit and any other means, aggrandize even more power and wealth" (*Hechizospells* 13).

There is no doubt that Sánchez's narrative poetry tells a story of Chicano *desmadrazgo* in the powerful key of tragedy. In addition to his own tragic experiences, his educational background included exposure to numerous works of darkly tragic literature. As a member of a Thespian society in prison, he participated in productions of Beckett's *Waiting for Godot* and Albee's *Zoo Story.* He studied Oedipus, Freud, Kierkegaard, and Dickinson, as well as the more modern canon that includes Lorca, Eliot, Sartre, Camus, Charlie Parker, Jack Kerouac, and James Baldwin.[33] Contemporary Chicano literature has developed under the influence of this modernist canon that brought forth expressions of loss and confusion as well as progress. The poetry of Gloria Anzaldúa and Lorna Dee Cervantes and the novels of Miguel Méndez, Alejandro Morales, and Aristeo Brito give abundant testimony of anguish and tragic loss. These Chicano authors improvised new forms and languages for a literature that is haunted by death and tragedy. Sánchez's work is part of this new form of literary tradition. For example, in the poem "Alan, my nephew," the poet comforts a young man whose war injuries have caused him to be institutionalized:

. . . I see terror
hiding
in your struggle to smile;

alan, my nephew, my ahijado   *godson*
whom I confirmed
within catholicism's regimen
years ago,
you 100% disabled youth of 20,

back
from the orient
where you wore army fatigues
and your mind became fatigued
by horrid realities
and they've branded you in this mental ward,
. . . .
but your release is beyond me,
for others make the rules:
. . . .
you ask me about Mando, is he making it?
yes, he also has a 100% disability process,
and the shrapnel in his brain is not totally excised,
and he, too, is a loved nephew, and he hurts
from irreparable/irreversible brain damage,
. . . .
in the computer mind of amerika
all Chicanos come from greaserville
and that is certainly one region,
not a big area full of states/cities/
regions . . . but he is well, now, alan,
not completely all that he used to be,
for when you lose a parcel of your brain
you never regain it,
but he will survive
and so will Katy (his wife), his twin
daughters, little danny and david his boys.

pero don't fret, alan,
you, too, shall survive
within your struggle to re-know

> yourself, yes, act brave,
> embrace your crazy uncle
> who laughs at everything,
>   eventhough I cry now inside,
>   you won't see the tears (*Hechizospells* 271–73).

To Sánchez it was unacceptable that the story of the "greaser" and the "meskin" should be nothing more than footnotes or melodramatic whispers in the annals of American literature, for he cries out a full-throated *cantogrito* that reveals undiscovered tragic sensibilities. He performed the *récits* of tragedy and the human condition in order to tell a story in which Chicanos played a significant role. According to Sánchez, "All literature is particularistic in expression, and generalistic in as much as it expresses such themes as love, hunger, war, slavery, and other human needs and conditions" (*Hechizospells* xi). He did not distrust universalizing discourses. He included them in his own theory of Chicano literature, treating them as a legacy of learning that, in one way or another, had been handed down, borrowed, or stolen by many generations. At the beginning of *Hechizospells* Sánchez states what the book is about. The section, "Notes on the Human Condition," opens with an essay titled "Hechizos: Pieces of life":

> This book is a series of glimpses at a multifaceted world; seething with anger and discontent; pulsating with love and hope; and inspired by the humanity of those who have shared moments with me. The barrios of my past live on, if only in the imagery coursing through my mind. The jadedness of prison and the callousness of tormented tourist trapping streets in North Beach, Ciudad Juárez, Hollywood, Times Square, and the French Quarter still shrill out dehumanization—lustfully, sordidly, just as the political beast we call society still shreds up our humanity in order to exploit us. . . .
>
> Thoughts/ideas/poetry/fiction/truth & fact, all these form the inner world(s) I inhabit. These are also the structure of this book. Brief llantos and lloridos and locuras and looks at a process . . . un proceso vital that has matter-of-factly known the anomie of prison/army, the desolation of poverty, the love of family [. . .] and the soulfulness of being within the multidimensions of life (4–5).

Hechizospells is a reprise and continuation of the autobiography begun in *Canto y grito mi liberación*. Many of Sánchez's themes such as his criticism of Amerika and his love of family, friends, and nature are familiar to readers of the first collection. In his painful/joyful autobiography Sánchez is demonstrating, like his *compa,* Abelardo Delgado, that human life, talent, and resources are being tragically wasted in Chicano communities. In his poem, "stupid america," Delgado directs the nation's attention to "that chicanito / flunking math and english / he is the picasso / of your western states / but he will die / with one thousand masterpieces / hanging only from his mind."[34] Sánchez, an ex-*pinto,* pachuco, and high school dropout, throws himself against the lowered expectations that lead to the familiar cycle of failure, destruction, and waste. But even as he denounces the foibles and cruelty of mainstream society, his main objective continues to be his *cantogrito* to *entelequia.* "Love is the key," sings the poet: "it is the force that propels us toward writing/painting/acting. To see squalor and not protest is to deny our humanity. To act with people toward nation building is to affirm our humanness and to show our love for progeny and all humanity. The racism and deprivation we have survived must be brought to an end, that our children and future generations might live more humane lives, able to create more with their lives" (*Hechizospells* xix).

Marvin Lewis declares *Hechizospells'* 321 pages a "monumental work not only in terms of size but also for the poetic time period which it covers, roughly 1961–1974." He also observes a poetic development between the two collections, suggesting that *"Hechizospells* is an expansion of *Canto y grito mi liberación."* Philip Ortego stated that *"Canto y grito mi liberación* was a cry of the poet's liberation; *Hechizospells* is a statement about the liberation of all mankind. With this book, the poet's vision of life has moved from the chronicling of the particular to the encompassing of the universal." Similarly, Francisco Lomelí and Donald Urioste believe that *Hechizospells* "proves to be more profound" and "continues, or better yet, amplifies the themes established in his first book, *Canto y grito mi liberación,* with a definite change in tone."[35]

But what is it exactly that makes *Hechizospells* more profound, more humane, or more compelling than *Canto y grito mi liberación?* Up until now none of its readers or critics has been willing to say. In the following section I show how the book attains a cathartic unity of the universal and the personal in and through tragedy.

Notes on the Human Condition

Hechizospells is divided into three main sections, the first of which is the introductory "Notes on the Human Condition." This part consists of seven prose pieces, including a letter, essays, satire, and fiction, most of which date from 1973 or 1974. This part is followed by a selection of some ninety poems that make up the bulk of the volume. As critic Marvin Lewis notes, the selection includes *pinto* poems from as early as 1961 to post-Movement writings from 1974. The third and final section is another group of poems, most of which are dedicated to the poet's third child, Pedro-Cuauhtémoc Sánchez, who died shortly after his premature birth on January 16, 1975. These poems date from October, 1974, to March, 1975.

Not unlike its burly, bearded author, the physical exterior of *Hechizospells* is boldly imposing. The composite Spanish/English title is emblazoned in red stylized script that dominates the front cover. The illustration below the title is an ink drawing of two hands conjuring a skeleton to life. The signs of life and death are juxtaposed on the dedication page as well, where names of the living and the dead appear among the poet's *carnales,* fellow-poets, and children. This opening presentation introduces the poet's meditation on life as an existential struggle in which youth, maturity, and death coexist as stages of the human process. But the normal process can easily be cut short by violence, by tragedy, or by illness, as we read in a long poem composed in ballad style that memorializes the death of Santos Rodríguez, a Chicano boy who was killed by a Dallas police officer. In the third section the poet recounts the brief struggle of Pedro-Cuauhtémoc Sánchez, who died of congenital heart disease.[36] The poet was unable to obtain the funds to pay for doctors and treatment that might have saved his son. Thus, the book's cover also signifies the opposition between the Culture of Life and the Culture of Death: "A legacy based on human worth and liberation, truth and dignity, and love and appreciation for life—with acceptance for the real-ness of death—is more meaningful and sanguine than a materialistic legacy. . . . We take but experience with us to the grave, and only the moments of sharing and love do we leave behind—for objects have a shorter life span than good memories. Money and objects merely facilitate mobility and momentary pleasures, but do not engender love nor a felicitous life" (*Hechizospells* xx).

Very early in the text the poet sounds a note of resignation that contrasts sharply with the urgency and desperation of much of *Canto y grito mi liberación.* In the five years between the two collections Sánchez gains considerable success and experience, but he seems to be a sadder and wiser man. He learns to moderate his exuberance and rebelliousness as he acknowledges the limits that life places on his words and actions. But the poet's resignation is not yet a surrender; it is a tragic realization that the journey, the road to a final victory and true freedom and justice, will be long, much longer than he can travel in a lifetime.

Canto y grito owed much of its inspiration to the Movement that promised a better future for Chicanos. Sánchez's criticism of the Movement was designed to be constructive and reformist and to make its leadership more effective and responsible. However, by the time *Hechizospells* was published in 1976, the Movement as many had conceived it—a male-dominated revolution to recover the lost land—had come to an abrupt end. Sánchez realized that without a cause capable of rallying all Chicanos, the rest of the journey would be a bitter and difficult one. While the determination to live on in struggle remained, there were moments when confusion reigned:

> confusion mixt
>   into circumlocution
> spiral of evolution
> stagnated/stunted,
> wary eyes
> seeking change
> via revolution,
> a hysterically historical
> human merry-go-round
> feeding on the discontent
> created by the power elite—
> and the dispossessed (*Hechizospells* 7)

Sánchez was, without apologies, a Chicano patriarch who would not live to see his people in possession of the promised land. If Aztlán was indeed their destination, it was his fate to be buried along the way, in a poor grave among the poor, and his books and poems were his gifts to their children.

Hechizospells' three sections allow Sánchez's tragic theme of life and death to be dramatically developed in three "acts." In this way, the formal structure of the book is also reminiscent of the classical tragedy, and very different from the open-ended narrative of *Canto y grito mi liberación,* which reveals no subordination of its material or clear sense of an ending amid the exhilaration which the poet and his community are experiencing. Five years later, however, shadows of death invade the Movement, the community, and the poet's own family, threatening to cast the future into darkness. Sánchez has been chastened by the collapse of the Chicano Movement and stunned by the death of his infant son. There is no surrender yet, he will continue to work and write, but the poet has been forced at last to think in terms of endings. Specifically with regard to the new collection, he must provide it with an ending as well as a beginning and something in between. In short, he must give the work a formal structure and unity, and a project this ambitious demands that he imagine his own end, his own mortality, which he has cheated on many occasions and has refused to acknowledge until now. The protean poet realizes that there is a limit to the future—his future. And so he discovers his theme—the Human Condition—and his project responds to that discovery in a number of ways. First, it recognizes death as a part of life. For every death there is a new birth, and his poetry, his *cantogrito,* recounts the anguish and joy of these incomprehensible *hechizos.*

Sánchez's use of theoretical discourse in the first section of *Hechizospells* also signals a break from his practice in *Canto y grito,* in which he did not preface his narrative with a theory of literature or with disquisitions on the human condition. One reason for this is that the task of publishing the book was part of the creative process of *Canto y grito mi liberación,* while cultural theory fulfills this role in *Hechizospells.* In both cases, Sánchez was an innovator: his goal was to challenge the standards of the mainstream, even as he defined the process for Chicanos. With his art, language, and ideas he wanted to set the standard for Chicano publishing, Chicano theory, and Chicano poetry. With *Hechizospells* Sánchez intervened in the reception as well as the production of Chicano literature. Again, his goal and the goal of other Chicano critics of the 1970s was to *chicanizar la crítica*—to nudge criticism and theory away from academic abstraction and make it more responsive to minority interests and Chicano forms of thought and expression.[37]

Yet Sánchez's project is far from narrow or ethnocentric. On the contrary, in *Hechizospells* his poetry is accompanied by his *ars poetica,* and the topic of both is the human condition, a powerful universalizing discourse that traces its modern legacy to the Renaissance and Michel de Montaigne, and its ancient roots to the Stoic philosophers. The discourse of the Human Condition brings Chicano literature into contact and into a contestatory relationship with a number of canonical genres and traditions, including the essay, the novel, biography, tragedy, and stoicism, all of which have been bequeathed to modernity by the Renaissance, and which in turn recovered them from the ancient, pre-Christian civilizations of the Mediterranean. Sánchez's theoretical essays do not attempt to deconstruct this literary heritage; instead they make a claim, they seek to participate and make a contribution that will *chicanizar* the canon and its tradition.

Hechizospells' tragic discourse is thus a means of incorporating a diachronic sensibility and perspective, or better, an effective temporal subtext, within a personal narrative that is concerned with the self-awareness, suffering, and maturity of a particular subject in a particular cultural context, namely the Chicano experience. The temporal subtext is that of the human condition, which is identified at various times with tragedy, Stoic resignation, or modern existentialism. However cultures or conditions may vary, our definition of tragedy stipulates that the *human* response to death, horror, and loss is "basically the same all over the world," and that it is inherent in history as an essential part of human nature. Tragic sensibility allows us to participate in the emotions and experiences of persons and cultures across time and space precisely because it is inherent in the human condition. The human, emotional response to tragedy is horror, pity, and anguish, all of which are resolved and purged when tragic art becomes the affirmation of the deepest suffering, when "we are able to include within ourselves, and to vindicate, even the deepest suffering."[38]

In 1933 the French novelist André Malraux published an influential first novel, *La condition humaine,* which was translated into English as *Man's Fate.* In his introduction to the translation Harold Bloom calls the novel "an achieved tragedy, with the aesthetic dignity that the genre demands."[39] *La condition humaine* is set in China during the Shanghai rebellion of 1927. In the second half of the novel a group of imprisoned revolutionaries is awaiting death by torture and execution. According to Lucien Goldmann, "It becomes obvious that the subject of *La [c]ondition humaine* is not only a chronicle of events in Shanghai; it is also, indeed, primarily, this extraordinary realization of the revolutionary community in the defeat of the militants and their survival in the revolutionary struggle that continues after their death."[40]

One might be tempted to compare this situation to that of Chicano militants who were facing the death of their Movement in the mid-1970s. When queried by interviewers about authors he had read, Sánchez frequently mentioned French existentialists such as Sartre and Camus, but I find no reference to Malraux or his novel. Nevertheless, the intertextuality of title and theme in *Hechizospells'* "Notes on the Human Condition" and Sánchez's interest in French existentialism suggest that he may have read *La condition humaine.* According to critic Roger Dial, in Malraux's novel, "The essence of man is anguish. . . . The mind conceives man only in the eternal, and the consciousness of life can be nothing but anguish." LeRoy Breunig observes that it is a cliché in France that "all of Camus and much of Sartre came out of the mold of Malraux's novels. For most readers today it is axiomatic that *La [c]ondition humaine* is a great existentialist novel."[41]

In any case, whether or not Sánchez was familiar with Malraux's novel, his interest in existentialism influenced his view of Chicano culture and his own role as an artist: "Seeing the Chicano struggle within a broader scope, as part of a global push for human liberation; sensing the hurt in our barrios; and realizing that we, too, must participate creatively and thoughtfully, I find myself propelled to write and write and write" (*Hechizospells* xv).

To understand the influence of existentialist authors on Ricardo Sánchez we must recall once again the transformation that foreign ideas and doctrines undergo as they come in contact with mestizo culture. We observe it today in the use of postmodernism theory by Chicano critics (see chapter 3). With respect to the Mexican Revolutionary period, we noted the "Mexicanization" of the ideas of Henri Bergson by Mexican philosophers and a similar transformation of the ideas of Karl Marx in the muralism of Diego Rivera. In this case as well, we must recognize a process of *chicanización* that tends to violate the European-ness of the foreign models. The intertextual adaptation of European styles, models, and discourses, such as Bergsonism, existentialism, and postmodernism, requires a prior reconciliation with the characteristics of mestizo culture. In this process both the foreign influence and the mestizo culture undergo a transformation or *transculturación*.[42] And to study the dynamics of reception and intertextuality between two mestizo cultures is to give an account of the different historical circumstances of the two cultures. This is necessary in order to understand the Chicano Movement's reception of Mexican theories of evolution and race via José Vasconcelos's *La raza cósmica,* or the often class-based appropriation of cultural forms such as the corrido, Roman Catholicism, and *indigenismo* by Chicano authors and artists. These intertextual practices reveal the strategies of continuity and hybridity that the Chicano *mestizaje* employed within an Anglo American context that disdained and neglected Mexico and Mexicans.

Although Ricardo Sánchez was influenced as a youth by the French existentialists and by the Beat poets, he was a Chicano/mestizo poet rather than a Beat or an existentialist. Sánchez adapted the tradition of European tragic literature to the extent that it provided a metaphor for the Chicano experience, although it cannot be the only metaphor. Responding to an interviewer, Sánchez conveys his sense of mestizo universality as *entelequia:* "The human condition is many diverse conditions, a composite of all, the sum of all, it is not one linear definition but many definitions—some linear, and some fragmented conceptualizations."[43]

Thus, in the first part of *Hechizospells* Sánchez employs the essay form to explore intellectual terrain that extends far beyond the Chicano timespaces of the *barrio, la pinta,* and the migrant stream, which we saw in *Canto y grito mi liberación.* Yet certain of his themes do not change: "[O]ne must ever struggle toward human liberation," and writing remains "an affirmation of one's culture and linguistic world-view" (*Hechizospells* x). In his preface to *Hechizospells* the newly minted Ph.D. is theorizing about the book. He is telling and also showing what Chicano literature is and can become: "The coming generations shall take today's creations and build on them perspectives which will stagger the imagination" (xviii). Before he presents his poems

Sánchez discusses technique and language and issues of regionalism and universalism. The unschooled people's poet has become someone with a stake in literature as an institution and in what critics and others say about it. The *vato loco* is not expected to appear as a sophisticated literary type, but Sánchez plays the role, sometimes with a straight face, at other times with tongue in cheek and a dose of *cábula*. His arguments combine mestizo wisdom with the apocalyptic, environmental paranoia of the 1960s counterculture that was extremely critical of modern technology and its amoral custodians. But Sánchez's writing continues to respond to the violence that is committed against the poor and the powerless; he has recovered his family life and self-respect, but past struggles remain in his memory and his writing:

> The realization of my having been formed by past experience coupled by hereditary traits assails me. Born into the conflicts bred by powerlessness, cursed by the constancy of insufficiency, and processed the whole of my life through the insufferable idiocies of inadequate schools, racist institutions, barrio barren-ness, tumultuous liturgical inculcations of hate (in the army), self-deprecation in jails and prisons, incessant vociferations of dogmatic/fanaticized true believerism, propagandized questing for liberation within the prism of my humanity, nurturing my paradoxical sense of chicanismo, and aware of the proverbial supplications of family and friends and their solemn right to survive however and at whatever the cost—just living becomes a compendium of the love/hate syndromes and circumnavigations that have historically afflicted humankind (*Hechizospells* 7).

Entelequial poetry is in the service of "a powerless people populating the vaguest of human/social/existential margins . . . the bleak reality of a people encaged in the neo-serfdom of chattel-peripheral-menial laborers in a complex technocratic system" (8). Sánchez is the self-appointed spokesman of this despised *pueblo,* as he extends his inquiry into the human condition and encounters new issues and another horizon of global challenges dealing with horrific scenarios engendered by nightmarish, futuristic technologies of oppression and other forms of institutionalized power that have no regard for the subject's personal or cultural identity. Chicanos must prepare themselves for an endless assault by new forms of objectification, degradation, dehumanization. But before the author can work himself into a hallucinatory state of paranoia and rage, as he often did in *Canto y grito,* he reacts to a memory arising from the past: WE HAVE MANAGED TO SURVIVE! (11).

The tragic reality of mere survival should not be enough for a proud people; but like Malraux's revolutionaries who are engaged in a struggle to the death, the survival of the struggle is equivalent to victory. *La raza* has confronted the threat, and, in confronting it, has temporarily checked its advance. The mad, fascistic, cold war conspiracy of technocratic paranoia will collapse of its own weight, yet Chicanos must continue to prepare for the worst and to believe in "dire hope": "Especially in the coming decades, when the anti-human/nixonian-orwellian-agnewian dialecticians get into full swing to realize their acerbic, manic goals of cloning and altering the human will through arbitrary biochemical/electronic experimentation and mass manipulation/thought control . . . does there exist—and has it ever existed?—a human quest, a light?" (*Hechizospells* 12–13). The poet seeks a path through the darkness to a steely new statement of purpose, and a call to arms: "It is vital to begin framing questions that shall plumb the very depths of the destructive processes. . . . The fight before us is even greater than any we have waged thus far" (12).

Amid the final days of the long Vietnam conflict and Richard Nixon's abortive and scandal-ridden second term, conspiracy theories and a generalized mistrust of power made possible the apocalyptic dread that characterized the mid-1970s: "-watergate, impeachment, or possible presidential resignation notwithstanding, the societal process is now beyond presidential decree!"(12).[44] Parodying Allen Ginsberg's vision of Moloch in *Howl*, Sánchez feigns fascination with the spectacle of power and evil and with his own rhetorical outpouring: "The technology for bio-chemical/electronic thought control exists. . . . The atomic bomb was created out of fear and deterrent, and it was wantonly used to decimate Hiroshima and Nagasaki. Menticide was developed and used in Korea much more effectively than the rack, and it is now being applied in a more sophisticated fashion . . . to alter the behaviour of inmates in prisons and mental wards, and there is talk of using it to restructure the minds/souls of children who are being classified as potential troublemakers—the children of the undesirables, i.e., ethnics, political dissidents, and questers of liberation" (*Hechizospells* 12).

From the abuses of power on a global scale the poet returns to the specificity of the Chicano context: "What of the movement!" he wonders as if recalling the hope that he and other Chicanos had placed in the solidarity of *raza*. "Is it real? Can its leaders be trusted (blindly) . . . ? One would be foolish, indeed, to unthinkingly relinquish power over one's destiny and blindly follow anyone. No—no leader can be trusted to remain true to any cause or people" (15). Although this categorical statement confirms that for Sánchez the Movement is finished, he retains hope that new and humane leaders will later emerge: "Can't the natural cadence of love and trust be the weapons to fend off oppression?" (17). Sánchez again declares his confidence in the people and their ability to "define their own world, analyze it and act—all they need is time/exposure/resources and less fear" (17). After completing this attack on the forces of nihilism, vanity, and ambition, the familiar themes of Chicano identity, language, and family re-energize the text as Sánchez sounds his most characteristic refrain: "Hacia la liberación popular / a testament to our being" (30). The Movement may be dead as a nationalist "Plan" and as a fantasy of Chicano (male) Power, but the struggle for *liberación* continues.

A composition in this first section entitled "La Pinta/Slammer/The Joint:/thoughts & ahuites" mirrors the internal structure of *Hechizospells* as the poet's imagination rearranges pieces and shards of memory into recollections in verse and prose, sight and sound. This composite text telescopes a poem dated October 28, 1969, six months after Sánchez's release from Huntsville prison, into an essay dated January, 1974. The poet's marginal note describes this as a coming together of *"continued feelings"* (31). Separately, each of the two texts represents *la pinta* from different emotional and temporal perspectives, with the pathos of the poem providing the occasion for the essay's critical reflection. This suggests that each "return" to the timespace of *la pinta* has different functional and emotional meanings, including anger, fear, and loss. On this occasion memory and imagination produce a truculent, hybrid composition in which the poem's narrative thread is blocked by the essay's impersonal monologic discourse composed of prosaic thoughts and opinions that are aptly described by the piece's title in English/*caló:* "thoughts and ahuites."

The prose pieces in this section tend to dwell on a critique of racism. They are angry and at times become enmeshed in sociological abstraction, polemics, and anecdotes that lack the contextualized density and economy of Sánchez's verse, to say nothing of the poetic interplay of sound, rhythm, and image. In "thoughts and ahuites" Sánchez delivers poetry mixed with sociology and a confessional mode juxtaposed with politics, so that neither the maudlin tears nor the brilliant images can claim purity or predominance because, at least in this section, they are all part of the search "hacia la liberación popular."

The fourth piece in this section, "Letter to Manuel Peralta: Melo," re-enacts some of the issues that were raised in the "Opened letter to my conscience," which appears at the beginning of *Canto y grito mi liberación*. This "letter," composed entirely in prose, continues the narrative thread of "thoughts and ahuites" but within the timespace of the migrant stream. The letter is dated October 21, 1969, in Washington, D.C., where the recently paroled convict was completing a journalism fellowship. A year later he would be in South Texas, where he composed the "Opened letter to my conscience." These two "letters" then, continue the technique of intertextual and temporal grafting that we saw in the "Pinta/ahuites" composite, except that the timespace of *la pinta* recedes as the migrant poet's location shifts from the affluence of the nation's capital to its "tragic valley" in South Texas. The "Letter to Manuel Peralta: Melo" continues the monologic and didactic style of the essays in this section, while the "Opened letter," as we saw earlier, develops a much more complex and polyphonic collage of voices and interests. But each of the pieces, in its own way, appeals to the conscience of the reader to consider the welfare of *raza* in the Movement and beyond. As Melo's correspondent states, "Even though I write this letter to you, it is also a letter to myself and other raza—in fact, to all humanity" (47). Here we witness the double movement of the poet's *entelequia* as it expresses concern for *la raza* and extends the meaning which the term "*la raza*" has for mestizos, to include "other raza[s]," or, in other words, the entire human *raza* ("all humanity").

The final three pieces in this section include "Caras y más-caras, A-men," an indictment of Movement officials; "It was after," a satirization of Chicano writers and poets; and "VACHA's chronchis night," a *pinto* version of the tragic dilemma faced by the protagonists in Malraux's *La condition humaine*. In a dramatic sketch of a parolee's paranoia, the protagonist of "Vacha's" is obliged by the parole officer to either give up his revolutionary activities or return to prison: "Maybe he'll kill me also, but I doubt it. Me, he wants me alright, but nice and legal so that I can rot in prison and die moment by moment. He'll be smirking when he can pin me down and have my parole violated; he'll be smiling when he sees me shuffling off to Huntsville, knowing that the cotton field guards will delight in stomping on me, demanding tons of white gold from me and making each moment of imprisonment more horrible than the sweetness of death. Yes, he wants me alive and imprisoned, but he'll have to kill me, for I won't go back—no way will I allow them to violate my parole" (*Hechizospells* 66). The parolee knows that only the tough and the shrewd can survive in that prison hell: "[M]an, you have to be strong to withstand that bitching Texas joint—even confirmed bank robbers have been broken there" (66). One of the deceased inmates of the *pinta* scenario is El Telo Pico: "He wanted to just be left alone, and he wound up alone, in the nut farm. He had been slapped around so much by guards and building tenders that he finally blew it, yes, just before he went on a religious kick and began his confessional rituals. Damn, but his voice still haunts me, the way he would undress in his cell and pray. . . . One night, bleeding and crying, Telo took off his belt and hung himself" (66).

This short tale of horror and obsession marks the transition from "Notes on the Human Condition" to the poetry selections, where we will encounter other victims like Telo, who "really didn't kill himself—the guards and their horrible system drove him to it" (69). For the *vato loco* in *la pinta* and on the streets, death can be swift and violent, and he may have little opportunity to reflect on the human condition. This chore is left to the survivors to plan and reconcile their lives and deaths.

Poetry in Exile

The main poetry section of *Hechizospells* begins where the previous section ends—in the timespace of *la pinta*. The first poem, "Tiers/tears," dated April 7, 1961, in the prison at Soledad, recalls another victim who could be the twin of El Telo Pico:

young hurting
chicanito,
he once shared
a cup of coffee,
told me his father
was también   *also*
del chuco,   *from El Paso,*
. . . .

              but los perros   *the dogs*
              lo golpearon   *beat him*
              and he cried
              upon that tier
              and somehow felt
              he'd lost
              his manhood (*Hechizospells* 72–73).

In the poem "Soledad was a girl's name," Soledad has become "a jagged prison world,"

     where hate
     is a common expletive,
     seems everyone hates,

seems everyone is a convict,
even guards and counselors
    do time here,
    everyday trudging into
    this abysmal human warehouse (77).

This poem flashes back chronologically, past Huntsville, Texas, the setting of "Vacha's chronchis night," to Soledad, California, in a movement that reveals *la pinta* as a timespace in which locations, conditions, and victims lose their specificity and individuality.

This poetry section begins with a reprise of the timespaces that we saw in *Canto y grito mi liberación:* the *pinta* of the early sixties, the barrios of El Paso, and the author's literary "migrant stream." Since the poet has presented much of this already, the time devoted to Soledad now will be brief, scarcely long enough to observe the *pinto* bantering with other inmates as he prepares for his parole date. He says good-bye, dreading the possibility of returning to prison: "don't give me no jive, ese, / about coming back" (76), and "eso sí compiras, no quiero regresar" [*that's for sure, pal, I don't want to come back*] (79). The parolee is back home in El Paso in the fall of 1963, "tasting freedom, / a freedom / that even now hides" (80).

The poem "Out/parole," deplores the exploitation of Chicanos and Chicanas and the lack of employment opportunities in the barrio. However, this is the only poem from that period, leaving the autobiographical record silent about a number of events, including Sánchez's first meeting with María Teresa Silva, their courtship and marriage, her first pregnancy, and the circumstances of his arrest for armed robbery. Rather than relive this period, there is an urgency to advance the narrative quickly to another time and place. The next poem, "Otra vez," from the summer of 1967, finds the poet back in prison at the Ramsey I farm in Huntsville, Texas, where he is resisting the guards' efforts to make him work:

. . . for the judge he said
i sentence you ricardo,
to do twelve years,
he didn't say a thing 'bout
rehabilitation through cotton picking (81).

The story of Sánchez's time in Ramsey I is told in the first section of *Hechizospells,* in the hybrid text "La Pinta/Slammer/The Joint:/ thoughts and ahuites," analyzed elsewhere in this book. This structure allows the poetry

section to advance the narrative past the years of reincarceration to the pro-
tagonist's next parole date in March, 1969. The poem, "Three days to go"
mentions something called "Chicano POWER," a revolutionary movement
that is supposedly helping *raza* to "build a new nación" (84). It is characteris-
tic of Sánchez's subversive chronology that upon his release from prison, his
discursive persona joins the movement whose demise he announced in the
previous section. As in other transitions, this return to the world is marked
by a return to family, friends, and the barrio in El Paso. Here, as in *la pinta*,
the poet encounters urgent needs and bureaucratic abuse. As in his previous
parole, he looks for an answer to the problem of survival, an answer that will
keep him out of prison. In "Splinterings," the poet expresses his willingness
to serve and advance a popular cause with his writing and oratorical skills,
insisting that

> it is up to you
>
>   and me
>
> to now unite
> it must be done in time,
> for destiny—fragmented & splintered—
> is growing thinner
> with
>
>   every
>
>   passing
>
>   moment
>
> and the time to start living
> is now (87).

Chicanos who inhabit the timespaces of *la pinta* and the barrio are pris-
oners of "a pre-ordained jet-age serfdom," a concept which the text will de-
code later. For now the poet must flee and "start living" in exile. One may
argue that the genesis of *Canto y grito mi liberación* is to be found in the
barrio where Sánchez grew up and where Carlos Rosas painted his mural,
Entelequia, or some might say that it was in *la pinta* that the poet discovered
a unique sense of time and space, as well as his poetic voice. But it is very
likely that the possibilities of that poetic outcry could never have been real-
ized in either of those timespaces but only "on the road," in the jet-age, intel-
lectual "migrant stream" familiar to the Beat poets who were Sánchez's con-
temporaries. Unable to remain in the barrio, fearing, as we have seen, the
revolving door back to *la pinta*, by July 1, 1969, Ricardo Sánchez was enrolled

in the Frederick Douglass Fellowship Program in Richmond, Virginia, where
he witnessed a different yet very familiar social reality:

> bleeding blackness
> coursing richmond's
> chimborazo park
> . . . .
> almost sinking
> in the oceanic poverty
> that gobbles up the masses,
> sometimes poetry and truth
> are very fragile straws
> but they do keep the faithful floating
> in spite of all the odds
> that herald our demise (*Hechizospells* 88).

In Virginia, the Texas poet notes certain differences of regional practice and
custom:

> rot-gut east texas mendacity
> is virginny honey-dripping subtlety
> so
> that I can only puke
> out the resin of your lying (90).

Sánchez refers to the pain endured by his wife and children in several po-
ems, among them, "Son: my love destroys you slowly," "Teresa," "Libertad
was born in primavera," and "Rikard." The poet's partner and consolation
throughout is his wife, Teresa. In one poem dedicated to her Sánchez does
not speak of their romantic first meeting but of the passion and need that
sustains their family through years of hardship, including his years in prison:

> in the midst of our pobreza [*poverty*]
> we bask in each other's arms,
> your warm, tender brown-ness
> calms the pandemonium in my loins . . .
>
> "amidst the barren steel of walls/bars/& tenderless nights,
> and hope fights on implacably. . . ."

we've turned the tide around,
nestled our realities
within the coverlets of love,
and soon another voice shall sing
its soft melodic tunes
and gird us with a smile (96–97).

The bitter epigraph to this poem, "even roaches sweat in hope," speaks to the torment and indignities that beset the migrant family in Virginia. But when their love bears fruit for a second time and Libertad-Yvonne is born in April, 1970, in Northhampton, Massachusetts, there is a joy that erases past defeats:

Libertad, sweet child
of bronze skin and glowing eyes,
tender one
with resilience and love
dancing out your smile,
whatever awaits you
we shall ever be there
not just to cuddle you
but to help you weather
storm and to share bounty and joy (107).

Rikard-Sergei was Sánchez's first child, born just after the poet was sentenced to prison in Huntsville, Texas. On October 4, 1969, when "Son: my love destroys you slowly" was composed, Rikard was four years old, yet father and son had been together all of six months:

it can be a rot gut society
when
little wide-eyed children
feel lash and confusion,
fear and retribution,
and
their dreams are
nightmarish glimpses
. . . .
it is pain,
my son, when your eyes

question
duelos and anxieties
and
you are only four—
how much more
will your tender soul hurt
when you are ten
and
know that life is
dying and death is living?

part of your hurt
is being born Chicano
in
an anglo-ideating culture
that chews up human-ness;

the other part
is being you,
son of my perturbations,
and feeling the anxious
welter that angers me
mirrored in your eyes;
and all we are
confuse you right now
and you adjust
(stifling young soul yearnings),
and
I love you, yet, cannot
keep you from knowledge's
hurting demeanor (94–95).

Sánchez gives voice to the story of Chicano migrant families and the fa-
thers whose paternal care is inadequate to protect their children from the
world. The repetition of the term "rot-gut" and other crude images of ab-
normal digestive function are concrete autobiographical references to the
physical and psychological turmoil that the poet is undergoing in exile. The
tensions and the pressure, the need and poverty that accompanied difficult
changes in living circumstances began to aggravate chronic health problems,
such as diabetes, that Sánchez was already suffering while in prison and per-
haps earlier. Sánchez's references to these symptoms provide biographical

data about the intestinal maladies that he had to contend with the rest of his life, presumably as a result of stress, poor diet, and toxic substances that he consumed both inside and outside of prison. He boastingly writes that:

> . . . I drink wildness
> by the gallon
> trying desperately to recoup my sanity
> . . . .
> inundated in sotol, tequila, y mescal (111).

There may be some hyperbole blended with the truth when Sánchez writes about his appetites. Nevertheless, in the early eighties, while he was living in Utah, he underwent surgery to remove a portion of his lower intestine, and his death in 1995 came as a result of generalized abdominal cancer.

The poem "This, too," dated October 3, 1969, represents the poet's most revealing self-critique to this date. It judges the possible errors he has committed as an activist and Movement figure. This confessional piece is set in the timespace of the migrant, as are the "Opened letter to my conscience" and "Flight: San Antonio, Houston, Atlanta, Richmond from El Paso . . ." from *Canto y grito mi liberación*. At stake here is the ethical and ideological integrity of the Movement, which is in the hands of individuals who claim leadership responsibility and enjoy special privileges. It seems appropriate that the setting for this discussion of political influence and corruption should be Washington, D.C.

The time and place of composition of "This, too" is similar to that of "Letter to Manuel Peralta: Melo," which appears in "Notes on the Human Condition," the first section of *Hechizospells*. Both were composed in October, 1969, and both cite Washington, D.C., as the place of composition. Another figure common to both pieces is Chicano poet Abelardo (Lalo) Delgado. The first paragraph of the "Letter to Manuel Peralta: Melo" reads in part: "Lalo Delgado and I were discussing you earlier this week in a street bar in this barbaric city" (*Hechizospells* 45). Likewise, the marginal note at the beginning of "This, too" provides a setting and a mood: "drinking beer with Lalo Delgado . . . in a musty/funky D.C. tavern" (100). The "Letter to Manuel Peralta: Melo" is a second-person critique of a Chicano comrade who has fallen victim to alcohol, drugs, and other behavior that threatens his well-being and standing in the Movement. Unlike many of Sánchez's personal attacks, this one is not harsh in tone, but admonitory and supportive. The poem, "This, too," however, criticizes the author and his companion(s) as they sit in a topless bar in the nation's capital:

to mad-eyed cabrones
visualizing conquests
        via flighty moods,
equating take-overs
        and revolutions
during beerlapping spree
        in a musty d.c. tavern
featuring topless lasses, mo (100).

The use of the Spanish slang word *cabrones* in this context implies a critical rather than a casual reference to pimps and other males who tolerate affronts to public or personal decency. The seriousness of the accusation is clear in the verses that follow:

nation
flowing
like a river of masqueraders
imbibing mendacity, dementing humanity:

                        we all
                        stand
                        accused,
                indicted . . . charged
                with inhuman perpetuity
                of sordid deeds & wishes,
yet,

we sit pompously
blinking, finking, drinking
stinking, thinking
plots
against our human-ness;
gorging to overcome
                ravenous primordiality—

this, too, is amerika,
when the dispossessed
rubberstamp their dispossession
by emulating their oppressors (100–101).

Sánchez is anxious about the corrupting influence of American politics. Self-censure becomes a way of attenuating the sense of guilt and self-loathing of the *vendido* or the "fat political coyote" of *I Am Joaquín*. Chicanos who would sell out their *carnales* merely open the way for the assimilation of Movement politics into the corrupt political culture of Richard Nixon's Washington. At the same time, the pious "Letter to Manuel Peralta: Melo" chastises a wayward comrade for his "autoeroticism, drug cultism, alcoholic binges, chronic tripping out, and self-glorification," behavior "that is castrating our movement" (45). According to his correspondent, Melo was "one of the first to question me upon my release from prison in March; you demanded of me my best—for you said that all Chicanos must strive to help their Raza find sanity and freedom, that I should never again live just for myself, that being a pinto had meant ego-tripping and disregard for our raza's well being and survival" (45).

In the letter the author entreats his friend (as well as himself and other *raza*) to reject this hypocrisy and heed his own advice: "Come back to us, bato. Re-coup your identity and let us all blaze a meaningful passageway to freedom for ourselves and raza" (46). Sánchez writes himself a part in this bit of political theater. He too is a leader attempting to bring people into the Movement with false integrity and vapid arguments. His authority to write the letter seems to place him in an awkward position, which he attempts to overcome by publicly airing his own indulgences and alerting Chicanos of the need to be vigilant with regard to their leaders. But in reality, Sánchez is dramatizing the decline of the Movement. These pieces demonstrate how the discourse of Chicano solidarity is undermined from within by the hypocritical behavior of the *políticos*. In 1969, two years after the publication of *I Am Joaquín*, he dramatizes how the Movement, at the level of its leadership, has lost its innocence and the confidence of its followers. As in the poem "Los Theys Are Us," the distinction between the good and bad, with Chicanos always on the side of the former, is no longer credible.[45] One year later Sánchez and Abelardo Delgado would be in Denver shouting, "Indict Amerika," and "stupid america," knowing that this really meant that "all of us stand indicted," because "this, too, is amerika" (*Hechizospells* 101).[46] Sánchez is saying of the Chicano Movement: this too is dirty politics, this too is American politics.

The poem "Flight . . . ," also from 1969, voices similar concerns about personal and collective goals: "I question / self-motives / and / one year journalistic fellowship / relegates La Raza, causa, etc., / to minor role / (if only temporarily) / and / mi alma [*my soul*] weeps out / its paradox" (*Canto y grito* 57). The paradox is that the flight to security and conventional levels of success outside the barrio occasions its own spiritual and moral dangers. Among these are assimilation into the majority culture, loss of identity, and a longing to return to the home culture. To become a writer the Chicano subject must assimilate and educate himself in the discourse of the Anglo, an operation that again leaves him confused and lost. He is a hybrid, torn between an essentialist love of "brown-ness" and an opportunistic appropriation of the Anglo's intellectual baggage. The poet feels "subtle oppression encroaching on our spirit. The awareness that barren-ness is seeking a foothold in my mind/soul leads me to love the brown, earthen beauty of my birthrights. From the honey-bronze loins of our creation to the bronze hurt in our barrios now comes the angered demand for total liberation, and out of love and a hectic sense of life do I feel my soul palpitate with pride, dignity, and love for our brown people, for our Raza ardientemente Chicana" (*Hechizospells* 47).

Sánchez's song of love for *la raza* is a total identification with his people. It functions like a discursive retreat into the honest poverty of the barrio to find solace and forgiveness, and comes after the poet's confession of guilt for enjoying the pleasures and freedom of the road. In the barrio he is haunted by his adventures on the road and in the Movement: "My ranting attracted other ranters, and we became a mutual-we-adore-us clique. We had the rants down pat. We were in—so in that we lost sight of the reality of our people. Hell, we had even lost sight of ourselves. We rapped about mercantile capitalism, its attendant hoopla horrors, the military-industrial complex . . . the schizoid factorial in minority students, and a number of other topics—all predesigned to achieve a certain response from the college types we rapped at. We were los prestigiosos—los elitistas del movimiento . . . Either we over-accented our voices while rapping and lecturing, or we became experts at gavacho modulation" (*Canto y grito* 151).

In the end, Sánchez was part of the critical onslaught demanding reform within the Movement while witnessing its demise. The significance of *Hechizospells* as tragic discourse is its search for answers and for solace in the face of this and other deaths. This work will continue to present a formidable challenge to critics with a limited command of Chicano English, Spanish, and *caló*. Unfortunately, many who are capable of understanding and analyzing the complexities of a work like *Hechizospells* prefer to devote their efforts to the growing body of Chicano literature in English. *Hechizospells* is only one example of a multilingual Chicano text that remains unsung, unread, and unacknowledged, almost as if it were a buried text. No doubt Abelardo Delgado was correct when he concluded his review with the following observation: "The ultimate judges and critics, after all, are the readers of this generation and of those generations to come. Sánchez, his writings, his genius have already suffered too much for being 'out of time.' They are so much ahead of our time that many look at them as foreign in nature. *Hechizospells* and Sánchez are not foreigners and are very much our contemporáneos."[47]

Luis Leal argues that Chicano literature has become "a significant part of minority literatures in the United States, and, at the same time, of literature in general. . . . Chicano literature by lifting the regional to the universal level has emerged from the barrio to take its place alongside the literatures of the world."[48] But to Ricardo Sánchez and Abelardo Delgado it seemed tragic that the creativity of Chicanos should remain buried and suppressed, just as it is a tragedy that bronze bodies should continue to suffer unwarranted abuse, hatred, and injustice. If the U.S. Constitution does not permit the poetry of a people to be banned, it has nevertheless allowed a people to be marginalized in the semi-obscure regions of a culture that recognizes the value of American literature in one language only—English.

The poem "Llorido lamento en extremo" ["Cry and Lament in Extreme"] exemplifies this problem. It is written entirely in Spanish, and, unlike similar poems in the collection, it is not addressed to a Mexican or a monolingual Spanish audience, or to any specific audience. Rather, it expresses feelings and ideas that the poet could communicate only in Spanish. According to Sánchez, some poems are written in Spanish or English or *caló* not because the audience demands that language but because the poet's creative process requires it. However, the problem remains: Who will hear and understand those poems and how can they find a place within an English-only tradition?

Poemas a Pedro-Cuauhtémoc

Hechizospells' final act is reserved for a few poems that are probably the most powerful in the collection. The poems are dedicated to the poet's infant son, Pedro-Cuauhtémoc, and dramatize the effort to recover the thread of life in a time of mourning. In the first of these poems, "Conocí tu realidad, hijito," Sánchez recounts his son's brief but courageous struggle for survival. The poem is composed in the second person:

conocí tu realidad, hijito,   *I knew your reality, my little son*
    esos quince días   *those fifteen days*
    llenos de esperanza, ansiedad,   *full of hope, anxiety,*
    y anhelo . . .   *and longing . . .*

    heroic struggles within the clinician nightmare of your
surviving a lifetime of two weeks in that intensive
nursing care catacomb, your fragile body caught
in hopeseared pain (*Hechizospells* 294).

The poet's words try to overcome the boundary between life and death as
they attempt to reach the lost one and find an outlet for the pain:

> you had a coronary, m'ijo,
> and the doctors said you must
> be transferred right away;
> we cried as you were taken
> to providence hospital,
> we raced the ambulance
> and went up to admissions,
> their cold and business voices
> spoke first about insurance,
> once more I realized
> the penury of being
> un bato sin trabajo   *a guy without a job*
> but Rafa said don't worry
>   we'd raise the money somehow (*Hechizospells* 296).

Here Sánchez relives the circumstances of his wife's first pregnancy a decade
earlier when he was also unemployed and resorted to armed robbery to get
the money that the family needed. He writes in *Canto y grito mi liberación:*
"Teresa, I watched anxiously the welling of you with our son, and I never
realized that I would come to know him only after he was four years old, for
once more I went to prison—two days before his birth, I stood alone in
my mind indicted for robbery, you meanwhile suffering the pangs of birth
deliverance, also alone . . . aloneness, the condemnation of humanity—
aloneness! robbery committed in anxiety and desperation; joblessness so I
pulled jobs—and you both waited while I spent tumultuous years pent up
in texas—ramsey prison farm no. 1" (78). Now, in 1975, he is finding it dif-
ficult to be a father to a son that is gone forever.

> we didn't raise the money
> and it was nip and tuck,
> you fought for two whole weeks;
> two more damn coronaries/
> convulsions shocked your body,
> even as we baptized you,
>   Katita, Rafa saw you,
>   they prayed outside your window,
> the priest, your mother, I,

we hoped and prayed for you . . .
the water hit your head,
its drops cascaded over
the tubing and the wires
which fed you glycerine,
your little chest's upheavals
protested all the gadgetry
you seemed to grope for freedom,
your little tautened fists
kept reaching for an outlet,
you stretched your downy legs
until your pain engulfed you (*Hechizospells* 296–97).

The recollection is total, as is the poet's identification with a tiny body in agony. In its lucidity and economy Sánchez's account of a child's death surpasses the autobiographical classic *Death Be Not Proud* (1949), by John Gunther. In that story the father has money to pay for the finest doctors and the best care. But Sánchez's voice reveals no bitterness for his impoverished condition, only shame and sadness. Gone is the "and no one seems to give a damn" refrain of *Canto y grito mi liberación*. All the poet's attention seems concentrated on his son's ordeal. But the newborn Pedrito-Cuauhtémoc did not live. He became a sad statistic even though, in his father's mind, he lived and died an epic struggle:

we hurried back to see you,
        Teresa, Rafa, I,
we held you to our beings
and saw our tears commingle.

your body was still warm,
tan tierno y tan firme,   *so tender and so firm*
that we could only hold you
with fragile lovingness;
. . . .
we KNEW that you were dead,
no longer of this world,
still we seemed to understand
that love has no dimensions,
we held you softly then (*Hechizospells* 297).

The family must continue to live in time as it seeks the reality of death be-
yond space and time:

> on February 4th
> we gave you back to the earth,
> your little coffin rests
> beside my father, brothers,
> Three Pedros rest there now,
>   my father and my brother,
>   alongside brother Sefy,
> three generations sleep (298–99).

With time the family will learn to accept its loss:

> more days shall come for us, we'll live through joy and hurt, and we'll
>   recall your visage until we, too, are gone . . .
>   Pedrito-Cuauhtémoc, m'ijo,
> como flor [*like a flower*] aborning in time's filament,
>   pedazo de amor   [*a bit of love*]
> caught in timorous fragility
>   twixt life and death,
> surviving but 15 days,
>   you visited us briefly
> in those days of hopeseared pain
>   and imprinted
> your life's beauty on our mindsouls . . .
> tierra y ceniza   *earth and ashes*
> y esperanza en la brisa,   *and hope in the mist,*
> I recall you beyond your lifespan
> from January 16th to 31st of 1975 . . .
> I recall you aunque la mente dice   *although the mind says*
> adiós, cariño, adiós hijito querido,   *good-bye, dear one, good-bye*
>   *beloved son,*
>   te recuerdo siempre   *I recall you always*
>   en tu vibrante vitalidad con sonriente duelo . . .   *in your vibrant*
>   *vitality with a*
>   *grieving smile*
>   *. . .*

>   tu padre (299–300).   *your father*

The loss of a loved one, especially a child, and the somber gravity of death itself require of the poet an elegiac decorum, a dignity that permits no rages of accusation against self or others. The second poem to Pedro-Cuauhtémoc, "Ni Xipe, chavito" is also in the second person and reiterates the sense of a lifetime relationship that has been tragically cut short, to be replaced by a contemplation of future memories that will never be:

> hijo   *son*
>   de los recuerdos y los anhelos,   *of the memories and dreams*
> cauterized in frenzied hopes
> toward horizons we would explore,
> spaces exist now
> where you would grope and gurgle,
> y tú ahora   *and now you*
> entre peñascos silenciosos   *'midst silent crags*
> eternalizing much that
> was left unsaid, undone . . .
>
> you were to be Pedro,
> rocklike strength
> coalescing
> with Cuauhtémoc,
> sylvan fighter,
> synthesizing
>
> mundos [*worlds*] alienated by reality's unsanity (301).

The pride of the poet and father in naming and celebrating his own creation/offspring is vanquished in the ground, as are the hopes of seeing the continuation, in this Chicano child, of the grandfather's lineage and the name of *la raza*'s heroic ancestor, the Aztec warrior Cuauhtémoc. The tragic death of Pedrito-Cuauhtémoc is thus symbolic of the death of the Chicano Movement as a patriarchal force; and the tragic life of the father, Ricardo Sánchez, proves again to be charged with profound meaning. His poetic testimony of the struggle for life and dignity will continue to be emblematic of the Chicano experience.

For Ricardo Sánchez, both Pedro-Cuauhtémoc and the Chicano Movement died in 1975. The Movement had lost the qualities of warrior strength that would have ensured its future; instead it had fallen into corruption and arrogance. In Greek tragedy this flaw is called hubris or pride, the male pride of strength and self-assertion, and, according to the *Dictionary of Literary*

Terms and Literary Theory (1991), "eventually hubris brings about downfall and nemesis." The death of the last Aztec emperor, Cuauhtémoc, was a tragedy that presaged the humiliation and defeat of the native peoples of Mexico. But the fruit of that tragedy, and many others that occurred in the centuries of colonization, was *mestizaje,* the blending of the "cosmic race," which was nourished by the life and death of many *mestizos y mestizas,* Asians, Africans, Europeans, and native men and women. It is because of that tragic legacy that the language and the struggle, *la lengua y la lucha chicanas,* persist on the borderlands of English and Spanish.

In this final section of *Hechizospells* the poet acknowledges the Chicana who, as mother and warrior, sustains the family and *la raza* itself in tragedy and adversity. In the poem "Coyúntate, mujer" he appeals to her to renew their love and solidarity in the trials that confront them, for the future is hers to share:

cauterized have we been
riding on the savage crests
de pasiones que hemos explotado,   *of passions that we have unleashed,*

lips and fingertips caressing
all universes,
todas partes del porvenir   *every part of our future*
se han venido   *has come*
cascading
sobre momentos enmielados   *upon sweetened moments*
lack of fear;
we've cast reservation
to all winds,
suckling out of being
a resonant affirmation
que nacimos todos   *that we are all born*
para seguir confirmando   *to go on confirming*
la vida   *life*
con cantogrito   *with our song/shout*
así quebrando   *and thus bursting*
encadenamientos sociales,   *our social chains,*
dejando rejas   *and leaving prison bars*
en las cenizas del pasado   *in the ashes of the past*
(*Hechizospells* 307).

The celebration of achievement and the pain of loss are shared by the couple, man and woman:

no, mujer,	*no, woman,*
no temo tu fuerza	*I do not fear your strength*
ni me escondo de tu ternura,	*nor do I hide from your tenderness,*
pues también he llorado	*for I too have wept*
mis duelos y cantado mis gritos	*with grief and shouted my songs*
cuando pésames o alegrías orgullosas	*when mourning or prideful joys*
han frecuentado mi vivir (308).	*have entered in my life*

Yet the poet knows that it is time for the Chicana to seek her own definitions, her independence and liberation, and he promises to support her with care and understanding, because women's struggle is a universal one:

tienes mente y alma,	*you have a mind and soul,*
puedes pensar y decidir	*you can think and decide*
los predilectos de tu vivir,	*the choices in your life,*
mereces tener dignidad,	*you deserve dignity,*
como creación tuya,	*as something that you create,*
algo que forjastes,	*something that you forged,*
y no como algo que un amo	*and not something that a master*
te permitió (310).	*allowed you*

Here Sánchez is saying that Chicanas must be full partners in the struggle. The two sexes together will share leadership and guard against the abuses that Sánchez has been criticizing all along. Thus, with the death of the Movement a new vision is born. Leadership will be placed in the responsible hands of men and women capable of working through the maze of conflicting interests and agendas. Yes, Pedro-Cuauhtémoc is dead, the Movement is dead, but from these losses come renewal and greater wisdom. There will be a victory, as we see in the poet's birthday song to his daughter, Libertad-Yvonne:

Libertad, be free.
Free as your name,
free as your heritage demands,
free as your soul must be
that you may grow

                    to reach the zany zenith
                        of your enfant's expectations . . .
        Libertad,
                    gurgle out
                        the joy
                            of
                                being

                                    live,
                    reach out
            and grapple
        with la vida,   and teach us
                            human-ness
        ("to my daughter, newly born . . ." n.p.)

On the other hand, during the next twenty-five years, as children grew to adulthood and began to raise children of their own, the advancement of justice for Chicanos would continue to be a struggle, a process of fits and starts, of both achievement and disappointment that left many goals unrealized and the future of Chicanos far from secure.

After his physicians informed him that he was suffering from terminal stomach cancer, Sánchez included a new selection of poems in the revised edition of *Canto y grito mi liberación: The Liberation of a Chicano Mind Soul* that was published by Washington State University Press in 1995. Sánchez had been teaching at WSU for several years, and he was granted tenure shortly before his death. The new material that he included in the revised *Canto y grito* represents a final statement on his life and death. As a writer, Sánchez was certainly prepared by experience to tackle the question of his own mortality. The tribulations of his life had been the raw material for his poetry, and terminal illness would not be an exception. There was a determination in his character that made him eager to confront the large questions that concern all artists regardless of culture or nationality: "The voice intoned with much finality: 'You have at best six months to live, without, or even with, Chemo-Therapy.' The Doctor looked sure of himself, the epitome of godliness dressed in powdery white shirt, pants and gloves blood spattered from my body. 'We opened up and found that we could not excise any cancer,' as the doctor continued his essay on my human condition. 'Inoperable stomach cancer which has spread to your liver and other major arteries and organs'" (*Canto y grito* 1995, 167).

So near the end of his life there is still in Sánchez the feistiness and quasi-mystical affirmation of pain and suffering, "y no temo ni el morir o el vivir" [*and I fear neither dying nor living*] (169), he boasts, "as I confront my pain and cancer/my spirit soars and sings" (170). Again, he sends a message beyond the grave to César Chávez and Manuel Acosta as he did to his son Pedro-Cuauhtémoc while in mourning: "Years ago, Manuelito Acosta, we shared tequilazos and you warned about a violent ending; I recall laughing and saying that a poet or artist must end life in a terrific struggle for survival. Can I survive? I marvel at the question as I strongly affirm that I can survive, I shall do so until my demise" (171). His narrative, too, continues as he awaits the next leg of his migrant's journey:

> told that I am nearing the terminal,
> my eyes scan the horizon for the bus
> or train or plane or even skateboard
> that I must entrain or even board
> in order to arrive at some cosmic stand (171).

As in *la pinta,* the poet questions his fate when time and his body become burdensome and his imagination can no longer soar:

> the clock feels heavy,
> my shoulders sense a weight
> that is less human, more freight
> . . . .
> so many messages about god arrive
> in the mail, there are so many gods,
> which one is the responsible one
> for my son's death, my diverticulitis,
> my stomach cancer, & the many other ills which have afflicted me and
>   mine (178–79).

The concern with tragedy and the human condition that we find in *Hechizospells* culminates in the new edition of *Canto y grito mi liberación.* We can say that Marvin Lewis understated the dynamism of *Hechizospells* when he referred to the book as a combination of "development and stagnation." Lewis observes that "the central image of desmadrazgo, or cultural violation, remains one of the overbearing features of *Hechizospells* as in Sánchez's earlier work."[49]

In this chapter I have tried to develop the critical direction suggested by

Lewis, Delgado, Bruce-Novoa, and others, while clarifying some of the issues that they raised. I have also sought to place Sánchez's notion of *desmadrazgo* within the larger meaning of the human condition *as tragedy,* a development that is not present in the first two editions of *Canto y grito mi liberación* but that is fully achieved in *Hechizospells.*

Conclusion

Ricardo Sánchez was a Chicano poet with a compulsion to see and communicate different truths, to speak different languages, to experience the suffering and celebration of the human experience within different timespaces. He was born in El Paso, Texas, and in the early 1970s he became known as a *pinto* poet who wrote from a Chicano perspective about the hellish conditions of *la pinta*—the Texas and California prisons that he inhabited for nine years. After his final parole from prison he journeyed to the East Coast, but after a year he returned to Texas to work with Abelardo Delgado on behalf of the Chicano Movement. During a visit to Denver Sánchez helped to publish *Los cuatro,* one of the first anthologies of Chicano poetry. On the basis of this early work he won notoriety as a protest poet and spokesman for the Chicano Movement. In this study I have argued that Sánchez was also a critic of the Movement, and I've tried to show that in this and other respects, critical studies have failed to understand the early work of this important poet.

My study of *Canto y grito mi liberación* and *Hechizospells* traces Sánchez's journeys through three interconnected Chicano timespaces. The first of these is the timespace of the barrio. For Ricardo Sánchez, this meant first and foremost the barrio of El Paso that was his birthplace as well as the birthplace of the pachuco identity. In Chicano communities during the 1950s and 1960s the pachuco was seen as a figure of social and linguistic rebellion. In the barrio young Chicanos like Sánchez learned to emulate the pachuco's defiant stand against authority, particularly Anglo American police authority. They also imitated pachuco speech, combining English and Spanish vernaculars in the underground argot called *caló* and the creative wordplay and one-upmanship called *cábula.* The heroes of Sánchez's youth were the *vatos locos* who moved back and forth between the barrio and a second timespace, that of *la pinta* or the prison. The career path of the young poet followed these role models into the timespace of *la pinta.*

It was Sánchez's writing that helped him to break out of the cycle of the barrio and *la pinta* and enter the timespace of the migrant stream, which his family and generations of Chicanos have populated as laborers, artisans, and itinerant entrepreneurs. However, Sánchez's life was to become a kind of intellectual migrancy sustained by poetic and oratorical skills that allowed him to travel widely and yet remain, in memory and imagination, within the timespaces that had formed him: the barrio and *la pinta.* Indeed, after nine years in prison, he came to see the world as a *pinta* that continued to frustrate his dream of liberation. Sánchez lived the life of an itinerant Chicano intellectual, combining his literary talent with an uncompromising critical sensibility.

It may seem contradictory that an ex-convict should try to impose a code of ethics, but Sánchez liked to combine such contradictory notions through the use of verbal constructions such as *timespace, cantogrito, mindsoul,* and *pensarsentir.* This form of Chicano poetic expression was pioneered by Alurista, who encountered it in Aztec poetry called *flor y canto.* Sánchez was undoubtedly influenced by this innovation, but when he merged words and concepts in this manner he was not emulating Alurista or Aztec poetry, nor was he trying to blur the differences between these notions. His strategy aimed to contextualize them within the barrio dualities of community and *desmadrazgo.* To this end, he set Chicano time against the linear time of mainstream society and placed before his audience a view of humanity's potential that was in conflict with entrenched ideologies of ethnocentrism and white supremacy. His poetry demonstrated the contradictions of a "free" society (such as the United States with its Bill of Rights and guarantees of free speech and free press) in which the powerful were still capable of silencing the ideas, voices, and languages of dissenters and minorities.

Ricardo Sánchez was this kind of dissenting voice. As Francisco Lomelí has written, "He preferred to defy all and any conventionalism known in literature. He honored no limits and knew no bounds."[1] At the end of his life Ricardo Sánchez's words and demeanor displayed the stoicism and strength of a warrior, a strength that had sustained him through many battles, tragedies, and setbacks in both his personal and public life. It would seem that his life was cut short, in what might have been the prime of his life and career. Clearly, the years of hardship and bitterness took their toll on Sánchez. Yet in those years he accomplished much that Chicano critics, particularly those trained in the Anglo American tradition, have failed to acknowledge. For example, his challenge to make critical discourse less abstract and more responsive to Chicano concerns (*chicanizar la crítica*) remains a project that Chicano criticism must ultimately address.

I have tried to show that Sánchez's sense of Chicano timespace defies American notions of time and shows a kinship with Mexican culture and philosophy, which recognize the coexistence of multiple timespaces. In Sánchez's autobiographical narrative we witness an intensely active life, including his years in prison. *Canto y grito mi liberación* and *Hechizospells* are personal narratives presented in the context of social and political upheaval. They tell of the emergence of Chicano identity in a variety of genres and discourses, from critical essays to journalistic pieces to folk ballads. This autobiography depicts both the joy and turmoil that affect all lives, but Sánchez's depiction is in dramatically intense doses. As a Chicano poet, Sánchez rebelled against the artistic, linguistic, economic, technological, and political values of U.S. society and lived to write about it. "Amerika" represented for him this sordid way of life, the source and cause of *desmadrazgo,* the social and historical tragedy of Chicano dispossession. Sánchez's response was to create new forms of poetic expression; I argue in particular that his notion of *entelequia* introduces a Chicano tragic aesthetic that is grounded in the classic as well as the modern traditions of Europe and America.

In his barrio childhood and the racist schools of El Paso, in the army, in Texas and California prisons, in his family life, in his travels throughout this country and abroad, Sánchez distilled the full range of the human condition. In his poetry he savors the pleasures of love, the joys of freedom, the pain of exile and solitude, and the sordidness of incarceration. He exults in his strength and refuses to live in fear. He feels the need to achieve the most and withstand the worst that a racist, capitalist Amerika can offer. Years after being told by teachers that he should aspire to being a janitor instead of a writer, he helps to found a new poetic movement. After being a high school dropout he goes on to earn a Ph.D. After spending the first four years of his eldest son's life in prison, he sees the second one die in infancy. After surviving surgery for diverticulitis and living for years with diabetes, he dies of stomach cancer at the age of fifty-four, leaving behind a family and a considerable body of Chicano literature that must be considered among the most important to date.

Sánchez's youth was marked by the frustrations of a hostile environment: chronic racism and the lack of educational and other positive opportunities in the barrio. Nine years in prison were not enough to break him; instead he committed himself to writing against the social injustices that threatened the lives of young Chicanos. In his youth his judgment at times failed him, yet he found the strength to go on and develop his poetic vision. Most critical studies of Sánchez's work have overlooked the fact that his poetry explored issues beyond his political activism in the Chicano Movement. Few have spoken of the tenderness he expressed for family and friends, for the harsh beauty of the desert and the natural and urban landscapes of Aztlán. His poetry reflects his interest in painting, culture, and music of various kinds, from Native American chants to Beethoven, to modern jazz and Tex-Mex *conjuntos*. The arts inspired the poet to resist the monocultural, monolingual vision of Amerika. His ferocity and outrage were thus a strength, but this was only one aspect of his character. He learned that these weapons could be turned against him, and over the years he was able to temper and control them.

Sánchez criticized leaders in general and Chicano leaders in particular when he felt that they betrayed values that he cherished and considered permanent. The Chicano Movement's inability to reform itself, and its eventual decline, moved Sánchez to create his Chicano poetics of *entelequia,* which was based on his experience of the linguistic and cultural reality of poor Chicano communities throughout the country. Sánchez visited many of these barrios, and he wrote about them in order to combat the unidimensional society that he called "Amerika."

Sánchez was one of the first Chicano writers to speak out in English, Spanish, and *caló* against the tragic destruction of Chicano lives in America. Others followed, but their voices too have been excluded by the monolingual definition of American literature that prevails in university departments of English. Sánchez's Chicano existentialism emerges from this threat to the survival of his culture and languages. His universality rests in part on his warning that the threat of holocaust and genocide are not foreign dangers but represent a historical American experience for Chicanos and ethnicities of color. I have argued that recent criticism ignores the breadth of Sánchez's work in its complexity and diversity. On the basis of flawed and specious theories, critics persist in misinterpreting Sánchez's place in Chicano literature. Viewing his poetry through the filter of these theories, they have failed to understand its languages and the unity that lies at the core of works like *Hechizospells.*

Too often the critical approach has been to briefly summarize a work or an author and then quickly move on to the next and the next in an attempt to produce broad surveys, general classifications, and sweeping generalities— none of which can describe or analyze the poetic developments that occur within the work of individual poets. It should now be clear that Chicano poetry presents a body of work that is too vast and complex to permit such easy summarization.

Appendix

Works of Ricardo Sánchez

Ricardo Sánchez's papers are housed in the Nettie Lee Benson Latin American Collection at the University of Texas at Austin and in the Special Collections of the Stanford University Libraries, Stanford, California.

"to my daughter, newly born. . . ." Unpublished poem, May 1, 1970. Manuscript in Ricardo Sánchez Papers, Department of Special Collections, Stanford University Libraries.

Obras. Pembroke, N.C.: Quetzal-Vihio Press, 1971.

Los cuatro. Edited by Ricardo Sánchez and Abelardo Delgado. Denver: Barrio Publications, 1971.

Canto y grito mi liberación (y lloro mis desmadrazgos). El Paso: Mictla Publications, 1971.

Canto y grito mi liberación: The Liberation of a Chicano Mind.. Garden City, N.Y.: Anchor Books, Doubleday, 1973.

"Fuente Onoria Soul/Mind Journey." *De Colores: Journal of Emerging Raza Philosophies,* vol. 1, no. 1 (winter, 1973).

"CUNA: poetics/prosa, cúmulo y cumbre toward a new definition of experientials." Ph.D. dissertation, Union Institute Graduate School, Yellow Springs, Ohio, 1974.

Hechizospells. Los Angeles: Chicano Studies Center/Publications Unit, University of California, 1976.

"Poema en 8 idiomas." *Caracol,* vol. 3, no. 3 (November, 1976).

"No, no fuistes." *Mango,* vol. 1, no. 2 (1977).

Milhuas Blues and gritos norteños. Milwaukee, Wisc.: Spanish-Speaking Outreach Institute, 1978.

"Entelequia III: An Original Screenplay." Salt Lake City: Chispa Productions and the University of Utah, 1978.

Brown Bear Honey Madnesses: Alaskan Cruising Poems. Austin: Slough Press, 1981.

"Letter to My Ex-Texas Sanity." *Revista Chicano-Riqueña,* vol. 10, no. 1–2 (spring, 1982).

"ENTEQUILA, entelechy, híjola pero Entelequía: prose-poem dedicated to Carlos Rosas, muralist/artist/compadre/& creator of *entelequía* apt mural at 6th & campbell." *Revista Chicano-Riqueña,* vol. 10, no. 1–2 (spring, 1982).

Amsterdam Cantos (y poemas pistos). Austin: Place of Herons Press, 1983.

Selected Poems. Houston: Arte Público Press, 1985.

Perdido: A Barrio Story. Austin: Rob Lewis/REM, 1985.

"Notas a Federico García Lorca (con festejos y disculpas)." *The Americas Review,* vol. 17, no. 1 (spring, 1989).

Bertrand and the Mehkqoverse: A XicAno Filmic Nuance. Austin: Slough Press, 1989.

Eagle-Visioned/Feathered Adobes: Manito Sojourns and Pachuco Ramblings. El Paso, Tex.: Cinco Puntos Press, 1990.

The Northwest Cantos—Part I. Moscow, Idaho: Palousian Poets Press/Palouse Arts Council, 1992.

Amerikan Journeys: Jornadas Americanas. Iowa City, Iowa: Rob Lewis, 1994.

Canto y grito mi liberación: The Liberation of a Chicano Mind Soul. Pullman: Washington State University Press, 1995.

Notes

Introduction. A Critical Approach to the Poetry of Ricardo Sánchez

1. Page citations for *Canto y grito mi liberación, Hechizospells, Los cuatro,* and other major poetry collections by Ricardo Sánchez will appear in parenthesis after the title or citation. Of the three editions of *Canto y grito mi liberación* published to date, the first (Mictla, 1971) appeared without page numbers. The two later editions (Doubleday, 1973, and Washington State University Press, 1995) did include numbered pages as well as revisions, additional poems, and other introductory material. In this study, citations for *Canto y grito mi liberación* correspond to the 1995 edition unless otherwise noted.

2. The term *pinto* is a Chicano vernacular expression for an inmate at a jail or prison (*la pinta*). *Pinto* poetry refers to an autobiographical genre within Chicano poetry in which the author deals specifically with his or her past or present experience of incarceration. Ricardo Sánchez, Raúl Salinas, Judy Lucero, and Reymundo "Tigre" Pérez are generally considered the leading exponents of *pinto* poetry in the 1960s and 1970s.

3. Lomelí, "Ricardo Sánchez," 751–54.

4. Leal, introduction to *Canto y grito mi liberación* (1995), 7.

5. Marcella Aguilar-Henson describes the relation between language and theme in Ricardo Sánchez's poetry, arguing that "Chicano poetry can be analyzed, by using traditional methods of analysis; namely, the study of images, metaphor and other formal elements" (Aguilar-Henson, "Angela de Hoyos and Ricardo Sánchez," 13).

6. See Candelaria, *Chicano Poetry,* 54–58; Pérez-Torres, *Movements in Chicano Poetry,* 106–107, 115–17, 149–50; Bruce-Novoa, *Chicano Poetry,* 48–68; M. Lewis, "Ricardo Sánchez and the Development of Chicano Poetry," 199–206; Tatum, *Chicano Literature,* 146.

7. See Candelaria, *Chicano Poetry,* 39–42 and 57–58, for her views on Sánchez's work as naïve.

8. Deleuze, *Bergsonism,* 116. See also Deleuze, *Nietzsche and Philosophy.*

9. Bakhtin, "Forms of Time and of the Chronotope in the Novel," 84. In the context of the literary work Bakhtin refers to these "timespaces" as chronotopes.

10. Sánchez quoted in Binder, ed., "Ricardo Sánchez," 171.

Chapter 1. The Autobiographical Project and the Movement

1. In her dissertation, Marcella Aguilar-Henson asserts that Ricardo Sánchez "has found his *raison d'être* in the Chicano Movement" (Aguilar-Henson, "Angela de Hoyos and Ricardo Sánchez," 93).

2. Binder, "Ricardo Sánchez," 162. In this interview Sánchez states that "my cultural identity was closely linked with the land orientation of my family, for our foods, norms, values, et al., were still those of people from *el norte de Nuevo México,* while my life outside the home was steeped in the brine of *pachuquismo.*"

3. Ibid., 168.

4. See Barker, *Pachuco*, 13–14.

5. Mazón, *The Zoot-Suit Riots*, 78.

6. Ibid., 8.

7. See Binder, "Ricardo Sánchez," 163, and Castillo, "Interview with Ricardo Sánchez," 23.

8. Sánchez quoted in Binder, "Ricardo Sánchez," 162.

9. Paz, *Labyrinth of Solitude*, 9.

10. McFarland, "Indelibly Chicano," 187.

11. Sánchez quoted in Binder, "Ricardo Sánchez," 168–69.

12. Castillo, "Interview with Ricardo Sánchez," 22–23.

13. Delgado, review of *Hechizospells*, in *Caracol* 4, no. 4 (Dec., 1977): 21.

14. Delgado, "This Is (Mi Compa) Sánchez," 20–21.

15. Candelaria, *Chicano Poetry*, 54.

16. Bruce-Novoa, *Chicano Authors*, 158.

17. Ricardo Sánchez, *The Publish-It-Yourself Handbook*, 63.

18. Ricardo Sánchez and Delgado, "Minority Publishers," 38–39.

19. Olivares, "Two Contemporary Chicano Verse Chronicles," 214–31. In his editor's note for this article, Olivares cites Robert F. Sayre's "Autobiography and the Making of America," in James Olney, ed., *Autobiography, Essays Theoretical and Critical* (Princeton, N.J.: University Press, 1980), 146–68.

20. Padilla, *My History, Not Yours*, 3. Bruce-Novoa analyzes Chicano poetry as a "response to chaos" and views the intentionality of Ricardo Sánchez's work as "literary autobiography" (Bruce-Novoa, *Chicano Poetry*, 219).

21. Beverly, "The Margin at the Center," 93.

22. Williams, "The Writer," 25, as quoted by Beverly in "The Margin at the Center," 91, 92.

23. Beverly, "The Margin at the Center," 97.

24. Sánchez quoted in Binder, "Ricardo Sánchez," 170.

25. Castillo, "Interview with Ricardo Sánchez," 32.

26. In 1982 Marcella Aguilar-Henson was able to write that "Ricardo Sánchez is one of the most studied Chicano writers, both in Europe and Latin America" (Aguilar-Henson, "Angela de Hoyos and Ricardo Sánchez," 143). However, she qualified this statement, noting that while "his work has been reviewed often, critics have generally failed to study its full impact" (91). In *Chicano Authors: Inquiry by Interview* Bruce-Novoa concludes that "Sánchez demands our attention, and perhaps only by giving it to him in an extreme to match his own will we begin to understand better his significance" (221). To my knowledge no other Chicano critics have undertaken this task.

27. See López, "Tres textos críticos chicanos," 185–88. See also Gonzales-Berry, "Chicano Literature in Spanish," 22–39.

28. See the selections in recent anthologies such as González, ed., *After Aztlán*, and Rebolledo and Rivero, eds., *Infinite Divisions*.

29. Moraga, *Loving in the War Years*, 129.

30. Padilla, *My History, Not Yours*, 239.

31. Not all Chicano historians are in agreement with this view. For a differing view, see Gómez-Quiñones, *Chicano Politics*. According to Gómez-Quiñones, there have been "incremental" gains: "Much had been accomplished, new problems had arisen, and past injustices still lingered, as did obstacles to progress. After two decades since the start of the Movimiento, these years of sustained conflict and struggle had yielded some positive results. . . . For many, the Movimiento provided hope for the future. At present, demographic growth and political and economic potentiality offer bases for both optimism and frustration. And during the 1980s, the Mexican community in the United States exhibited both persisting and changing realities" (*Chicano Politics*, 189–90). Mario T. García straddles the fence as well: "Both the Mexican-American Generation and the Chicano Generation—as expressions of lead-

ership—attempted in their own distinct styles to confront and challenge the historically exploited positions of Mexicans in the United States. Neither generation fully succeeded. Yet each advanced the struggle. Each passed on and added to a legacy of Mexicans as historical actors struggling to achieve self-determination" (M. García, *Mexican Americans,* 301). García echoes Padilla's pessimism with regard to the decline of educational opportunity: "Educational reform . . . has been a disastrous experience in the 1980s. Today, more Chicano children than in the last three decades find themselves in segregated and inferior schools" (301–302).

32. Tatum, *Chicano Literature,* 146. Primarily on the basis of Sánchez's collaborative effort in *Los cuatro* (1971), Cordelia Candelaria's 1986 study, *Chicano Poetry,* places the poet in an early, underdeveloped stage of Chicano poetry. In the 1980s the theory of chronological development was used primarily by critics in departments of English to argue in favor of a more refined Chicano poetics. Rafael Pérez-Torres's 1995 monograph, *Movements in Chicano Poetry,* represents a continuation of this neo-positivist, teleological criticism.

33. See Karrer, "Gender and the Sense of Place," 237–45, and Grandjeat, "Ricardo Sánchez," 33–43. Grandjeat points out the changes that are evident in Sánchez's work during the 1980s, and Karrer calls for "a renewed dialogue between Chicanas and Chicanos on a new footing" ("Gender and the Sense of Place," 244).

34. In his introduction to Ricardo Sánchez's *Selected Poems* Nicolás Kanellos refers to Sánchez as "the minotaur poet . . . a genius whose real existence and poetic creations merge, leaving only a very fine line between life and lyric poetry" (Kanellos, "Ricardo Sánchez—Minotaur," 7). Juan Bruce-Novoa claims that "as an extremist [Sánchez] suffers at times from overkill, especially with respect to certain persons within the Chicano Movement whom he repeatedly attacks" (*Chicano Authors,* 219, 21).

35. In his preface to Ricardo Sánchez's *Amerikan Journeys: Jornadas Americanas,* Rob Lewis notes that Sánchez "does not write individual poems as such, each with an autobiographical content and representing in at least a conventional sense a closed and complete work of art. Rather, he composes an ever enlarging autobiography of which any poem is a slice or section" (iv).

36. Kanellos, "Ricardo Sánchez—Minotaur," 7; Bruce-Novoa, *Chicano Authors,* 219.

37. Ortego, "An Appreciation of *Hechizospells,*" 75.

38. M. Lewis, "Ricardo Sánchez and the Development of Chicano Poetry," 203.

39. Marvin Lewis is on target when he states in his article that "critical attention to Sánchez has been negligible although he is one of several major Chicano poets" (ibid., 199).

40. Ortego, introduction to *Canto y grito mi liberación,* 21. In a review of *Hechizospells* Richard Vásquez states that "the book evinces an abiding hatred for and desire for revenge against the Anglo-American society . . . a feeling that was more prevalent if not popular among Chicanos in the late 1960s" (*Los Angeles Times,* "Books," Dec. 5, 1976, 20). A more insightful review by John H. Haddox called it "a rich new fusion, a vital confluence, a new perspective that joins diverse elements of life and culture without confounding or confusing them" (*El Paso Times,* "Books," Oct. 31, 1976). Vásquez also complains that the author "seems to take delight in forcing the reader to the dictionary with arcane and multi-syllabic words, a dubious intellectual achievement which at best detracts immeasurably from the book's readability" (review of *Hechizospells, Los Angeles Times,* "Books," Dec. 5, 1976, 20). Abelardo Delgado notes that "not many have the patience or desire to weed through to uncover the genius which is undoubtedly envuelto in those writings" (Delgado, review of *Hechizospells, El maizal* 1, no. 2 [Jan., 1978]: 8–9).

41. Candelaria, *Chicano Poetry,* 72, 137 (as cited in Pérez-Torres, *Movements in Chicano Poetry,* 274 n. 5).

42. Limón, *Mexican Ballads, Chicano Poems,* 2, 3.

43. Ibid., 2; Pérez-Torres, *Movements in Chicano Poetry,* 5.

44. Pérez-Torres, *Movements in Chicano Poetry,* 5.

45. Ibid., 106, 107, 117, 116.

46. Ibid., 106. Marvin Lewis claims that one poem, "Oye Pito, ésta es: la vida bruta de un boy," is capable of summing up "the poetic attitude toward Chicano existence" (M. Lewis, review of *Hechizospells, Revista Chicano-Riqueña* 5, no. 3 [summer, 1977]: 54).

47. Pérez-Torres, *Movements in Chicano Poetry*, 7–8.

48. Candelaria, *Chicano Poetry*, 77–78.

49. Pérez-Torres, *Movements in Chicano Poetry*, 100.

50. Ibid., 4.

51. Gary Soto quoted in Binder, ed., "Ricardo Sánchez," 198.

52. Padilla, *My History, Not Yours*, 240.

53. Ortego, "The Chicano Renaissance," 294–307.

Chapter 2. The Languages of Ricardo Sánchez

1. Ricardo Sánchez, "Chicano Literature," 2.

2. Nevertheless, in Ricardo Sánchez's *Selected Poems* (1985) editor and publisher Nicolás Kanellos has tried to offer a collection of Sánchez's autobiographical English-language poems.

3. Ricardo Sánchez, "Chicano Literature," 2.

4. Aguilar-Henson, "Angela de Hoyos and Ricardo Sánchez," 146.

5. Haro, review of *Canto y grito mi liberación, Library Journal* 1 (July, 1973): 2108–2109.

6. Candelaria, *Chicano Poetry*, 73.

7. Ricardo Sánchez, "Poema en 8 idiomas," 13. Sánchez describes this poem as "un esqueira de experimental writing in octolinguistics . . . simón que yesca, ese, a poem in 8 languages: Español, French, Tarahumara, caló, Nahuatl, and one word in Italiano, paisan. . . . it is a cabulistic trip, ese, about a viaje into and out of the navajo nation. . . . navajo is a beautiful language"(13).

8. Deleuze and Guattari, *Anti-Oedipus*, 39.

9. Anzaldúa, *Borderlands/La frontera*, 59.

10. Rebolledo, *Women Singing in the Snow*, 172–73.

11. Lomelí and Urioste, *Chicano Perspectives in Literature*, 28.

12. Ortego, introduction to *Canto y grito mi liberación* (1995), 21.

13. Bloomfield and Dunn, *The Role of the Poet in Early Societies*, 19–20. Aguilar-Henson points out the "phonetic techniques—alliteration and chant-like incantations" that characterize the musicality of Sánchez's poetic language. She notes that "Sánchez stresses rhythm, rhyme, and, hence, musicality, both in the poetic and in the narrative" (Aguilar-Henson, "Angela de Hoyos and Ricardo Sánchez," 112, 188).

14. Ybarra-Frausto, "The Chicano Movement and the Emergence of a Chicano Poetic Consciousness, 104; Keller, "Literary Stratagems Available to the Bilingual Chicano Writer," 263.

15. Rosaura Sánchez, *Chicano Discourse*, 36, vii, iv.

16. Rebolledo, *Women Singing in the Snow*, 171–72.

17. Ibid., 171, 172, 215.

18. Rosaura Sánchez, "Spanish Codes in the Southwest," 44.

19. See Candelaria, *Chicano Poetry*, 77–78.

20. Trujillo, "Linguistic Structures in José Montoya's 'El Louie,'" 150.

21. Ricardo Sánchez and Abelardo Delgado edited *Los cuatro*. This anthology includes the work of Ricardo Sánchez, Abelardo Delgado, Reymundo "Tigre" Pérez, and Magdaleno Avila.

22. See Candelaria, *Chicano Poetry*, 39–42, 57–58.

23. Limón, *Mexican Ballads, Chicano Poems*, 128. See also Candelaria, *Chicano Poetry*, and Bruce-Novoa, *Chicano Poetry*, 48–68.

24. Limón's study theorizes the anxiety of patriarchal influence within a line of Chicano poetry that descends from a master precursor: the corrido or Mexican folk ballad. Limón states that *I Am Joaquín*

demonstrates "a seeming total abandonment, actually a full repression, of the precursor, in favor of a new beginning" (Limón, *Mexican Ballads, Chicano Poems*, 120). Because Limón is interested in establishing a direct line of patriarchal influence from the corrido, he does not trace the influences that flow between this new precursor and its "ephebes."

25. Limón, *Mexican Ballads, Chicano Poems*, 128, 124–25.

26. Ricardo Sánchez, "Some Notes on 'Entelequia III,'" i.

27. Limón, *Mexican Ballads, Chicano Poems*, 181.

28. Ibid., 180.

29. "El chamizal" is an island in the Rio Grande between El Paso and Juárez that has been claimed by both the United States and Mexico.

30. Muñoz, *Youth, Identity, Power*, 75–78.

31. Candelaria, *Chicano Poetry*, 57; Bruce-Novoa, *Chicano Poetry*, 157.

32. Rodolfo "Corky" Gonzales, *I Am Joaquín/Yo soy Joaquín, An Epic Poem*, was published in 1967 by the Farm Workers Press. All subsequent page citations will be from this edition.

33. "El plan espiritual de Aztlán," quoted in Anaya and Lomelí, eds., *Aztlán*, 1.

34. Muñoz, *Youth, Identity, Power*, 86.

35. See Bruce-Novoa, *Chicano Poetry*, 56, 59, and Limón, *Mexican Ballads, Chicano Poems*, 124–25. According to Bruce-Novoa, "The poem's purpose is propaganda, consciousness-raising, not intellectual analysis or 'high culture.' . . . The poem's main thrust is to rescue Chicanos from an enveloping chaos due to the loss of their land" (*Chicano Poetry*, 49).

36. Sánchez quoted in Binder, ed., "Ricardo Sánchez," 171–72.

37. Bruce-Novoa, *Chicano Poetry*, 48.

38. Romano, "The Historical and Intellectual Presence of Mexican Americans," 34; Paz, *Labyrinth of Solitude*, 141.

39. See Romanell, *The Making of the Mexican Mind*, 57–58.

40. Romano, "The Historical and Intellectual Presence of Mexican Americans," 32–34.

41. Contreras, "Existential Phenomenology and Its Influence on Mexican and Chicano Philosophy," 18–19.

42. Madrid-Barela, "In Search of the Authentic Pachuco," 35–36, 37.

43. Hernández, *Chicano Satire*, 27.

44. Montoya quoted in Bruce-Novoa, *Chicano Authors*, 128.

45. Paz, *Labyrinth of Solitude*, 13.

46. Paz, *Claude Lévi-Strauss o el nuevo festín de Esopo*, 88.

47. Anderson Imbert, *Historia de la literatura hispanoamericana I*, 340 (my translations). According to Anderson Imbert, the Peruvian critic Alejandro Deústua (1849–1945) was "uno de los introductores de Bergson en América."

48. Ibid., 477. In his imaginative essay *Ariel* (1900), addressed explicitly to the youth of América, Rodó defended Latin America's culture against Anglo Saxon pragmatism and imperialism that had triumphed in the 1898 Spanish-American War and placed the former Spanish colonies of Cuba, Puerto Rico, and the Philippines under U.S. control.

49. Ibid., 478.

50. Contreras, "Existential Phenomenology and Its Influence on Mexican and Chicano Philosophy," 11–12.

51. Paz, *Claude Lévi-Strauss o el nuevo festín de Esopo*, 57.

52. Fuentes, *La nueva novela hispanoamericana*, 21.

53. Paz, *The Labyrinth of Solitude*, 13.

54. Ibid., 12; Monsiváis, "Los chicanos," 46.

55. Paz, *The Labyrinth of Solitude*, 11.

56. Canclini, *Culturas híbridas,* 13 (my translation).

57. Aguilar-Henson, "Angela de Hoyos and Ricardo Sánchez," 143; Ferrari, introduction to *Obra poética completa,* 9–10.

58. R. Lewis, preface to *Amerikan Journeys,* by Ricardo Sánchez, 3.

59. Ortego, "An Appreciation of *Hechizospells,*" 77; Sánchez quoted in Binder, ed., "Ricardo Sánchez," 171–72.

60. Sánchez quoted in Binder, ed., "Ricardo Sánchez," 171–72; Limón, *Mexican Ballads, Chicano Poets,* 91–92.

61. Leal, "Sin fronteras," 113.

62. Madrid-Barela, "Towards an Understanding of the Chicano Experience," 185, quoted in Villanueva, *Chicanos,* 18; Paz, *The Labyrinth of Solitude,* 9–10.

63. Villanueva, *Chicanos,* 17–18.

64. Contreras, "Existential Phenomenology and Its Influence on Mexican and Chicano Philosophy," 144. The author goes on to state that "Chicano culture, though it represents an adaptation of its original culture to the environment of the United States, is perhaps in more direct contact with its sources than the culture of any other immigrant group in the United States. The political aspects of Mexican culture are noteworthy in this context, since it was a culture forged in revolution. Names such as Juárez, Zapata, Villa, and Cárdenas are household words, not only in Mexico, but also in the 'barrios' of California and the Southwest. Informal traditions of story telling (oral traditions), songs (corridos), holidays, etc., keep this particular history alive even among the illiterate and semi-literate members of the Chicano community" (150).

65. "The Plan of Delano," by César Chávez for the United Farm Workers, quoted in Valdez and Steiner, eds., *Aztlán,* 200.

66. Unamuno, *The Tragic Sense of Life,* 89.

67. Leibniz, "A Specimen of Dynamics," 119.

68. Bloomfield and Dunn, *The Role of the Poet in Early Societies,* 110–11.

69. Ibid., 118; Deleuze, *Nietzsche and Philosophy,* 20; Bloomfield and Dunn, *The Role of the Poet in Early Societies,* 4.

70. Bloomfield and Dunn, *The Role of the Poet in Early Societies,* 115; Candelaria, *Chicano Poetry,* 77. Marcella Aguilar-Henson states that "Ricardo Sánchez creates a unique musical poetic world vision based on an oral tradition" ("Angela de Hoyos and Ricardo Sánchez," 147).

71. Sánchez, "Some Notes on 'Entelequia III,'" i.

72. Ricardo Sánchez, "Chicano Literature," 12.

73. Deleuze, *Bergsonism,* 107.

74. Rosaura Sánchez, "Postmodernism and Chicano Literature," 7–8.

75. Deleuze, *Bergsonism,* 17; see also 17–21.

76. Ibid., 13. According to Deleuze, this method "has its strict rules, constituting that which Bergson calls 'precision' in philosophy. Bergson emphasizes this point: Intuition, as he understands it methodologically, already presupposes *duration*" (13).

Chapter 3. The Recovery of Chicano Discursive Timespace

1. See Padilla, *My History, Not Yours,* pp. 239–40.

2. Pérez-Torres, *Movements in Chicano Poetry,* 173.

3. See M. García, *Mexican Americans,* and R. Garcia, *Rise of the Mexican American Middle Class.*

4. M. García, *Mexican Americans,* 273. See G. Sánchez, *Forgotten People;* Castañeda, *Our Catholic Heritage in Texas;* and Campa, *Hispanic Culture in the Southwest.* See also M.. García, *Mexican Americans,* 231–90.

5. Paredes, "The Origins of Anti-Mexican Sentiment in the United States," 139, 158.

6. Acuña, *Occupied America,* 26.

7. Robinson, *Mexico and the Hispanic Southwest in American Literature,* 166.

8. Webb, *The Texas Rangers,* 14, cited in Paredes, *With His Pistol in His Hand,* 17.

9. Paredes, "The Origins of Anti-Mexican Sentiment in the United States," v–vi; see also the work containing that essay, Romo and Paredes, eds., *New Directions in Chicano Scholarship.*

10. Lomelí, "The Chicano Reinvention of America," 212.

11. Leal, "The Problem of Identifying Chicano Literature," 5.

12. For "anxiety about authenticity," see Pérez-Torres, *Movements in Chicano Poetry,* 173.

13. Leal, "The Problem of Identifying Chicano Literature," 2, 3, 5.

14. Ricardo Sánchez, "Chicano Literature," 12.

15. According to Bakhtin, these differences "explain the simultaneous existence in literature of phenomena taken from widely separate periods of time, which greatly complicates the historico-literary process" ("Forms of Time and of the Chronotope in the Novel," 85).

16. Candelaria, *Chicano Poetry,* 77; Ortego, "An Appreciation of *Hechizospells,*" 73.

17. Bloomfield and Dunn, *The Role of the Poet in Early Societies,* 6. In addition to his praise of *chicanismo* and of *carnales* such as Dr. Reymundo Gardea, who provided financial support for Mictla Publications, and his attacks on Amerika and corrupt *movimientistas,* Sánchez included the elegiac "Recuerdo" in memory of his father, Pedro Lucero Sánchez, in *Canto y grito mi liberación.* There is another in *Hechizospells* for Santos Rodríguez, a young Chicano shot and killed by a police officer in Dallas, Texas, as well as an entire section dedicated to his own son, Pedro-Cuauhtémoc Sánchez, who died in infancy.

18. Bloomfield and Dunn, *The Role of the Poet in Early Societies,* 21.

19. See Curtius, *European Literature and the Latin Middle Ages,* 417–35, 468–73; Deyermond, *Historia de la literatura española,* 32–33, 232–33; Menéndez Pidal, *Poesía juglaresca y orígenes de las literaturas románicas,* 334. Menéndez Pidal finds "el espectáculo juglaresco en el origen de las literaturas románicas." According to Bloomfield and Dunn, "Oral poetry is composed by improvisation, and often preserved by memory, frequently with the help of formulaic expressions, and it circulates by means of performance" (*The Role of the Poet in Early Societies,* 14).

20. See Valdez, *Luis Valdez—Early Works,* 168–99; and these works by Alurista: *Floricanto en Aztlán, Nationchild Plumaroja,* and *Timespace Huracán.* See also Morales Blouin, "Símbolos y motivos nahuas en la literatura chicana," 179–90, and Vallejos, "Mestizaje."

21. Anaya and Lomelí, eds., *Aztlán,* ii–iv; Leal, "In Search of Aztlán, 8–9.

22. For "El plan espiritual de Aztlán," see Anaya and Lomelí, eds., *Aztlán,* 1–5. See also Padilla, "Myth and Comparative Cultural Nationalism," 111–34.

23. "El plan espiritual de Aztlán," in Anaya and Lomelí, eds., *Aztlán,* 4.

24. Armas and Zamora, introduction to *Flor y Canto IV and V,* 10. Bloomfield and Dunn observe that "when we study early societies, we are dealing with oral literature, literature that by its very nature is transient, evanescent, but self-renewing. Although in decreasing number, societies still survive where oral literature flourishes, . . . almost all of them have been affected by book culture to the extent that they have been removed from anything that could be called their primal state." The authors give the example of the African "Xosa poets who compose orally and also write poetry down, even though it may not be the same kind of poetry." The hybridity and temporal heterogeneity of Chicano experience is exemplified by the collective celebrations of oral culture at the Floricantos, and the publication of the poetry and proceedings of the festivals in book form. Bloomfield and Dunn point out transitional stages of development from orality to literacy and from rural to urban settings: "The breaking up of these societies by the process of urbanization, even more than the arrival of the book itself, threatens the survival of their unique culture" (Bloomfield and Dunn, *The Role of the Poet in Early Societies,* 13, 14). The emergence of Chicano cultural and political activism in the 1960s did take place in an atmosphere of crisis and confrontation, what Juan Bruce-Novoa termed a "response to chaos" in which "society totters on the brink of the abyss" (*Chicano Poetry,* 14). But rather than viewing this rural-to-urban, oral-

to-literate transformation as the extinction of a culture, we might consider the shift to be merely an indication that Chicanos were emerging from a long period of social invisibility.

25. Armas and Zamora, introduction to *Flor y Canto IV and V,* 10.

26. Alurista, introduction to *Festival de Flor y Canto II,* 13.

27. Pérez-Torres, *Movements in Chicano Poetry,* 173.

28. Rosaura Sánchez, "Postmodernism and Chicano Literature," 7.

29. Deleuze, *Bergsonism,* 22; see also Bakhtin, "Forms of Time and of the Chronotope in the Novel."

30. Rosaura Sánchez, "Postmodernism and Chicano Literature," 7–8. Chicano novels such as *Bless Me, Ultima, The Road to Tamazunchale, Victuum, So Far from God,* and others continue to demonstrate a rejection of these imposed ideologies.

31. Rosaura Sánchez, "Postmodernism and Chicano Literature," 10.

32. Ibid., 11.

33. Lomelí, "The Chicano Reinvention of America," 217, 220.

34. Grandjeat, "Doxy and Heterodoxy in the Emerging Chicano Critical Discourse," 321, 314.

35. Ibid., 320 (my emphasis). See also Quintana, "Ana Castillo's *The Mixquiahuala Letters,*" 72–83.

36. Grandjeat, "Doxy and Heterodoxy in the Emerging Chicano Critical Discourse," 316 (my emphasis).

37. Ibid., 314; Lomelí, "The Chicano Reinvention of America," 221.

38. Vásquez, review of *Hechizospells, Los Angeles Times,* "Books," Dec. 5, 1976, 20.

39. Delgado, introduction to *Canto y grito mi liberación,* 23, 15.

40. Erasmus, *The Praise of Folly and Other Writings,* 53.

41. Anzaldúa, *Borderlands/La frontera,* 89–90.

42. Pérez-Torres, *Movements in Chicano Poetry,* 91.

43. Anzaldúa, *Borderlands/La frontera,* 91.

44. Karrer, "Gender and the Sense of Place," 240. Karrer rightly points out that "there is no Chicano middle class in *Borderlands.*"

45. Bloomfield and Dunn note that "praise and blame will not work if they are not just and true to things as they are," and again, "It is not a matter of praising or blaming *anyone;* the claim must, above all, be true" (*The Role of the Poet in Early Societies,* 11, 7).

46. See Castillo, "Interview with Ricardo Sánchez," 22, regarding the poet's study of Freud.

47. The repudiation of Freudian psychoanalysis is a topic of Deleuze and Guattari's *Anti-Oedipus:* "The whole of psychoanalysis is an immense perversion, a drug, a radical break with reality, starting with the reality of desire . . . that is why, inversely, schizoanalysis must devote itself with all its strength to the necessary destructions . . . when engaged in this task no activity will be too malevolent" (313–14).

48. Deleuze, *Bergsonism,* 61. Deleuze also observes that "we have great difficulty in understanding a survival of the past in itself because we believe that the past is no longer, that it has ceased to be. We have thus confused Being with being-present" (55). He explains that "Bergsonian duration is, in the final analysis, defined less by succession than by coexistence" (60).

49. Bergson, *Creative Evolution,* 236–37, cited in Deleuze, *Bergsonism,* 33, 86. My use of the composite "timespace" in this study acknowledges an analysis of pure duration as memory and subjectivity prior to its actualization as Chicano timespace.

50. Kanellos, "Ricardo Sánchez—Minotaur," 7.

51. See Franklin, *Prison Literature in America.* The author notes that "the mere fact that prisoners are creating literature is nothing new. Many significant figures in European and American culture have been incarcerated as criminals" (233).

52. Dostoyevsky, *Notes from a Dead House,* 323–24. In a letter to his brother quoted on the book jacket, Dostoyevsky said of the work: "*Notes from a Dead House* has taken quite a definite shape in my mind . . . There will be the serious, the gloomy and the humorous, the convicts' peculiar lingo and the

portrayal of characters *never heard of* in literature before, and the touching" (emphasis in original). The prison memoir was originally published in 1861.

53. Byron, *Cervantes*, 391, 392.

54. Rom. 8.18–23.

55. According to Lomelí and Urioste, "un evidente fluir psíquico le otorga a su poesía una espontánea fuerza masculina que tiene sus raíces en el anarquismo del bato loco" (*a stream of consciousness technique lends his poetry a spontaneous masculine vigor that has its roots in the anarchic code of Chicano gang culture*) ("El concepto del barrio," 28).

56. My emphasis. This phrase appears in both "Stream" (45) and "Reo eterno" (73).

57. Sahagún, *The Sun, Moon, and Stars, and the Binding of the Years*, 21–22; León-Portilla, *Los antiguos mexicanos*, 57–60.

58. Pérez, *Free, Free at Last*, 28.

59. Bakhtin defines a chronotope as "the intrinsic correctedness of temporal and spatial relationships that are artistically expressed in literature . . . [the chronotope] expresses the inseparability of space and time (time as the fourth dimension of space)." Although his essay focuses on time and the chronotope in the novel, the critic allows that the concept may be extended to other genres: "the chronotope [is] a formally constitutive category of literature . . . [in which] the primary category in the chronotope is time" ("Forms of Time and of the Chronotope in the Novel," 84–85).

60. Gómez-Quiñones, *Mexican American Labor, 1790–1990*, 242.

61. See Griswold del Castillo, *The Treaty of Guadalupe Hidalgo*. Poems such as "Poema para los californios muertos" by Lorna Dee Cervantes and "Un Trip through the Mind Jail" by Raúl Salinas document the destruction of Chicano barrios.

62. See Barrera, *Race and Class in the Southwest*.

63. See Sandos, *Rebellion in the Borderlands*.

64. Sánchez quoted in Salazar, "Ricardo Sánchez," 15.

65. Deleuze and Guattari, *Anti-Oedipus*, 32; see also 36–50.

66. See Nabokov, *Tijerina and the Courthouse Raid*, for Reies López Tijerina's takeover of "government lands."

67. See Bruce-Novoa's influential article, "The Space of Chicano Literature" (reprinted in the volume of essays entitled *RetroSpace*), 93. In the second half of the decade Sánchez's philosophy no longer rallied the troops of the Movement. It was not until the 1980s, when the male-dominated wing of the Movement had been largely discredited, that Sánchez's notion of the "decade of the Chicano" was appropriated by Raúl Izaguirre, director of the National Council of La Raza, who designated the 1980s as the "Decade for the Hispanic." According to Rodolfo Acuña, Izaguirre's forecast and his terminology excluded many poor and working-class Chicanos. See Izaguirre, "The Decade for the Hispanic," 2 (cited in Acuña, *Occupied America*, 413).

68. Deleuze, *Bergsonism*, 34.

69. *The Encyclopedia of Philosophy* (1967), s.v. "time."

70. Deleuze, *Bergsonism*, 116. In a new afterword titled "A Return to Bergson," dated July, 1988, Deleuze states that "to continue Bergson's project today, means, for example[,] to constitute a metaphysical image of thought corresponding to the new lines, openings, traces, leaps, dynamisms, discovered by a molecular biology of the brain: new linkings and re-linkings in thought" (116–17). (The original edition, *Le bergsonisme*, was published in France in 1966.)

71. Deleuze, *Bergsonism*, 85.

72. Bergson quoted in ibid., 27.

73. Deleuze, *Bergsonism*, 27.

74. *The Encyclopedia of Philosophy* (1967), s.v. "time."

75. Kant, *Critique of Pure Reason*, 29.

76. Bergson quoted in Deleuze, *Bergsonism*, 28.

77. Foucault, *The Order of Things*, 225. Foucault does not include metaphysics or intuition among the "human sciences." However, he does document the merging of space and time within a composite history: "From the nineteenth century, History was to deploy, in a temporal series, the analogies that connect distinct organic structures to one another. This same History will progressively impose its laws on the analysis of production, the analysis of organically structured beings and, lastly, on the analysis of linguistic groups. History *gives place* to analogical organic structures, just as Order opened the way to *successive* identities and differences" (219).

78. With regard to Adam Smith, Foucault writes that, "for the economist, what is actually circulating in the form of things is labour—not objects of need representing one another, but time and toil, transformed, concealed, forgotten. . . . As for the fecundity of labor, it is not so much due to personal ability or to calculations of self-interest; it is based upon conditions that are also exterior to its representation: industrial progress, growing division of tasks, accumulation of capital, division of productive labour and non-productive labour" (*The Order of Things*, 225).

79. Bakhtin, "Forms of Time and of the Chronotope in the Novel," 84.

80. In a similar manner, Sánchez and Alurista have indicated the meaningful interconnectedness of concepts such as *cantogrito* and *mindsoul.*

Chapter 4. In the Movement and Beyond

1. Bruce-Novoa, *Chicano Poetry*, 151; Tatum, *Chicano Literature*, 146; Vento, introduction to *Milhuas Blues and gritos norteños*, iv.

2. Bruce-Novoa, *Chicano Poetry*, 157; Valdez, *Luis Valdez—Early Works*, 10.

3. See Muñoz, *Youth, Identity, Power*, 75–78. See also "El plan espiritual de Aztlán" in Anaya and Lomelí, eds., *Aztlán*, 1–5.

4. Gómez-Quiñones, *Chicano Politics*, 189–90.

5. According to Carlos Muñoz, Jr., there have been "different levels of assimilation into both the class structure and dominant culture. In addition to class differences, there have been and continue to be internal cultural differences . . . As a result, the multicultural, multiracial, regional, generational, and class character of the Mexican American people has contributed to the uneven development of political consciousness" (Muñoz, *Youth, Identity, Power*, 9–10).

6. Ibid., 86, 172.

7. Ibid., 4.

8. Tino Villanueva notes that "muchos de nuestros mayores hoy día prefieren llamarse *Mexican American*, o sea, mexicano-norteamericanos. Pero habría que añadir que dicha preferencia obedece también a que los ya mayores, y aun los de mediana edad sumados a un determinado número de jóvenes, repudian, en general, el fervor social y la actitud protestataria de quienes declaran ser chicanos, tachándolos injustamente de 'gritones locos militantes'" (*nowadays many of our elders prefer to call themselves Mexican American. But we must add that this preference is due to the fact that elderly persons, and even those who are middle-aged, as well as a certain number of young people, generally repudiate the social activism and confrontational attitude of those who call themselves Chicanos, unjustly labeling them as "crazy, screaming militants"*) (Villanueva, *Chicanos*, 15–16).

9. M. García, *Mexican Americans*, 298.

10. Ibid., 300.

11. Candelaria, "The 'Wild Zone' Thesis as Gloss in Chicana Literary Study," 21.

12. Rebolledo, *Women Singing in the Snow*, 71.

13. Cervantes, "Para un revolucionario," in *The Third Woman*, ed. Dexter Fisher, 381–82.

14. Ricardo Sánchez, "a donde llegaste," "a César lo suyo," and "dirge chicaneaux: a canto for César . . . ," in *Amerikan Journeys*, 37–53.

15. See Villanueva, *Chicanos*, 7–8.

16. Tatum, review of *Hechizospells, World Literature Today* 51, no. 3 (summer, 1977): 421; Delgado, review of *Hechizospells, El maizal*, vol. 1, no. 2 (Jan., 1978): 8–9.

17. Zimmerman, "Ricardo Sánchez," 369.

18. Sánchez, "Fuente Onoria Soul/Mind Journey," 64.

19. Ricardo Sánchez, personal interview by the author, El Paso, Tex., Sept., 1992.

20. Muñoz, *Youth, Identity, Power*, 7.

21. Ricardo Sánchez, "Some Notes on 'Entelequia III.'"

22. Here I am thinking of poets such as Anne Sexton, Sylvia Plath, Robert Lowell, and the Beat poets.

23. Witt, *Existential Prisons*, 2–3. Witt argues further that "the concentration camps of World War II are also part of a continuum in the human mind's consciousness of imprisoning spaces and of forces that imprison. Much of modern European language and literature has reflected a mode of consciousness modified by the camp phenomenon as well as by other imprisonments of war while not bearing the direct testimonial influence of Holocaust literature" (3).

24. Stan Steiner's *La Raza* was published in 1970. In 1972 Knopf published Luis Valdez and Stan Steiner's *Aztlán: An Anthology of Mexican American Literature*. Valdez collaborated with Steiner, notwithstanding Sánchez's and Delgado's objections.

25. Ricardo Sánchez and Delgado, "Minority Publishers," 38, 39.

26. Genaro Padilla provides a valuable historical contextualization. He quotes Pablo de la Guerra, a native Californian who became a member of the state legislature under the American regime: "It is the conquered who are humbled before the conqueror . . . They are foreigners in their own land. I have seen seventy and sixty year olds cry like children because they have been uprooted from the lands of their fathers. They have been humiliated and insulted. They have been refused the privilege of taking water from their own wells" (Padilla, *My History, Not Yours*, 15).

27. According to Octavio Romano, "*The Pachuco movement was one of the few truly separatist movements in American History*. Even then, it was singularly unique among separatist movements in that it did not seek or even attempt a return to roots and origins. The Pachuco indulged in *self separation from history*, created his own reality as he went along even to the extent of creating his own language" (Romano, "The Historical and Intellectual Presence of Mexican Americans," 39, emphasis in original). Arturo Madrid-Barela traces the literary and historical origins of the pachuco to the so-called "Zoot Suit" riots of 1943 in Los Angeles. Like Romano he cites *The Labyrinth of Solitude* by Octavio Paz, who observed pachucos as "instinctive rebels . . . [whose] attitude reveals an obstinate, almost fanatical will-to-be, but this will affirms nothing specific except their determination . . . not to be like those around them. The pachuco does not want to become a Mexican again; at the same time he does not want to blend into the life of North America" (Paz, *Labyrinth of Solitude*, 14, cited in Madrid-Barela, "In Search of the Authentic Pachuco," 36; see also 31–60).

28. Madrid-Barela, "In Search of the Authentic Pachuco," 52.

29. Grajeda, "The Pachuco in Chicano Poetry," 46. Grajeda cites a historical study which represents pachucos as "precursors of more recent young and militant . . . Chicano groups such as the Brown Berets" (258 n. 5).

30. Ibid., 46. The subject of pachuco gangs has more recently appeared in feature films such as Edward James Olmos's *American Me* (Universal, 1992). Like some of Sánchez's later work, Olmos's work in the film is a highly critical view of the deterioration of the Movement and its leaders and is intended to have a strong effect on audiences: "Unless the *vatos* in the gangs change the direction they're headed, and the children are headed, you're talking about a dead culture" (Edward James Olmos interview, "The American Me Generation," *SF Weekly*, Mar. 4, 1992, 15). The film depicts Hollywood's apocalyptic vision of post-Movement *pintos* involved in organizing the drug trade in the barrio, while omitting the

"excuses" of racism which we find in Sánchez's representation of the pre-Movement pachucos: "The horrors of the Amerikan dream and the awesomeness of racist reality forced Chicanos to seek escape. Drug cultism became an avenue for blotting out the dream—that vicious dream with its multi-headed dis-realities" (*Canto y grito* 35).

31. Like Grajeda's study, Rafael Pérez-Torres's *Movements in Chicano Poetry* omits all mention of Ricardo Sánchez's many poems that depict the pachuco, the *vato loco,* and their *caló* vernacular.

32. Grajeda, "The Pachuco in Chicano Poetry," 47.

33. Ibid., 46 (my emphasis), 47.

34. Ibid., 47.

35. As Francisco Lomelí and Donald Urioste note in an early article, "Sólo le queda su chicanismo como sentido espiritual que ha resistido sin rendirse. Por esta razón, caracteriza la existencia chicana del barrio como algo vivido intensamente" (*All that remains is his spiritual sense of Chicanismo which has resisted and refused to surrender*) ("El concepto del barrio," 27–28).

36. Bakhtin, "Forms of Time and of the Chronotope in the Novel," 84–85.

37. Lomelí and Urioste note the double effect of *la pinta* and the barrio on Sánchez's literary development: "El encarcelamiento tuvo un profundo efecto en su formación filosófico-artística porque sintió que ese ambiente hermético lo iba desintegrando interiormente . . . [u]na nota distintiva de *Canto y grito mi liberación* es la falta de idealización del barrio chicano. Está pintado como realidad paradójica" (*The period of incarceration had a profound effect on his philosophical and artistic development because he sensed a personal disintegration taking place within that enclosed environment. . . . [A] distinctive aspect of* Canto y grito mi liberación *is its refusal to idealize the Chicano barrio. It is depicted as a paradoxical reality*) ("El concepto del barrio," 27–28).

38. Sánchez, *Publish-It-Yourself Handbook,* 62.

39. Candelaria, *Chicano Poetry,* 54.

Chapter 5. *Hechizospells* as Tragedy

1. *Dictionary of Literary Terms and Literary Theory,* 3rd ed., s.v. "tragedy."

2. Ibid.

3. Ibid.

4. Tatum, "Contemporary Chicano Prose Fiction," 241–42.

5. Lomelí, "*Peregrinos de Aztlán* de Miguel Méndez," 49.

6. Ubilla-Arenas, "*Peregrinos de Aztlán:* De la crítica social al sueño humanista," 72.

7. Ibid., 72–73.

8. Miguel Méndez, "Posibilidades literarias del autor de habla hispana en U.S.A," paper presented at the Festival Flor y Canto, Austin, Tex., fall, 1974, quoted in Ubilla-Arenas, "*Peregrinos de Aztlán:* De la crítica social al sueño humanista," 73.

9. Lomelí, "*Peregrinos de Aztlán* de Miguel Méndez," 46.

10. Miguel León-Portilla describes Nezahualcóyotl's writings as those of a man in a state of existential angst, "tormented because he sees that everything in the world itself is like the plumage of a bird that rends itself, conscious of change and death." Nezahualcóyotl was a poet and philosopher, the lord of Texcoco who "was preoccupied constantly with the problems of becoming, time, and the divinity" (León-Portilla, "Pre-Hispanic Thought," 5, 14).

11. Richard Rodríguez characterizes Mexico and California as tragic and comic cultures, respectively. See Rodríguez, *Days of Obligation,* xvi.

12. See José Ferrater Mora's *Unamuno.*

13. See Ricard, *The Spiritual Conquest of Mexico,* and Gutiérrez, *When Jesus Came, the Corn Mothers Went Away.* See also Acuña, *Occupied America,* 344–45, 430–33.

14. According to Lomelí and Urioste, Sánchez "projects a type of Chicano existentialism of the

individual in the act of liberating himself through the creative process which becomes aesthetic sustenance for others" (*Chicano Perspectives in Literature*, 32).

15. Deleuze, *Nietzsche and Philosophy*, 11.

16. Haar, "Nietzsche and Metaphysical Language," 27–28.

17. Bruce-Novoa, *Chicano Authors*, 219.

18. Lingis, "The Will to Power," 47.

19. Tomás Ybarra-Frausto theorizes that *rascuachismo* is essentially an intuitive response: "Rasquachismo [*sic*] is a sensibility that is not elevated and serious, but playful and elemental. It finds delight and refinement in what many consider banal and projects an alternative aesthetic—a sort of good taste of bad taste" ("Rasquachismo: A Chicano Sensibility," 155; see also 155–62).

20. Deleuze, *Nietzsche and Philosophy*, 11.

21. Ibid., 17.

22. Leal, "Literary Criticism and Minority Literatures," 158–59.

23. See Calderón and Saldívar, *Criticism in the Borderlands*, 1.

24. Leal, "Literary Criticism and Minority Literatures, 158, 159.

25. Lomelí, "An Overview of Chicano Letters," 106–107.

26. Faulkner quoted in Block, "Malraux, Faulkner, and Tragedy," 59; Malraux quoted in Dial, "Elements in *The Conquerors* and *Man's Fate*," 103.

27. Block, "Malraux, Faulkner, and Tragedy," 59–60.

28. Ibid., 59.

29. See Castillo, "Interview with Ricardo Sánchez," 22–33.

30. Leal, "Literary Criticism and Minority Literatures," 153.

31. Bloomfield and Dunn, *The Role of the Poet in Early Societies*, 4.

32. Haar, "Nietzsche and Metaphysical Language," 28.

33. See Castillo, "Interview with Ricardo Sánchez," 22–33.

34. Delgado, *Chicano*, 32.

35. M. Lewis, "Ricardo Sánchez and the Development of Chicano Poetry," 203, 54–55; Ortego, "An Appreciation of *Hechizospells*," 77; Lomelí and Urioste, *Chicano Perspectives in Literature*, 33.

36. Bruce-Novoa, *Chicano Authors*, 225–26.

37. For more on the development of this critical perspective see issues of the journal *Carta Abierta*, which began publication in 1977.

38. Haar, "Nietzsche and Metaphysical Language," 28.

39. Bloom, introduction to *André Malraux's* Man's Fate, 1.

40. Goldmann, "The Structure of *La condition humaine*," 56.

41. Dial, "Elements in *The Conquerors* and *Man's Fate*," 103; Breunig, "Malraux's *Storm in Shanghai*," 69.

42. See Rama, *Transculturación narrativa en América Latina*. Rama analyzes José María Arguedas's novel *Los ríos profundos* to demonstrate the mutual influence between the *mestizo* and Quechua cultures of Peru. Arguedas's short story "Yawar fiesta" is also an excellent example of *transculturación*.

43. Sánchez quoted in Binder, "Ricardo Sánchez," 172.

44. Hunter S. Thompson's *Fear and Loathing on the Campaign Trail '72* (San Francisco: Straight Arrow Books, 1973) and *Fear and Loathing in Las Vegas* (New York: Random House, 1971) as well as his pieces in *Rolling Stone* magazine purveyed a white counterculture brand of "Gonzo journalism" saturated with apocalyptic nihilism and dread that reflected the political climate of the early 1970s.

45. For the poem "Los Theys Are Us," see Montoya, *Information*, 163–64.

46. For "Indict Amerika," see *Los cuatro*, 39–41.

47. Delgado, review of *Hechizospells*, *El maizal* 1, no. 2 (Jan., 1978): 9.

48. Leal, "The Problem of Identifying Chicano Literature," 5.

49. M. Lewis, "Ricardo Sánchez and the Development of Chicano Poetry," 199; M. Lewis, review of *Hechizospells, Revista Chicano-Riqueña,* 5, no. 3 (summer, 1977): 54.

Conclusion

1. Lomelí, "Ricardo Sánchez," 752.

Works Cited

Acuña, Rodolfo. *Occupied America: A History of Chicanos.* 3rd. ed. New York: Harper Collins, 1988.

Aguilar-Henson, Marcella. "Angela de Hoyos and Ricardo Sánchez: A Thematic, Stylistic, and Linguistic Analysis of Two Chicano Poets." Ph.D. diss., University of New Mexico, 1982.

Alurista. *Floricanto en Aztlán.* Los Angeles: Chicano Studies Center, University of California, 1971.

———. Introduction to *Festival de Flor y Canto II.* Albuquerque, N.Mex.: Pajarito Publications, 1979.

———. *Nationchild Plumaroja: Poems 1969–1972.* San Diego, Calif.: Toltecas en Aztlán, Centro Cultural de la Raza, 1971.

———. *Timespace Huracán: Poems 1972–1975.* Albuquerque, N.Mex.: Pajarito Publications, 1976.

Anaya, Rudolfo, and Francisco Lomelí, eds. *Aztlán: Essays on the Chicano Homeland.* Albuquerque: University of New Mexico Press, 1989.

Anderson Imbert, Enrique. *Historia de la literatura hispanoamericana I. Colonia. Cien años de república.* Mexico City: Fondo de Cultura Económica, 1982.

Anzaldúa, Gloria. *Borderlands/La frontera: The New Mestiza.* San Francisco: Spinsters/Aunt Lute, 1987.

Armas, José, and Bernice Zamora. Introduction to *Flor y Canto IV and V: An Anthology of Chicano Literature from the Festivals Held in Albuquerque, New Mexico, 1977, and Tempe, Arizona, 1978.* Albuquerque, N.Mex.: Pajarito Publications/Flor y Canto Committee, 1980.

Bakhtin, Mikhail M. "Forms of Time and of the Chronotope in the Novel." In *The Dialogic Imagination: Four Essays by M. M. Bakhtin.* Austin: University of Texas Press, 1981.

Barker, George. *Pachuco: An American-Spanish Argot and Its Social Functions in Tucson, Arizona.* Tucson: University of Arizona Press, 1950.

Barrera, Mario. *Race and Class in the Southwest: A Theory of Racial Inequality.* Notre Dame, Ind.: University of Notre Dame Press, 1979.

Bergson, Henri. *Creative Evolution.* 1907. Translated by Arthur Mitchell. New York: Henry Holt & Co., 1911.

———. *Duration and Simultaneity.* 1922. Translated by Leon Jacobson. Indianapolis: Bobbs-Merrill, 1965.

———. *Matter and Memory.* 1876. Translated by Nancy Margaret Paul and W. Scott Palmer. London: George Allen & Unwin Ltd., 1911.

Beverly, John. "The Margin at the Center: On 'Testimonio' (Testimonial Narrative)." In *De/Colonizing the Subject: The Politics of Gender in Women's Autobiography.* Minneapolis: University of Minnesota Press, 1992.

Binder, Wolfgang, ed. "Ricardo Sánchez." In *Partial Autobiographies: Interviews with Twenty Chicano Poets.* Erlangen, Germany: Palm & Erlangen, 1985.

Block, Haskell M. "Malraux, Faulkner, and Tragedy." In *Witnessing André Malraux,* edited by Brian Thompson and Carl A. Viggiani. Middletown, Conn.: Wesleyan University Press, 1984.

Bloom, Harold. Introduction to *André Malraux's* Man's Fate, edited by Harold Bloom. New York: Chelsea House, 1988.

Bloomfield, Morton, and Charles Dunn. *The Role of the Poet in Early Societies.* Cambridge: D. S. Brewer, 1989.

Breunig, LeRoy C. "Malraux's *Storm in Shanghai.*" In *André Malraux's* Man's Fate, edited by Harold Bloom. New York: Chelsea House, 1988.

Bruce-Novoa, Juan. *Chicano Authors: Inquiry by Interview.* Austin: University of Texas Press, 1980.

———. *Chicano Poetry: A Response to Chaos.* Austin: University of Texas Press, 1982.

———. "The Space of Chicano Literature." In *Retrospace: Collected Essays on Chicano Literature, Theory, and History.* Houston: Arte Público Press, 1990.

Burgos-Debray, Elizabeth, with Rigoberta Menchú. *I Rigoberta Menchú: An Indian Woman in Guatemala.* Translated by Ann White. London: Verso, 1984.

Byron, William. *Cervantes: A Biography.* New York: Paragon House, 1988.

Calderón, Héctor, and José David Saldívar, eds. *Criticism in the Borderlands: Studies in Chicano Literature, Culture, and Ideology.* Durham, N.C.: Duke University Press, 1991.

Campa, Arthur L. *Hispanic Culture in the Southwest.* Norman: University of Oklahoma Press, 1979.

Canclini, Néstor García. *Culturas híbridas: Estrategias para entrar y salir de la modernidad.* Mexico City: Grijalbo, 1989.

Candelaria, Cordelia. *Chicano Poetry: A Critical Introduction.* Westport, Conn.: Greenwood Press, 1986.

————. "The 'Wild Zone' Thesis as Gloss in Chicana Literary Study." In *Chicana Critical Issues.* Berkeley, Calif.: Third Woman Press, 1993.

Castañeda, Carlos E. *Our Catholic Heritage in Texas, 1519–1936.* 7 vols. Austin: Von Boeckmann-Jones, 1936–1958.

Castillo, Rafael. "Interview with Ricardo Sánchez." *Imagine,* vol. 1, no. 2 (1984).

Cervantes, Lorna Dee. "Para un revolucionario." In *The Third Woman: Minority Women Writers of the United States,* edited by Dexter Fisher. Boston: Houghton Mifflin, 1980.

Contreras, Jesse A. G. "Existential Phenomenology and Its Influence on Mexican and Chicano Philosophy and Philosophy of Education." Ph.D. diss., University of California, Berkeley, 1984.

Curtius, Ernst Robert. *European Literature and the Latin Middle Ages.* Princeton, N.J.: Princeton University Press, 1953.

Deleuze, Gilles. *Bergsonism.* Translated by Hugh Tomlinson and Barbara Habberjam. 1966. New York: Zone Books, 1991.

————. *Nietzsche and Philosophy.* Translated by Hugh Tomlinson. 1962. New York: Columbia University Press, 1983.

Deleuze, Gilles, and Félix Guattari. *Anti-Oedipus.* Translated by Robert Hurley, Mark Seem, and Helen R. Lane. Minneapolis: University of Minnesota Press, 1983.

Delgado, Abelardo. *Chicano: Twenty-five Pieces of a Chicano Mind.* Denver: Barrio Publications, 1969.

————. Review of *Hechizospells,* by Ricardo Sánchez. *Caracol,* vol. 4, no. 4 (December, 1977).

————. Review of *Hechizospells,* by Ricardo Sánchez. *El maizal,* vol. 1, no. 2 (January, 1978).

————. "This Is (Mi Compa) Sánchez." Introduction to *Canto y grito mi liberación,* by Ricardo Sánchez. El Paso, Tex.: Mictla Publications, 1971 (also in 1973 and 1995 editions).

Deyermond, A. D. *Historia de la literatura española: la Edad Media.* Barcelona: Ariel, 1973.

Dial, Roger. "Elements in *The Conquerors* and *Man's Fate.*" In *André Malraux's Man's Fate,* edited by Harold Bloom. New York: Chelsea House, 1988.

Dostoyevsky, Fyodor. *Notes from a Dead House.* Translated by A. Navrozov and Y. Guralsky. 1861. Moscow: Foreign Languages Publishing House, n.d.

"El plan espiritual de Aztlán." In *Aztlán: Essays on the Chicano Homeland,* edited by Rudolfo Anaya and Francisco Lomelí. Albuquerque: University of New Mexico Press, 1989.

The Encyclopedia of Philosophy. New York: Macmillan, 1967.

Erasmus (Desiderius). *The Praise of Folly and Other Writings.* Edited and translated by Robert M. Adams. 1508. New York: Norton, 1989.

Ferrari, Américo. Introduction to *Obra poética completa,* by César Vallejo. Madrid: Alianza Editorial, 1982.

Ferrater Mora, José. *Unamuno: A Philosophy of Tragedy.* Translated by Philip Silver. Berkeley: University of California Press, 1962.

Foucault, Michel. *The Order of Things: An Archaeology of the Human Sciences.* New York: Vintage Books, 1970.

Franklin, H. Bruce. *Prison Literature in America: The Victim as Criminal and Artist.* New York: Oxford University Press, 1989.

Fuentes, Carlos. *La nueva novela hispanoamericana.* Mexico City: Joaquín Mortiz, 1969.

García, Mario T. *Mexican Americans: Leadership, Ideology, and Identity, 1930–1960.* New Haven, Conn.: Yale University Press, 1989.

Garcia, Richard A. *Rise of the Mexican American Middle Class: San Antonio, 1929–1941.* College Station: Texas A&M University Press, 1991.

Goldmann, Lucien. "The Structure of *La Condition humaine.*" In *André Malraux's* Man's Fate, edited by Harold Bloom. New York: Chelsea House, 1988.

Gómez-Quiñones, Juan. *Chicano Politics: Reality and Promise, 1940–1990.* Albuquerque: University of New Mexico Press, 1990.

———. *Mexican American Labor, 1790–1990.* Albuquerque: University of New Mexico Press, 1994.

Gonzales, Rodolfo. *I Am Joaquín.* Illustrated by Yermo Vásquez. Delano, Calif.: Farm Workers Press, 1967.

Gonzales-Berry, Erlinda. "Chicano Literature in Spanish." Ph.D. diss., University of New Mexico, 1978.

González, Ray, ed. *After Aztlán: Latino Poets of the Nineties.* Boston: Godine, 1992.

Grajeda, Rafael. "The Pachuco in Chicano Poetry: The Process of Legend-Creation." *Revista Chicano-Riqueña,* vol. 8, no. 4 (fall, 1980).

Grandjeat, Yves-Charles. "Doxy and Heterodoxy in the Emerging Chicano Critical Discourse: Metacritical Notes on *Criticism in the Borderlands.*" In *Écrire la différence: Interculturalism and the Writing of Difference.* Bordeaux, France: Bordeaux University Press, 1993.

———. "Ricardo Sánchez: The Poetics of Liberation." In *European Perspectives on Hispanic Literature of the United States,* edited by Genevieve Fabre. Houston: Arte Público Press, 1988.

Griswold del Castillo, Richard. *The Treaty of Guadalupe Hidalgo: A Legacy of Conflict.* Norman: University of Oklahoma Press, 1990.

Gutiérrez, Ramón A. *When Jesus Came, the Corn Mothers Went Away: Marriage, Sexuality, and Power in New Mexico, 1500–1846.* Stanford, Calif.: Stanford University Press, 1991.

Haar, Michel. "Nietzsche and Metaphysical Language." In *The New Nietzsche: Contemporary Styles of Interpretation,* edited by David B. Allison. Cambridge, Mass.: MIT Press, 1985.

Haro, Robert P. Review of *Canto y grito mi liberación,* by Ricardo Sánchez. *Library Journal,* vol. 1 (July, 1973).

Henderson, Bill, ed. *The Publish-It-Yourself Handbook.* Yonkers, N.Y.: Pushcart Book Press, 1973.

Hernández, Guillermo E. *Chicano Satire: A Study in Literary Culture.* Austin: University of Texas Press, 1991.

Izaguirre, Raúl. "The Decade for the Hispanic." *Agenda* (January/February, 1980).

Jameson, Fredric. *The Seeds of Time.* New York: Columbia University Press, 1994.

Kanellos, Nicolás. "Ricardo Sánchez—Minotaur." Introduction to *Selected Poems,* by Ricardo Sánchez. Houston: Arte Público Press, 1985.

Kant, Immanuel. *Critique of Pure Reason.* Translated by F. Max Muller. 1781. Garden City, N.Y.: Anchor Books, 1966.

Karrer, Wolfgang. "Gender and the Sense of Place in the Writings of Gloria Anzaldúa and Rolando Hinojosa." In *Gender, Self, and Society: Proceedings of the IV International Conference on the Hispanic Cultures of the United States,* edited by Renate von Bardeleben. Frankfurt: Peter Lang, 1993.

Keller, Gary D. "Literary Stratagems Available to the Bilingual Chicano Writer." In *The Identification and Analysis of Chicano Literature,* edited by Francisco Jiménez. Tempe, Ariz.: Bilingual Press/Editorial Bilingüe, 1979.

Leal, Luis. "In Search of Aztlán." In *Aztlán: Essays on the Chicano Homeland,* edited by Rudolfo Anaya and Francisco Lomelí. Albuquerque: University of New Mexico Press, 1989.

———. Introduction to *Canto y grito mi liberación: The Liberation of a Chicano Mind Soul,* by Ricardo Sánchez. Pullman: Washington State University Press, 1995.

———. "Literary Criticism and Minority Literatures: The Case of the Chicano Writer." In *No Longer Voiceless,* by Luis Leal. San Diego, Calif.: Marin Publications, 1995.

———. "The Problem of Identifying Chicano Literature." In *The Identification and Analysis of Chicano Literature,* edited by Francisco Jiménez. Tempe, Ariz.: Bilingual Press/Editorial Bilingüe, 1979.

———. "Sin fronteras: (Des) mitificación en las letras norteamericanas y mexicanas." *Mexican Studies/Estudios mexicanos,* vol. 9, no. 1 (winter, 1993).

Leibniz, G. W. "A Specimen of Dynamics." In *Philosophical Essays,* edited and translated by Roger Ariew and Daniel Garber. Indianapolis: Hackett, 1989.

León-Portilla, Miguel de. *Los antiguos mexicanos.* Mexico City: Fondo de Cultura Económica, 1987.

———. "Pre-Hispanic Thought." In *Major Trends in Mexican Philosophy.* Notre Dame, Ind.: University of Notre Dame Press, 1966.

Lewis, Marvin A. Review of *Hechizospells,* by Ricardo Sánchez. *Revista Chicano-Riqueña,* vol 5, no. 3 (summer, 1977).

———. "Ricardo Sánchez and the Development of Chicano Poetry." Pp. 199–206 in *Twenty-seventh Annual Mountain Interstate Foreign Language Conference, Oct. 1977,* edited by Eduardo Zayaz-Bazán and Manuel Laurentino Suárez. Johnson City, Tenn.: Research Council of East Tennessee State University, 1978.

Lewis, Rob. Preface to *Amerikan Journeys: Jornadas Americanas,* by Ricardo Sánchez. Iowa City, Iowa: Rob Lewis Publisher, 1994.

Limón, José. *Mexican Ballads, Chicano Poems: History and Influence in Mexican-American Social Poetry.* Berkeley: University of California Press, 1992.

Lingis, Alphonso. "The Will to Power." In *The New Nietzsche: Contemporary Styles of Interpretation,* edited by David B. Allen. Cambridge, Mass.: MIT Press, 1985.

Lomelí, Francisco A. "The Chicano Reinvention of America: Is Cultural Essentialism Dead? Or, Breaking the Gridlock on Poetics of Indifference." In *Écrire la différence: Interculturalism and the Writing of Difference,* edited by Jean Beranger, Jean Cazemajou, Jean-Michel LaCroix, and Pierre Spriet. Bordeaux, France: Bordeaux University Press, 1993.

———. "An Overview of Chicano Letters: From Origins to Resurgence." In *Chicano Studies: A Multidisciplinary Approach,* edited by Eugene E. García, Francisco A. Lomelí, and Isidro D. Ortiz. New York: Teachers College Press, 1984.

———. "*Peregrinos de Aztlán* de Miguel Méndez: Textimonio de Desesperanza(dos)." In *Miguel Méndez in Aztlán: Two Decades of Literary Production,* edited by Gary D. Keller. Tempe, Ariz.: Bilingual Review/Press, 1995.

———. "Ricardo Sánchez." In *Reference Guide to American Literature.* Detroit: St. James Press, 1994.

Lomelí, Francisco A., and Donaldo W. Urioste. *Chicano Perspectives in Literature: A Critical and Annotated Bibliography.* Albuquerque, N.Mex.: Pajarito Publications, 1977.

———. "El concepto del barrio en tres poetas chicanos: Abelardo, Alurista y Ricardo Sánchez." *De Colores: Journal of Emerging Raza Philosophies,* vol. 3, no. 4 (1977).

López, Miguel R. "Tres textos críticos chicanos: la generación del ochenta." *Nuevo Texto Crítico,* vol. 4, no. 8 (1991).

Madrid-Barela, Arturo. "In Search of the Authentic Pachuco: An Interpretive Essay." *Aztlán,* vol. 4, no. 1 (1974).

———. "Towards an Understanding of the Chicano Experience." *Aztlán,* vol. 4, no. 1 (spring, 1973).

Malraux, André. *Man's Fate.* Translated by Haakon M. Chevalier. New York: Modern Library, 1934.

Mazón, Mauricio. *The Zoot-Suit Riots.* Austin: University of Texas Press, 1984.

McFarland, Ron. "Indelibly Chicano: An Interview with Ricardo Sánchez." *Americas Review,* vol. 23, no. 3–4 (fall/winter, 1995).

Méndez, Miguel M. *The Dream of Santa María de las Piedras.* Translated by David William Foster. Tempe, Ariz.: Bilingual Press/Editorial Bilingüe, 1989.

———. "Posibilidades literarias del autor de habla hispana en U.S.A." Paper presented at the Festival Flor y Canto, Austin, Tex., fall 1974.

Menéndez Pidal, Ramón. *Poesía juglaresca y orígenes de las literaturas románicas.* Madrid: Instituto de Estudios Políticos, 1957.

Monsiváis, Carlos. "Los chicanos." *Cultura Norte* (July/August, 1987).

Montoya, José. *Information: Twenty Years of Joda.* San Jose, Calif.: Chusma House, 1992.

Moraga, Cherríe. *Loving in the War Years: Lo que nunca paso por sus labios.* Boston: South End Press, 1983.

Moraga, Cherríe, and Gloria Anzaldúa, eds. *This Bridge Called My Back: Writings by Radical Women of Color.* Watertown, Mass.: Persephone Press, 1981.

Morales Blouin, Elga. "Símbolos y motivos nahuas en la literatura chicana." In *The Identification and Analysis of Chicano Literature,* edited by Francisco Jiménez. New York: Bilingual Press/Editorial Bilingüe, 1979.

Muñoz, Carlos, Jr. *Youth, Identity, Power.* London: Verso, 1989.

Nabokov, Peter. *Tijerina and the Courthouse Raid.* Albuquerque: University of New Mexico Press, 1969.

Olivares, Julián. "Two Contemporary Chicano Verse Chronicles [Jimmy Santiago Baca and Tino Villanueva]." *Americas Review,* vol. 16, no. 3–4 (1988).

Ortego, Philip D. "An Appreciation of *Hechizospells* by Ricardo Sánchez." *MELUS,* vol. 7, no. 2 (summer, 1980).

———. "The Chicano Renaissance." *Social Casework,* vol. 52 (May, 1971).

———. Introduction to *Canto y grito mi liberación,* by Ricardo Sánchez. El Paso, Tex.: Mictla Publications, 1971 (also in 1973 and 1995 editions).

Padilla, Genaro M. *My History, Not Yours: The Formation of Mexican American Autobiography.* Madison: University of Wisconsin Press, 1993.

———. "Myth and Comparative Cultural Nationalism." In *Aztlán: Essays on the Chicano Homeland,* edited by Rudolfo Anaya and Francisco Lomelí. Albuquerque: University of New Mexico Press, 1989.

Paredes, Américo. *With His Pistol in His Hand: A Border Ballad and Its Hero.* Austin: University of Texas Press, 1958.

Paredes, Raymund. "The Origins of Anti-Mexican Sentiment in the United States." In *New Directions in Chicano Scholarship,* edited by Ricardo Romo and Raymund Paredes. La Jolla: Chicano Studies Program, University of California, San Diego, 1978.

Paz, Octavio. *Claude Lévi-Strauss o el nuevo festín de Esopo.* Mexico City: Joaquín Mortiz, 1967.

———. *The Labyrinth of Solitude: Life and Thought in Mexico.* 1950. Translated by Lysander Kemp. New York: Grove Press, 1961. Originally published as *El laberinto de la soledad* (Mexico City: Cuadernos Americanos, 1950).

———. *Sor Juana Inés de la Cruz o las trampas de la fe.* Mexico City: Fondo de Cultura Económica, 1990.

Pérez, Reymundo "Tigre." *Free, Free at Last.* Denver: Barrio Publications, 1970.

Pérez-Torres, Rafael. *Movements in Chicano Poetry: Against Myths, Against Margins.* New York: Cambridge University Press, 1995.

"Plan of Delano." In *Aztlán: An Anthology of Mexican American Literature,* edited by Luis Valdez and Stan Steiner. New York: Knopf, 1972.

Quintana, Alvina. "Ana Castillo's *The Mixquiahuala Letters:* The Novelist as Ethnographer." In *Criticism in the Borderlands,* edited by Héctor Calderón and José David Saldívar. Durham, N.C.: Duke University Press, 1991.

Rama, Angel. *Transculturación narrativa en América Latina.* Mexico City: Siglo Veintiuno Editores, 1982.

Rebolledo, Tey Diana. *Women Singing in the Snow: A Cultural Analysis of Chicana Literature.* Tucson: University of Arizona Press, 1995.

Rebolledo, Tey Diana, and Eliana S. Rivero, eds. *Infinite Divisions: An Anthology of Chicana Literature.* Tucson: University of Arizona Press, 1993.

Ricard, Robert. *The Spiritual Conquest of Mexico.* Translated by Lesley Bird Simpson. Berkeley: University of California Press, 1966.

Robinson, Cecil. *Mexico and the Hispanic Southwest in American Literature.* Tucson: University of Arizona Press, 1977.

Rodríguez, Richard. *Days of Obligation: An Argument with My Mexican Father.* New York: Viking, 1992.

Romanell, Patrick. *The Making of the Mexican Mind: A Study in Recent Mexican Thought.* Lincoln: University of Nebraska Press, 1952.

Romano, Octavio, V. "The Historical and Intellectual Presence of Mexican Americans." *El Grito,* vol. 2, no. 2 (winter, 1969).

Sahagún, Fray Bernardino de. *The Sun, Moon, and Stars, and the Binding of the*

Years. Book 7 of *General History of the Things of New Spain: Florentine Codex*. Translated by Arthur J. O. Anderson et al. Santa Fe, N.Mex.: School of American Research, 1953.

Salazar, Anthony. "Ricardo Sánchez: Pachuco, Poet, Ph.D., and Scriptwriter." *Caracol*, vol. 4, no. 10 (June, 1978).

Salinas, Raúl. *Un Trip through the Mind-Jail y otras excursiones: Poems*. San Francisco: Editorial Pocho-Che, 1980.

Sánchez, George I. *Forgotten People: A Study of New Mexicans*. Albuquerque: University of New Mexico Press, 1940.

Sánchez, Ricardo. "Chicano Literature: An Evolving Linguistic Pyramid." *Nosotros* (June, 1972).

—. *The Publish-It-Yourself Handbook*. Edited by Bill Henderson. Yonkers, N.Y.: Pushcart Book Press, 1973.

—. "Some Notes on 'Entelequia III.'" In "Entelequia III, An Original Screenplay." Manuscript. 1978. Ricardo Sánchez Papers, Department of Special Collections, Stanford University Libraries.

Sánchez, Ricardo, and Abelardo Delgado. "Minority Publishers." *Publishers' Weekly*, March 15, 1971.

Sánchez, Rosaura. *Chicano Discourse: Socio-Historic Perspectives*. 2nd ed. Houston: Arte Público Press, 1994.

—. "Postmodernism and Chicano Literature." *Aztlán: Chicano Journal of the Social Sciences and the Arts*, vol. 18, no. 2 (1987).

—. "Spanish Codes in the Southwest." In *Modern Chicano Writers: A Collection of Critical Essays*, edited by Joseph Sommers and Tomás Ybarra-Frausto. Englewood Cliffs, N.J.: Prentice-Hall, 1979.

Sandos, James A. *Rebellion in the Borderlands: Anarchism and the Plan of San Diego, 1904–1923*. Norman: University of Oklahoma Press, 1992.

Steiner, Stan. *La Raza*. New York: Harper, 1970.

Tatum, Charles. *Chicano Literature*. Boston: Twayne, 1982.

—. "Contemporary Chicano Prose Fiction: A Chronicle of Misery." In *The Identification and Analysis of Chicano Literature*, edited by Francisco Jiménez. New York: Bilingual Press/Editorial Bilingüe, 1979.

—. Review of *Hechizospells*, by Ricardo Sánchez. *World Literature Today*, vol. 51, no. 3 (summer, 1977).

Trujillo, Ignacio Orlando. "Linguistic Structures in José Montoya's 'El Louie.'" In *Modern Chicano Writers: A Collection of Critical Essays*, edited by Joseph Sommers and Tomás Ybarra-Frausto, Englewood Cliffs, N.J.: Prentice-Hall, 1979.

Ubilla-Arenas, Cecilia. "*Peregrinos de Aztlán:* De la crítica social al sueño humanista." *La Palabra: Revista de Literatura Chicana*, vol. 1, no. 2 (fall, 1979).

Unamuno, Miguel de. *The Tragic Sense of Life*. Translated by J. E. Crawford Flitch. New York: Dover, 1954. Originally published as *Del sentimiento trágico de la vida en los hombres y en los pueblos* (Madrid: Renacimiento, 1912).

Valdez, Luis. *Luis Valdez—Early Works: Actos, Bernabé, and Pensamiento Serpentino*. Houston: Arte Público Press, 1990.

Valdez, Luis, and Stan Steiner, eds. *Aztlán: An Anthology of Mexican American Literature*. New York: Knopf, 1972.

Vallejo, César. *Obra poética completa*. Madrid: Alianza Editorial, 1982.

Vallejos, Thomas. "Mestizaje: The Transformation of Ancient Indian Religious Thought in Contemporary Chicano Fiction." Ph.D. diss., University of Colorado, 1980.

Vasconcelos, José. *La raza cósmica*. 1925. Reprint, Mexico City: Espasa Calpe Mexicana, 1976.

Vásquez, Richard. Review of *Hechizospells*, by Ricardo Sánchez. *Los Angeles Times*, "Books," December 5, 1976.

Vento, Arnold. Introduction to *Milhuas Blues and gritos norteños*, by Ricardo Sánchez. Milwaukee: Spanish Speaking Outreach Institute, University of Wisconsin, 1978, 1980.

Viezzer, Moema, with Domitila B. de Chúngara. *Let Me Speak! Testimony of Domitila, a Woman of the Bolivian Mines*. Translated by Victoria Ortiz. New York: Monthly Review Press, 1979.

Villanueva, Tino, ed. *Chicanos: Antología histórica y literaria*. Mexico City: Fondo de Cultura Económica, 1980.

Webb, Walter Prescott. *The Texas Rangers*. Cambridge: Houghton Mifflin, 1935.

Williams, Raymond. "The Writer: Commitment and Alignment." *Marxism Today*, vol. 24 (June, 1980).

Witt, Mary Ann Frese. *Existential Prisons: Captivity in Mid-Twentieth-Century French Literature*. Durham: Duke University Press, 1985.

Ybarra-Frausto, Tomás. "The Chicano Movement and the Emergence of a Chicano Poetic Consciousness." *New Scholar*, vol. 6 (1977).

———. "Rasquachismo: A Chicano Sensibility." In *Chicano Art: Resistance and Affirmation*, by the CARA National Advisory Committee and edited by Richard Griswold del Castillo, Teresa McKenna, and Yvonne Yarbro-Bejarano. Los Angeles: UCLA Wight Art Gallery, 1991.

Zimmerman, Enid. "Ricardo Sánchez." In *Chicano Literature: A Reference Guide*, edited by Julio A. Martínez and Francisco A. Lomelí. Westport, Conn.: Greenwood Press, 1985.

Index